Human Process and Group Dynamics Training

Human Process and Group Dynamics Training

Quest of Being a Trainer for Impacting Changes

By

Nagendra P. Singh

SAMSKRITI

In Association with Aseed-idmat New Delhi

SAṀSKṚITI
C – 9020, Vasant Kunj, New Delhi – 110070
Visit www.samskritibookshelf.com

ISBN: 978-81-8734-74-9

Typeset by SNGT Publishing Services Pvt. Ltd.
Published by M. Sengupta for Saṁskṛiti, New Delhi.
Printed by Roma Chakraborty,
D-630 Chittranjan Park, New Delhi-110019
chakraborty.roma@gmail.com

To

Dedicated to late Dharni P. Sinha a noted Human Process Trainer and OD Guru, one of the founders of ISABS and founder chairman Advisory Council of IDMAT. And all other group process trainers who have slogged with me in search of my quest of 'Being'

Some Comments From Eminent Professionals

"The book is a perceptive and insightful work on the complex phenomenon of group process based learning for personal development and behavioural change at different levels, and facilitation process for such change, attempting to blend the Western and Eastern thought on the subject. The deeply insightful real life personal statements have well illustrated and enriched the cognitive analysis and understanding of the human process in learning and personal development. The key issues in group process facilitation related to Person, Role, and Skills have been critically examined. It is an interesting, perceptive, and provocative original work."

Prof. Abad Ahmad,
Former Pro-Vice Chancellor and Dean FMS,
University of Delhi, and Former Member of Board, ISABS.

"Dr N. P. Singh has given a very valuable direction to the thinking about facilitation processes by integrating them with Indian thought. It should prove to be of great value to the practitioners of behavioural science in India and be an inspiration to the practitioners in other non-western countries."

Prof . Rajan Gupta,
Management Development Institute,
Gurgaon

"The book is a classical analysis of human process learning with a foucs on identity search and quest of being. The indepth analysis of trainers behviour, their attitude and pedagogial orientation has been discussed at length with special focus on sensitivity training experiences and group dynamics with live cases and meaningful illustrations."

Deepak Bharara,
Director-Corporate HR,
Lanco Infratech Limited

"A serious and in depth work that connects the reader with the quest of unfolding oneself. The book is supported by cases and several life examples of small group encounter learning.
I am sure the book will be read by all those who are interested in art and science of Human Process Training."

Kirpal Singh,
Former President ISABS,
Director Kirpal Associate New Delhi

"This is a signature contribution on T-Group relevance and the 'process of Becoming 'with specific focus on entrepreneurship. It is a unique blend of research , case studies, theory and is deftly woven with life journeys' of individuals and also dealing with complex issues of self concept, identity and self image. This is going to be of immense benefit to process learners and practitioners, as well as individuals interested in their own personal growth from any field."

Sudhir Kumar Aggarwal
General Manager SAIL and Regional Coordinator ISABS

"This is an incredible piece of work by the author that blends oriental overtones with extensive research covering more than 250 Indian trainers from diverse background assessing their training styles, self image and their pedagogical preferences with several live cases. Group dynamics training for impacting change has been the focal point of the book."

Rita Sengupta Director BS,
National Institute of Entrepreneurship and
Small Business Development (NIESBUD),
MSME Govt of Inida.

Contents

Prologue

Human Process and Group Dynamics Training

Origin

The human process laboratory has been synonymous to T group training. That was launched quite some time back and is rooted with history of NTL training initiative. It may be interesting to note that concept of group dynamics training was born with its own branding of personal growth laboratory during early seventies. Later, it was taken to professional development support programme under the banner of ISABS[1]. It was a newly born baby with active collaborations of selected few professionals of those days (Somanth, Pulin, Dharni, Udai, Francis and Ishwar Dayal, Prayag and Abad Ahmad). They had gone to attend the NTL conference at Bethel USA. After their return from USA they

[1] Indian society of Applied Behavioural science

launched something similar model of group dynamics training in India. Founding international leaders of such a group centric training called it as group training or training groups.

"NTL's history began with the vision of Kurt Lewin, founder of modern social psychology. In 1946, Lewin, then Director of MIT's Research Center for Group Dynamics, concluded from his experiences that increased awareness of self and others could be accomplished through facilitated group dialogue in Training Groups (or T-Groups) that advocates open-minded appreciation and inclusion of differences. Lewin also concluded that T-Groups who learned by experience, rather than lecture and reading, provided high potential for diagnostic study, evaluation and, most important, for changing behaviors[2].

As stated above, they coined an important method of adult learning that was discovered during their first conference and it needed further development. This was action-research at its best. It was during 1947 as per document of NTL[3] bulletin, clinical psychologists were added to the staff to help persons experiencing stress in the training groups (later it was called T Groups). T group thus became acronym to *training groups* and got its own credibility as a brand due to special 'human interaction and process centric focus'. It was a clear Inter-play of group dynamics that could drive a person towards working on clinical issues as well. It was thus known in India as personal growth laboratory (P G lab) in early days. It was different than normal clinical mode of handling group behavior and help confront group dynamics to address interpersonal issues and self related issues.

Pulin Garg being very strong with clinical background, made strong impact on its branding with different focus who later departed from ISABS during seventy nine and created separate organizational identity. ISABS maintained its core on human process focus with less of clinical design. Thus training group (t-group) survived as the key domain of group dynamics training despite the fact that group dynamics training has been addressed even without any T group approach in different parts of the world. The book has been the outcome of several such small group experiences of T group facilitators that has been placed in to a multitude of collective cognitive mapping chapter in the first section of the book.

---

[2] Extracted from www.NTLInstitute.org

[3] NTL Bulletin has printed detailed history of what made T-group term gain its popularity over the years.

Human Process

The word human process has generally been characterized by the typical 'chemistry' of human interactional pattern in a group setting. What and how human beings tend to relate and what do they say, why and how do they build a tentative or sustained social or emotional relationship during a group work setting in a given learning environment.

Duality of 'content and process' is very important in a learning environment. Organisations, very often, see it in a dichotomy. That is very unfortunate. It can not be seen separately, rather both are closely inter-related and interdependent to each other. Organisation process therefore demands clarity of such an interplay while moving in to its growth curve and change programme. The emphasis on content shows the thrust on what is to be done rather than how things are to be done. Udai[4] (2002) made elaborate analysis on concept of process dwelling the difference between 'what and how' part of group behvaviour. Thus process was concerned with overall dynamics which underlie most of the content and question of changes. The process also relates to individual awareness of various aspects of one's personal life that are directly concerned with self actualization and effort in pursuing those goals. There could be several levels of process clarity that need understanding during group work. Udai has discussed in detail on various facets. *"It may be an existential process–person centric, interperson–empathatic process, role-coping process, group–evolution process, intergroup–collaborative process, organization-decision making process and environmental process and community–social awareness process. It also raises concerns of value process. Society, in general, holds key of several organizations that are engaged in social change and development. Most often, it has been noted that poor awareness to social processes would impact the very survival of such organizations' existence".* Therefore, sense of social responsibility has emerged as an area of critical concern in today's context at organizational level.

It is strongly believed that our sensitivity and clarity of human process would add value to our interpersonal and social competencies as a trainer and facilitator. The dilemma for many trainers have been -at what level they should work and how far they move forward in building process diagnostic skill in addition to other facilitative competencies. It does

---

[4] Udai Pareek, 'Process the neglected Dimensions in the organisations' ed. Brick of foundation published by ISABS 2002

demand confronting one self, learning to accept and define one's goal and value. The book has gone in to detailed analysis of small group setting where several trainers and participants' self disclosure of their respective 'learning journal' have made a difference to meaning of trainers growth. The self acceptance and authenticity suggests you to be yourself while being a trainer of T-group. Thus first section of the book offers touch stone of be yourself–the person. Dharni's significant contribution has made detailed analysis on observation dimension prescribing *'what to observe in the group-content and process'. The first section of the book does steer us on self exploration process of a person at existential level in an organization.* Of course, I have placed many life cases of old friends and group mates with whom I have worked. Many of them volunteered to disclose their identity and name but quite a few have remained anonymous with names changed in the text[5].

Person, Role and Skills

The structure of the book originates from the history of one's quest of being and becoming a person. It suggests that in order to be a trainer or guru in whatever field of specialization one belongs to, they need to go for relentless search for learning and education. Veterans[6] have arrived not because of age but due to their quest for learning and striving hard work as a trainer. The book presents a piece of aggregated self-exploration of the author while working with small groups in India.

I guess I began the project of writing on the theme from 2003 and completed this project in present format in almost more than seven years. It was my sheer lethargy and too many things on my hand. The note therefore elucidates cases of several small group work led by experienced T group trainers in addition to my own. Therefore, Cognitive mapping drawn by several learners on personal existential process would highlight the clarity of being yourself. "What is different about you than others that equips you to act as an effective T group trainer I have put myself

[5] Section one also contains author's own entrepreneurial struggle in search his freedom to be.

[6] Indian Veterans Prof Ishwar Dayal, Udai Pareek, Somnath chattopadhaya, Abad Ahmed, Gourango Chatopadhyay, Dharni Sinha, TV Rao and many others (whose names may not find place due to economy of space at this juncture) in the field of applied be-hvaioural science and group dynamics training have done great deal of work with their theories and research at different point of time in various areas of their operation.

on mat with self exploration while examining my goal congruence." The extensive analysis of case study would take us to deeper clarity of human process at existential level and role centric coping process. Role and skills are equally important for a T group trainer having chosen to step in to such a profession though each person brings a different learning climate in the group. Of course there is evidence of growing desire to be authentic as a trainer all around us in the emerging popular culture of T group setting. In pursuit of professional excellence the dichotomy of the trainer as a person and his skills are equally important to impact the change process

The person–being, his inner clarity and growth issues would decide the nature of group dynamics. Case analysis, therefore, offers a variety of intense moments on related aspects. Professional development approach by professional bodies like ISABS and others are generally seen as a *skill building programme* rather than building a person that he or she is meant to be. The person, role and one's skills are integral to impact making process. Controversy and debate at several point of time has not changed the document of PDP[7] in content but process and dynamics has undergone a sea change due to new breed of trainers taking over front seat and those who founded have gone in hybernation[8]. What I mean here is the person–the trainer matters more than the rules and guidelines laid by a system for small group training. There is a strong need to revisit news concerns of behavioural change programmes. The book does not elaborate on related issues but makes a provocative analysis at several places that may need attention. I have not discussed the organizational issues and its perspectives that has been the breeding ground for large number of Indian process trainers in the country over the years. But trainers in general, their modalities and styles have touched the foundation of the book impacting behavioral change programme through group dynamics training. The chapter on 'Freedom to be' in the section one has placed limited case examples but the depth of analytical support of ISABS secondary data base of early stage makes an interesting

[7] Professional development programme (pdp) document of ISABS has clear design of what to cover in a given phase of learning programme.

[8] Somanth and Deepankar Roy have done extensive work during late eighties but have kept themselves away from the organizational role relationship and its impacting process for quite sometime. Effort to streamline the professional excellence has already begun over the years. Uma Jain's initiative in this regard deserves mention. ISABS has also launched separate modular programme on organization development bringing freshness and varieties to the organization.

revelation. We know that many are in the race of seeking freedom as viable career pursuit of trainer consulting path. Ironically, word freedom is a misunderstood and misplaced notion for many.

What makes me a group facilitator or trainer?

"Freedom exists in self restraint. In human society there are rules and an order by which we live and work. There is rhythm and reason, direction and purpose. Thus running away from responsibilities is not freedom". When all is said and done the freedom[9] needs to be determined by our values, ethics and code of conduct and finally our mental outlook and state of being. Many people hold several roles from organizational point of view or otherwise as a group dynamics and human process trainer. How much we are sensitive and responsive of our roles is a matter of introspection.

The section two describes 'what makes you as a trainer'. The skills' as group dynamics trainer would largely depend on the diagonostic or observational skills blended with clarity of process dynamics. The seemingly inexorable rise of human process labs in India in recent past has created mass production of T group trainers. Of course the growing demand with corporate and social sector has yet to make full utility of its relevance and merit. Eventually trainers identity, his authority to influence, and power of being may place a new horizon of skills expected of a trainer. There is a growing belief that every body need not step into the T group profession. Learning to learn and your sense of satisfaction for what you do or how you do, builds the facilitators' style.

This section also examines in great detail learning style and its blend of eastern and western philosophy approach on learning cycle principle. The deeper analysis of process on self level and description on sensitivity training or T group training was taken up on great length. Author's rich experience and self exploration beyond sensitivity describes an interesting mix of trainers clarity on self and his pursuance on goal.

The multi thematic set of defined competencies or skill of a T group trainer or facilitator has been a matter of debate for quite some time. NTL and many other process organizations have viewed it differently as a cluster of <u>*skill set*</u>. Some of them may be placed as below for our comprehensive understanding.

---

[9] *SGI quarterly-A Budhist forum for peace ,culture and education* july 2011 number 65 PP12-13

Skills	Dimensions	Attributes
1	Interpretive and Intuitive skills	Being observant and diagnostic to the group situation and understand the gravity of group dynamics and its undercurrents
2	Confrontative skill	Ability to share or express any authentic uneasy feeling and maintaining the mutual dignity of the person in a given situation
3	Empathetic and communicative skill	Able to place oneself in others' shoe and feel from others' point of view
4	Sensitive interpersonally and Interpersonally	Understanding individual and group perspectives
5	Elasticity and perseverance	Persevering towards group growth despite setbacks and odds of different emotional nature
6	Balancing and enabling skill	Supportive and enabling skill. By being neutral
7	Innovativeness with skills of handling diversity	Ability to address diverse culture, and styles with innovativeness

Sapt-Gunas of T -Group Trainers

Above *gunas* have been discussed at different level in the book .We have drawn insight from varieties of live experiences and miniature cases. Our vedantic literature has revealed three major *gunas* viz *satwic*, *rajash*, *tamasha*. Above *saptgunas* may be repositioned in multiple ways but in comprehending our roots of self, eventually, the quality of person matters more than skills perse in ultimate race of becoming a trainer. The book has spoken about the dichotomy but that needs more research and extensive longitudinal case studies. That we have not done in process science till date. Now we are ready for that, I guess.

Trainers Self-Image, Methodology And Challenges

The third section combines with extensive research data analysis of more 250 trainers profile scattered all over India. Quantitative research support was taken up to support some of the observation and hypothesis made in first and second section of the book. Quantitative and qualitative blend of the book makes an interesting mix to explain as to how trainers development assumes significance in a backdrop of his skill building process. It was found that self image, choice of method and one's ability to deal with ambiguity encourages him to design and handle unstructured mode of training compared to other mode. T group being highly unstructured mode of learning approach demands greater attention on quality of trainer as a person, his role and professional competencies.

Data was collected from corporate, social and public sector background. Majority of them had T group and process training background. However response of other trainers were collected to gather an insight for comprehensive analysis. Theoretical model propounded by 'Lynton and Pareek (1967)' was reestablished in order to test the hypothesis. Trainer-participant interaction indicated the trainer's interaction with participant presented a different pattern of relationship building that defined quality of trainer being–the person as well. Most often trainers were satisfying their own need than learners' need and professionals growth issues of learners during training, regardless of the feeling and climate of the group. Therefore, *Task oriented trainers* seem to have landed in high content focus of learning climate than addressing the underlying process concerns of T group learning goal.

Group oriented trainers were generally found to be concerned about *participants–participant's* interaction. They would encourage a group to evolve its own culture and norms conducive to their learning. Self oriented trainers were defined as those whose entire focus was on depicting their control and command over the subject, regardless of the need and expectation of the participants. Training styles and interactional pattern has been analyzed to establish a clear relationship between self image, clarity of goal and style. A comparative glimpse of underlying assumptions of trainers from T group and non T group (other schools of behavioural science) background with their belief and manifest behavior would also offer an interesting readings at the concluding part of research summary. Future direction of group dynamics training has also made an interesting insight of the book. Last chapter has taken us towards theoretical and practical issues of T group training supported by review of literature.

Findings of case studies and cognitive analysis of several trainers behavior, their skill and approach has set a foundation of learning on group dynamics and human process issues far beyond T group training. With expanding focus on training institutions at various level and for different purpose the quality of group dynamics trainers, their orientation, mindset and skills assume great significance. The book demands greater sensitivity on their part in order to play a change agent's role in the society with strong commitment and dedication. Training profession may be viewed as a pastime and routine profession. However, there are many who have made it an incredible impact in their work life because of their passion to what they do and clarity of why they are in. My salutations to them.

I am deeply touched by Professor Abad Ahmad Delhi University and Prof. Rajan Gupta, MDI Gurgaon for their patience to read the manuscript in parts and pieces to help me improve the document. It has been painful exercise to read one's own work number of times yet I did it with support of my friend Madhu Sengupta of Saṁskṛiti and his editorial team who extended their unabiding interest to publish the same with IDMAT. There are many colleagues of mine from ISABS fraternity who have contributed their input in making my work complete.

I have acknowledged their input and placed their contributions but there are many whose names could not appear in the manuscript-my children, Kusum my wife and my lovely grand children Annanya, Manya, Tanya, they have taught me to drive on the turbulent path of my life and enabled me to complete the task. Their association has repaired the cracks and holes of the life with renewed energy and vigor. The journey continues in the quest of my being. I feel I could have done better.

Nagendra
Jan. 2012

SECTION – I

What Makes Me A Full Person - The Quest of Being

World may call me a Facilitator or a trainer associated in any field of development but my quest of being is unending. My willingness to learn as I interact with every new group has set a strong learning foundation of my life...Yet I have miles to go before I become a full person.'

Chapter-I

Quest of Being – A Journey Within

Where the mind is without fear and head is held high
Where the knowledge is free
Where the world has not been broken into fragments by narrow
Domestic walls….
Where clear streams of reasons has not lost its way in to dreary
desert sand of bad habits in to heavens of freedom..

Ravindra Nath Tagore (Religion of Man: London 1961 P.105)

"The self is never born. It never dies either; having been born it never ceases to be again. Unborn eternal and everlasting self stays in your identity that is not slain when the body is slain."

Bhagavad Gita (chapter2:20)

EVOLUTION

Eastern philosophy never differs on the moot point that individual's *karma* is the most significant essence of one's being. Therefore, how one can question the death of one's being that is essence of one's *karma* wrapped in one's identity. The transformation of 'the matter—the body' from one shape to another is not beyond the percepts of metaphysics alone. But the impacts of karma of human being is the truth that creates a world of new reality for every individual since each one is different and his karmas are different. One reaps the fruits of the seeds that he sows.

Common behaviour scientific knowledge strongly influenced by western school of thought examines and studies the self purely at behavioural level. The deep process work advocated and practiced by *applied behavioural science professionals from Indian Society for Applied Behavioural Science (ISABS), National Training Laboratories (NTL), many other human process centric professional bodies particularly in India and also in other parts of the world attempt to examine the self at three levels viz. opinionated self, attidinal self and core self that forms the bottom of the self concept and one's overall self-esteem. Of course* it is a very practical and pragmatic commonsense view. History of applied behavioural science is littered with unpaid promissory notes from the basic research of fundamental psychology. But process scientists have made far more counter-intuitive frame of basic research. Cognitive theories have been repelled and human process learners have defined their own cognitive mapping in pursuit of their growth. Layers of self awareness perceptible at three levels and human being's struggle to deal with internal incongruence is dealt with greater intensity that is based on small group work insight by many of the process driven scientists that we know of them in their journey of being; whether they are process trainers, consultants or facilitators occupying multiples roles in their own work life.

But many believe that our identity dies with the body's decay? Body indeed is perishable and it has to decay. How can there be death of actions or deeds that we perform every day. Deeds create an impact, either temporary or permanent. For example, work done by Gandhiji in India or Abraham Lincon in USA has its own impact even today in the society. Tagore's or Mother Teresa's contribution—their deeds or Karma would stay for ever in the heart and mind of people. Of course, imprint of one's Karma (deeds) varies from its nature and the magnitude. The pursuit of psychological analysis by behavioural scientists does not confine to contemporariness of individual action and its immediate impact. Though it may appear to be the word 'action', it is generally understood, in common parlance, a substitute of 'Karma or deeds'[1].

[1] It may appear as borrowed term from Buddhist or Hindu Philosophical doctrines. However, its meaning does not differ whether we call it 'action karma or deeds'.

'Being' Beyond the Body

The search for being the *persona*, has been a matter of in-depth self-examination for those who are inward looking. But those who are outwardlooking, it means nothing. For some, core of the personality is the 'being' or identity is the 'being'. From the ancient times there have been atheist and agnostic thinkers in India and all over the world who denied the existence of any such thing like soul or being after death or after the decay of body. They believe in nothing that can not be perceived by the senses. The law of psychic phenomena[2] has revealed that spirit never dies after the decay of the physical body. Orthodox science or materialistic logical frame of mind that denies the existence of soul as an entity also denies the existence of mind, life or intelligence as distinct from the results of matter, governed by physical forces and chemical actions where death is cessation of life—an inevitable end which all beings come to.

But science fails to answer: 'whether death of conscious life imply the death of physical organs' life? The fact is that cells and tissues have their own life, they do not die immediately after the death of a person. There have been cases where life did exist in its part but whole was dead. Many civilizations preferred to preserve the body intact and safe, with the hope that soul would be back to the body to dwell in after some time. Egyptians had believed that if body is not mutialated soul would dwell in. Thus burial and mummification was also taken as best practice. Essentially, there are two principle factors in the body. The one is mind, another is vibration of *prana* (breathing). It describes the vibratory state of cells and tissues that is governed by the forces of mind. It is a part of physical science doctrine that motion produces motion "How can we maintain that molecular motion of the brain cell that produces consciousness or intelligence? Therefore, ***vedanta*** philosophy teaches that source of consciousness can not be found in matter but stands independent of it. What we call matter is only the medium through which consciousness manifests itself.'[3] Gita reaffirms "as we throw away our old garments and put on new ones, so the living soul after using the body which is gross physical garment, throws it away, which is worn out and moves to new one."

---

[2] Swami Abheyananda, a known thinker and strong follower of swami Vivekananda has profusely quoted Thomas Hudson's work on psychic analysis related to spiritualism. *(Life beyond death, RK Mission 2005)*

[3] Ibid

To me Karma is kind of being one has enveloped within and beyond over the years from the childhood till the death (physical decay of body). Impact of deeds does not decay but looses its vitality and the shape over the passage of time. Our Karma remains like one's deeds and contribution of our lifetime achievements. Logically speaking, having attained the state of being, how can it move to the state of non-being. The concept of 'being and non-being' therefore does not arise.

"I am there forever by my deeds and action
You see it or do not
You feel it or not
Choice is that of your karma"

Statement of a Buddhist monk may be simplified here in a typical group dynamics setting when we pick up revelations of many ISABS professionals through their creative poetic expressions of being[4]. Thus self need not be comprehended as born or not born. The self is not an entity like that. Practically speaking, process learners in pursuit of their mission to work with themselves through small group method or sensitivity training may not be from basic education background of psychology. Most of them, from pure psychological school of background find it difficult to get out of their cognitive frame before they connect with emotive processes of group and one's own behaviour. Emotive process during the small group work demands multiple ways of looking at life or behaviour. Each person may be true in his own way. Yet truth is unkown to others unless person himself discovers what he or she is upto? Why one behaves the way he does? 'Eye of beholder' offers the half truth as others see him. The book has gone far beyond clinical review of human behaviour during small group learning with the psycho-analysis of individual self-identity being the value addition of several case studies and illustrations.

Silent Me

True sensitivity is better expressed in silence than in words. Even when we use words of comfort, they would be effective only if they are rooted in silence. A spiritual approach can help here. When our words stem from the depth of inner silence,

[4] For details see 'Rhythm & Rhymes' (ed.Nagendra Singh) published by ISABS 2004 Delhi. This is written by participants after they went through small group experience.

their eloquence is soothing; it heals. We can experience a communion, a oneness of being that binds us together for no other reason than that we are in each other and both of us are in God.

---Christopher Mendonca

I have seen myself more vivid and crystal clear in my silence. Silence gives me power to reflect and re-examine. I have been most active inside me in my silence than what others see me during my interactive moments.

Seemingly 'self' does not make sound yet it does. It makes so much noise that we stop listening to our own voice. I recall my short community session at NTL work few years back in Bethel, USA. An early morning session in a cross cultural setting.

"It was a great moment to examine my self that I could not do in my normal T–group session. I was so caught up in mundane issues that I have never located the silent little me a great resource with an inward clarity. I need to give pause to my life. Activities have taken over my life, its meaning and purpose of all that I have been engaged in", Henery, General Manager of a USA company shared in the group at the end of the day. Trainers'[5] *ability to deal with silence in a T–group session is considered to be a powerful skill in facilitation process.*

However, meditation, reflections and Dhyana are essentially instruments of self analysis through a guided principle of learning. The silence observed during small group work often becomes a very powerful intervention and also shows milestone for the group journey in terms of self exploration. "*The first day of silence in small group work was so restless and boring but on second and third day such moments became so enriching. I could see myself and go into trans to connect with myself within and examine the feedback that others had given to me", Mona, a professional development group learner shared in her group learning journal at the end of the week*'s experience. I recall a pre-breakfast session that I conducted on ***"listening to you inner voice***" *with an intercultural group of mostly American participants. It was an experience of closed*

---

[5] *I am aware of several of my colleagues in ISABS whose ability to convert silence into powerful learning insights have been remarkable. Example of Late Dharni and Sujits' style of intervention during silence have been classical model for many. Sujit Bhattacharjee's ability to live with groups' silence and move within everyone during that process with remarkable level of empathy and connectivity was an incredible power that he possessed.*

eyes with absolute silence in dhyan mudra (posture of concentration) that made a humming noise on a rhythmic note. It touched the soul of many who attended. The Group was asked to listen noise while they were requested to extend their imagination to move beyond the physical body. It was a step by step, rhythmic and cogent move to reconnect with universe in one's silence. One of them wrote a powerful quote from Bible of Humanity [6] out of his experience after the session was over;

"What a happy age of ours! The soul of the earth is harmonized by telegraph lines united in its present…though the lines of history and its comparison of different eras, it offers a sense of fraternal past." He shared that experience listening had offered the joy of knowing that soul has lived in the same spirit. I am a Christian by birth but I strongly believe that religion is comprised within the realm of spiritual activity but; spiritual activity is not contained within religion", he added.

Let us ask therefore, I told, "Am I the creator of the religion that bind people together in different bundles or am I piece of skeleton with flesh and blood bundled together unwilling and helpless to move out of the bundle to serve the humanity. Can I extend my reach and connect to world within—the subconscious self. Yes I can if I listen to its iner noise."

We fully agree that convergence of self exploration process may reach the doorstep of spirituality. Meaning of self exploration, on a pure rudimentary basis is, it sets a persons inward looking. Thus ability of a person to live with oneself in the moments of group silence brings new insights of self. Most of the poetic insights like the one below has opened new dimensions of self with all authenticity less during our small group process[7] work.

Searching self in silence
A blissful mirrored countenance,
An escastic experience,
Helps one in touch with one
Honestly, candidly, blatantly.

---

[6] Michelet Jules "Bible of Humanity" 1877. Trans Vincenozo Calfa. New York, J W Bouton.

[7] Indian Society for Applied Behavioural Science(ISABS) is strongly focused on small group process work. Its recent publication *(Rhythems and Rymes 2004 op cit)* as compilation of poetic insights of several learners has touched the soul of the author in taking out this piece.

When self with self
Opens, interacts, communicates
Unknown unravels, uncertain ensures:
Unfathomable surfaces,
One reaches out to oneself.

Silence on many occasions
Unbearable and lonely:
Yet one is never empty or lonely
If one is one with one s

Silence entices, attracts, engulfs
Evokes sensitivity
Overwhelms emotions
Invokes self identity
Overpowers commotion
To pregnate and bear self
Share selfcare self and heal self"

Gita a *revered Hindu epic says it very forcefully that "self is eternal, non-ending and all pervasive." In the present book, my attempt is to take you to a selective journey of metaphors on self analysis by different curious learners of life.*

The metaphysics of 'self understanding' need not be viewed as an extraction for religious percepts, nor I intend to do so. The philosophy of 'being' is common in all religion & thus there cannot be any different way of understanding and analysing 'self' from one to another religious frame.

I took pain of reading several reports written by our colleagues and also reviewed the compilation by Mahaveer and Sudhir in addition to other inputs with whom I had worked in their journey of deep process work at the self and group level.

Lonely me

It has been a great experience to examine on the issue of one's loneliness. However, the loneliness has been a very critical issue for many at different stages of one's life. One needs to differentiate between solitude and loneliness, the later is dysfunctional state of being, whereas, former state may remain a productive moment. ***Loneliness is a state where person is***

wrapped up so much with his own self that he pays no attention to how others experience him. I never realized how others become so lonely within until I met Preeti, who worked with me through small group sessions.

Preeti a young lady even after a wonderful happy married life appeared to be a lonely person. She was empty, alone and kept searching for jobs to engage herself after her husband used to go to office. Her 5 months old child was left to her mother-in-law, who enjoyed to being the care taker and satisfy her own quest for love. But Preeti kept changing jobs where she used to be busy but detached, uninvolved and remained anxious and depressed. Priority and planning was adversely affected. She used to be tense and showed her irritation and anguish to peers and could not make a sustained relationship in any of her jobs. At home in a typical joint family atmosphere she was lonely doing her task and nursing the baby, "I am a private person. I love being alone and handle my things by myself. I am very secretive and confidential." Though she was staying with several members of family but she could not build a meaningful relationships with anyone except her own husband and baby. She was choosy in relationship. "I need to go for a long drive, but I can not do it myself. My husband makes fun of me. He treats me as a child and I hate it. I am not a kid that people have built impression about me." She broke into tears and blocked herself. "I do so much in my office but somebody else gets promotion and reward. The boss says that I need to build relations with people not with task alone."

The lonely person finds difficult to locate any solution to his emptiness. He does gets engaged in something that does not satisfy him eventually. It is interesting to note that such a person would look for help passively and express his/her craving for love "*please take me on your lap, I am hungry for love and care. The more I get the more I need. Yet I do not know how to give to myself*", Preeti wrote in her learning journal in a very poetic manner as a powerful discovery of self. The question that she used to ask why the world turns away its back to fill in her insatiable needs. "*Because I never learnt to give to myself nor to others yet kept seeking love and affection all along the life.*"

Somebody told her in the lab "I must salute your husband for being so caring and able to understand your lust for love and attention. I fear what might happen to him after sometime by carrying such a big burden for so many years."

In solitude there is no feeling of deprivation. The person is continuously in touch with himself. He is engrossed within and is in touch with his feelings. He may not need an interaction with others. It is an exhilarating and intense experience to be with oneself so enriching and rewarding. Solitude is self nourishing state whereas loneliness is toxic and self inducing. *Search for a being is a state where one needs to make a paradigm shift from the level of one's emptiness and loneliness. Loneliness also drives a person to a workaholic mindset. Study of several social organizations of repute in course of my diagnostic intervention, has revealed skewed work life imbalance largely for many women and men sucked into the issues that they are engaged with.*

> *Happiness is like a butterfly which, when pursued, is always beyond our grasp, but, if you will sit down quietly, may alight upon you.*
>
> ***Nathaniel Hawthorne***

Me and Parts of me

Of course the 'colour and contours' of one's values and belief may have different religious roots. Philosophy of life and death and understanding of being is common to all. Thus it brings convergence of clarity on me and parts of me[8]. I have not been a student of psychology during my graduation but I loved watching and studying human behaviour. I used to write short stories depicting how people behave in a given situation. I was a science student but enjoyed arts of life and living. Of course, I was a creative guy from a local standard to outsmart many in my class because of my high sensing skills. One day my professor of economics in the university made a stunning remark after seeing my stage play that I had written and directed. "You are misplaced here, better you work on deep human psychological issues through your script and playwrite." "Traditional career is not your world," he added. I was touched but had no guts to take unknown path. I joined Delhi for my master and doctoral work where I had chance of meeting Udai and Prof G C Rai a veteran of educational psychology. They were teaching in department of extension education at IARI, a deemed university of international repute. I fell in love with the subject and no sooner I became the subject of myself. I wanted to chase Udai Pareek who had just moved to Indian Institute of Management, Ahemedabad. I met Pulin, Indira and many others

[8] "Friendship with God"depicts an entertaining reading to support the above.

during my early labs. But turning point of my life goal was after my first experience with Sujit Bhattacharjee. He became my mentor, my guru and role model in my early days. I worked with him in a couple of small group works quite before ISABS offered me the selection lab. There were many friends and colleagues of early days who made great impact in shaping my change process.

I could decipher that inability to recognize one's feelings takes people to disconnected relationship in the group learning setting. Therefore, first task of a person in group learning method is to feel the feelings of oneself and others in order to have empathetic relationship.

Donald Walsch, a noted Christian philosopher and well known author by being friendly with God through conversation and his touching dialogue may take us to a deep memory lane of our deeds and childhood action followed with insightful probing question of 'alter ego' friendly God. If we revisit Gita the well known Hindu epic, **Arjuna's** conversation with **Lord Krishna** closely resembles a similar phenomenon where the impact of relationships on Arjuna with his kith and kin has blocked him to address the present reality of battleground. Lessons drawn from the life meaning based on the childhood experience in a 'T-group' setting or in any encounter group-process learning situation does give a powerful message, of to be or not to be.' Meaning of 'here and now' in transitional process of life defines the reality of present neither past nor future. Thus focus in small group work has been learning from here and now. The impact of 'why do we say, what we say and how we say to each other at what stage of the group life "? Desire to bring changes, therefore, begins from awareness of location as to where do we stand in terms of our relationship with inner and outer world in the present reality. Awareness of present location of self drives us to recognize and own our feelings and behaviour. If we are not aware of our feelings at a given point of time, then we land up in a game of self-denial process. Krishna had to work very hard with Arjuna to help him fight against his learnt self-denial.

"In order to change something, you must first accept that it is there. In order to love something, you must do the same thing…You cannot love the part of yourself that you claim is not there, that you disown. You have disowned many parts of yourself that you do not wish to claim. In disclaiming those parts of yourself, you have made it impossible to totally love yourself—and thus, to totally love another.[9]

---

[9] Ibid

'Search of being is process of discovering me and its part. Owning the full and part of me sets a journey towards inner connectedness. Seeking light is a search for being but it can not happen unless we reduce our inner darkness. Deeds of my child hood are parts of me. Impact that I had on me because of parent's way of relating with me, handling my tantrum and sulking behaviour have become parts of me. Search of being therefore is a process of accepting and holding the parts of me. In the small group experience I had many such moments of my own.

An observer's diary of log book and learners' journal documents makes an interesting revelation.[10]

Nalini went on to her trip on self disclosure. She struggled very hard to stay in touch with group, but continued describing all that had happened to her, what her mother did by scolding, judging and comparing with her elder sister. She was very much on her past trip to describe and explain her behaviour. Group intervened and asked her if she was complaining against her mother for whatever she did to you hence whatever you are doing to your kids. As if sins of the mother were visited upon the daughter. Nalini broke and could connect.

The darkness inside and searching an answer for what she is doing to herself and to the relationship that is being created by her around, is an attempt of a quest for a being—an authentic being. Is Nalini a person who is integrated, aware and able to be in touch with herself and others as well?

Another participant of advance lab, Mahesh writes in his diary that, "*I learnt to deny myself. The first mode of self-denial was my failure to recognize the feelings. Quite often I was unable to accept and hold the same since I did not like to be what it was. Ironically, I disagreed with feedback given by the members in the group – they said I was rigid, frozen, stubborn. I denied, resisted to explore. Others persisted with same feedback time and again. I was wondering why trainer has been after my blood along with many in the group. Is it true what they say about me? It could not be since I had learnt to deny from within, so how could I accept things from outside.*

It took years after I had finished my phase A and was asked to observe a group process. I found my alter ego. She was exactly like me. But she owned what she was going through. She confronted with her inner

[10] Name has been changed to maintain anonymity.

darkness while accepting all that people said. She accepted embraced but disliked to be what it is. It was too late for me to say anything to her since the lab was over. She was my facilitator. I went to my room cried for hours in loneliness. How deceit and conceit I have been. I never accepted certain parts of me and thus became insensitive to myself and to others. I chose not to opt for T group training as career yet I continued my journey for professional development.

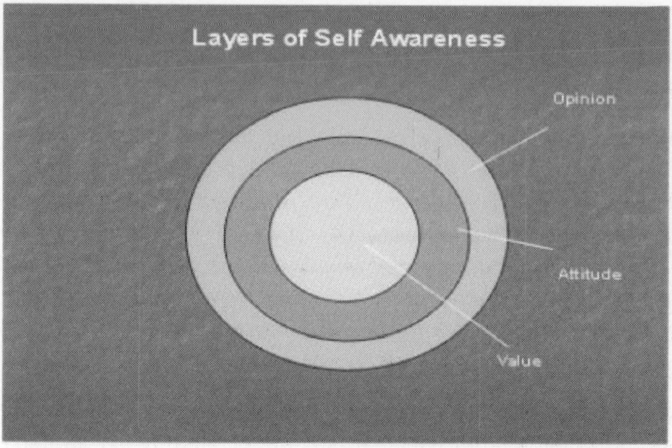

My awareness of being and its multiple facets gave a deeper insight of journey within and beyond. My interactions and intense work with large number of interns and small group members took me to a dive of personal odyssey, giving birth of this book dedicating to process learners of ISABS. *I grew, step by step, from my birth till date. I never realized that I have grown until my yearnings for the growth was felt*. The quest for learning about oneself is central to ISABS professional development program. Many have segued to their new phase of creative self in their struggle to look for their new being. Those who have examined their identity in their growth process, have gone through their identity crisis, search and research process and have come to terms with themselves in a new role relationship. They have hopefully discovered themselves and seen a mirror of new kind. Quest of search and freedom to be what they wanted to be has driven many process learners to the threshold of entrepreneurial of role of relationship in the world of their own. The next chapter begins with exploratory study taken up by the author based on primary and secondary data available with ISABS.

My role as Dean for several years and presidentship of the ISABS—the professional body helped me to pay exclusive attention to related issues that have been bugging my mind for quite sometime. Many of my fellow friends have contributed to my endeavour in their own way. Inspiration from Udai and Rolf at different point of time drove me to take up the task. Initial work of Sudhir and Mahaveer on my request also motivated me to enrich and develop the plan of new book in my search of ***being and becoming***.

Chapter II

In Search of Freedom to be

Many, who attended T-group labs over the years, decided to review their life journey and role relationship within and beyond even in the organization. It is estimated that about 40 percent organizations which nominated their staff to ISABS had a hidden grudge against such training, for not having retained their employees who were groomed towards personal growth process. It was found in our survey that quite a few of the professional members who completed their professional journey and created their own entrepreneurial identity as freelancers have quit their secured organizational role. The paper describes some of the critical concerns and insights on related matter. The questionnaire mode supported by informal interface with selected professional members provided interesting clues to examine my hypothesis. It highlights the quest of entrepreneurial being that many process trainers have displayed. Yet one wonders if it was the strength of process trainers to test themselves or move to their freedom to be? Of course, some of them felt the 'heat' of 'boiling pot'. They could not endure and jumped out to float in an entrepreneurial ocean.

Genesis

I picked up hardly thirty five respondents with the help of T T Srinath who could not pursue the study due to his other priority. Questionnaire were sent to 75 respondents. Only 18 had responded but remaining agreed to fill in during the national event. Thus thirty five professional members including six interns could respond maintaining anonymity. It was discouraging to move further keeping in view the small sample, nevertheless, the compelling need to explore the inner dynamics and my own drive enabled me to complete the task. Of course, research has never been priority for the ISABS as an organization, except for a few who are passionate to talk about without adequate action. I moved with ease at my own pace to expand the quality of interface to complete the analysis and examine hypothesis[11]

Assumptions and Postulates: It seems that search of freedom and liberation from the organizational role has been the compelling concern for people to launch research studies on entrepreneurial identity by many eminent scholars of early days[12]. Let me place it below for self examination and review. Findings of the study, blasted some of the assumptions, despite the limited sample size.

- Greater the process exposure and human sensitivity, lower is the commercial and entrepreneurial acumen.
- Longer the association with process training function through ISABS or otherwise, greater inclination for affiliative and social networking skills.
- Higher the social networking skill, greater is propensity to capitalise on emerging consulting opportunity for training and allied areas with client organisations of ISABS.
- Greater the personal interest goal of process trainers to succeed as freelancer or entrepreneur, lower is their professional association with ISABS and well its being except the occasional linkage.

---

[11] Study was supported by Asian Society for Entrepreneurship Education and Development but ISABS facilitated the data collection process. T T Srinath extended support in the early stage of data collection but got busy on his other priority. (The original version of this paper was published in 'Here and Now' bulletin of ISABS 2010 in two series)

[12] Udai Pareek and Manohar Nadkarni's classic work on related theme gave foundation of redesigning achievement motivational training programme of David Maclleland, particularly the Indian approach. Prayag also made a significant addition on social achievement aspects of training design. Later, *many Indian trainers and known behavioural science motivation trainers drew their strength from ISABS. My professional association with Somnath, Sujit and Nadkarni for several years on testing process of Achievement motivation training Model has a profound impact on my being.*

- Greater the risk orientation and quest for freedom from set organizational role boundaries, higher is compulsion to delink and launch at one's own.
- Process insight and its adequacy through professional recognition by ISABS has opened unknown area of role identity and life space to test their hidden strength with greater grip on locus of control.

Generally speaking, entrepreneurial urge is closely associated with high achievement motivation orientation. Process skill has never been found positively associated with entrepreneurial goal setting behaviours. If we trace the history, Manohar followed by Somnath were the only two freelancers who kept their head high plunged into enterprising role. Both set the learning foundation on entrepreneurial identity. Later, T. V. Rao and others joined the race. History reveals that Akhouri encouraged the reorientation of process trainers on achievement motivation process. It was taken up by several training institutes of eminence. Sujit, Akhouri, Manohar and T.V. Rao along with many other behavioural science trainers made a significant contribution evolving the foundation of identity based cognitive structure through achievement motivation intervention. I recall many ISABS trainers that went through such a course at NIESBUD[13] including Deepankar and Ramesh along with other professional members. Today, they are well known freelancing consultants in the process work. There was little documentary evidence to connect and test our hypothesis on the above. However, we did try to explore the unknown area and verify some of our assumptions.

Several studies were taken up by interns at different points of time to complete their PDP (Professional Development Programme) requirement. Very few could stand as a piece of recognized research document worth mentioning due to paucity of funds and time available to interns earlier. The recent initiative by the ISABS Board to encourage professional members as well as interns has yet to attract people to take up research ventures in depth. Some of the professional members like Prayag, Udai

[13] National Institute of Entrepreneurship and Small Business Development based at Delhi. Dr. Akhouri the then ISABS president and Ex-executive Director Niesbud, encouraged many process trainers to undergo achievement motivation training. I recall having spent sometime in such a training module along with him. Of course many process trainers saw it as new acquired competency. Is it the new acquired competency that a new entrepreneurial opportunity to drive these trained training with brand mileage? I have illustrated the analysis with some examples and cases who have volunteered to offer their response for the study.

and T.V. Rao have tried their best to motivate our team to take research projects of different nature. But we hardly moved an inch due to our visible apathy to innovate[14]. Every new president has been committing himself to push research agenda. I also joined their struggle as a part of presidential fraternity with an appeal to make things happen to promote the movement than what it is. *The paper is an evidence to support our effort to locate the search of identity that people have made in different organizational roles culminating into an entrepreneurial being.*

This awareness of potential danger in such entrepreneurial model suggests a slow degradation and eventual destruction of the enterprise[15]. In a static environment perhaps, such discordance may pass muster, for a while. Some of the trainers felt that setting a company or an enterprise becomes very complex process. Deepankar in his early days spent a few intimate moments of his growth process with me while departing from Engineers India at his mid age career.

He said, "I do not want to come in conflict with my freedom and complexities of managing and handling multiple roles of running an enterprise. I would like to test my flow than to get constricted in other pressure." It was clear choice of being a freelancer and self-employed guy. Uma Jain who spent long innings with public sector and social organization decided to detach herself finally from those boundaries and started operating as a new social entrepreneur breed. Dilemma of being freelancer versus entrepreneur has been visible in many cases. 'I do not have to get in to all that stuff of earning for so many people and get worried to pay cheque to those who work for me. It is too tiring and complex. I do not want to load myself at this juncture of my career, K. K Mehta spoke with a great sense of relief for whatever he has been engaged as process consultant.

But in a rapidly-altering situation, defined by heterogeneity (differences in needs and behaviour of organization constituents), hostility (cut-throat competition, resource shortage), the strain is visible. In this changing scenario, the emergence of the new-age entrepreneur is interesting.

---

[14] Studies on entrepreneurial identity in the early eighties by several social scholars supported the observation that Indians are very good in expanding the tested models of West than to innovate out of their passion. Economist felt a common pattern of developing society whereas psychologists see it as a lurking fear and sense of doubt of its acceptance by others. (Singh Nagendra 1981 "Entrepreneurial Identity", Indian Management 2:3)

[15] *Author has preferred to place his own being into third person than to look at as first person. Many respondents decided to remain anonymous therefore names of professional numbers have been used on selective basis.*

The new-age entrepreneur described as 'opportunistic' is fast outpacing the craftsman. He exhibits breadth of education and training, high social awareness and involvement, a high confidence in dealing with the social environment and an awareness and orientation towards the future. He is a catalyst of change, does not accept the boundaries of structured situations, is able to carry out new combinations, instrumental in discovering new opportunities, all of which make for the uniqueness of the entrepreneurial function.

Selective Cases and Insights

Let me illustrate the case of T. T Srinath whose entrepreneurial goal shifted after his process exposure through ISABS. It is a case of ***an Entrepreneur shifting to New Life Role after Process Insight.***

When I first read parts of David McClelland's (1961) book "The Achieving Society" I was charged by the thought of a small-scale entrepreneur's drive for Self-Employment, as being a consequence of the need to achieve. While getting in touch with the drivers that push a person to self-employment, one realizes, as a research says (Brockhaus–1982), that much of the impetus comes from risk disposition, a sense of self-worth and the need to self-determination. The realization that a job would rob a feeling of fullness that allows an entrepreneur to stray into the world of enterprise creation.

As an entrepreneur authors the enterprise, he quickly realizes that he cannot be separated from it, like 'the dancer from the dance' (Carland – 1988), the two being meshed, and this becomes self-limiting. Small-scale entrepreneurs, particularly the technocrats, the self-styled businessmen and small-scale manufacturers symbolize the 'craftsman' (Smith–1967), narrow in education and training, low in social awareness and certain limitedness in dealing with the environment. This, however, does not take away from them an 'internal-focus', that supersubscribes their character. They are a bundle of conflicts–'men of action and ideas' (Shumpeter–1931), with a desire to take responsibility for their decisions, the desire to own their own business as it offers economic freedom, a reliance on self, a willingness to accept challenges and a need to be their own boss. Against this is often high anxiety, poor organization, bordering on self-destruction at times? In many ways, it is 'an enigma' to many.

From They To Me:

When they start, they do so with a lot of pride, with a sense of hope and a surging need to build and leave a legacy. But in a society characterized by traditional values, they experience status deterioration and a certain psycho-social disequilibrium leading to a situation of depletion of self-esteem. Anger, anxiety contributes to a state of 'retreatism' (Kets De Vries – 1977), reflected as it does in instability. This, thus, leads to a gradual change and virtual transformation of their personality.

Social influences and lack of recognition as the entrepreneur makes his initial foray into the world is tinged with periods of disorientation, without apparent goals, encountering difficulties in acceptance of his ideas, succinctly almost 'deviant' in behaviour. He turns 'reactive'. People often say that his threshold of tolerance is low, his attention span limited and his need for gratification immediate. What is not available as data to all who comment is the bubbling of frustration, largely because of a sense of perceived deprivation in the formative years, a sense of impulsivity, a persistent feeling of dissatisfaction, rejection and powerlessness and forces contributing to an impairment and depreciation of his sense of self-esteem. The preparatory period is thus compromised by authority conflict, difficulty in organizational socialization and predictive job-hopping. The stage is being set to move from being helpless to acting the role of control. The only way of re-establishing contact with his reality, demonstrated by his ability to create meaning is to design his own 'enterprise'. His dealing with the organization is intense. But this very fact of psychological immersion, the key ingredient of initial success leads to a state of dysfunctionality. He becomes autocratic, refuses to delegate, lacks interest in conscious, analytical forms of planning and is often impulsive.

But he is bold, contributing to quickness of action and risk predilection. However, he suffers from an inability to distinguish between operating day-to-day decision-making and more long-term strategic moves. The horizon becomes restricted because of a flaky sense of prioritization spending unequal time on trivia and major strategic requirements. Within the organization, power depends on proximity to him and changing mood swings create an uncertain environment. Subjective and personal criteria becomes a yardstick for measurement and control. There is some role conflict and role ambiguity. Withdrawal or avoidance behaviour and reduction in communication among employees also becomes symptomatic. "Whatever may be the dilemma, there has been impact of process training on my being."

Case Two: Impact of Process On Me and My Role

It was in late eighties that I decided to be at my own. I have been pursuing my entrepreneurial dream for quite some time the right time to venture was not available until I forced myself to jump. It was a short overseas mission that gave me the financial backup to make my plan viable.

My senior colleague Somnath at MDI (Management Development Institute, Gurgaon) and veteran Process trainer and one of the founders of ISABS had great impact on my being in carrying out my new avatar. Of course, he always discouraged me and Deepankar for such a freelancing venture. I took my own independent path after I spent leadership role at EDI Lucknow. Having returned from overseas mission of UN job I quit and started floating. It was a final kick to my secured job.

In order to trace the fire within, let me go back to my journey with ISABS. For more than ten years, I have been on the Board of ISABS at different points of time. I was holding roles of different nature in the given organizational structure of ISABS. The urge to work with myself and the passion to explore new meaning of my life was driven by ISABS provoked by first personal growth lab of 1975 at Bangalore at Hotel Harsha. It was an exhilarating and fascinating experience to walk over the thorny roads of life. It is needless to mention here that the meaning and purpose of my life changed after I became aware of my being. ISABS adolescence during the late 70s was a traumatic experience, but it was refreshing to discover gaining a new lease of my life as I moved on. A search for freedom, autonomy, and independence and counter dependence in changing the contours of role relationship of workplace turned out to be a place of conflict with coexistence of peace and escape. Of course, I kept moving in my workspace from one role to another. Role relationship in the organizational context has been of a varied nature as I grew in my life. I suffered from trauma of abuse and varied tribulations of life at different points of time much before I moved to my entrepreneurial being and I launched an organization of my own with a dream to create my own space of freedom and autonomy and began testing my own urge to excel. I was like a child with creative feats of high order, always wanting to matter by doing something different through arts, poetry, dramatics, etc. Later, I picked up the path of academic excellence. A restless being with creative mindset could not stay with one role at a time in workspace. The organization (ASEED) grew by leaps and bounds and has come to stay with its own identity in the last seventeen years. I have begun fading out with my distinct succession planning process on a painful but rewarding journey. My exposure and work in ISABS has been a driving force in helping me search my identity, re-establish or re-create myself in a new entrepreneurial being. The focus in this compilation is more on how many of us have dealt with themselves and with their peers to address issues beyond task and normal work life as a part of their discovery of new being through ISABS experience.

Fall Out of Process Learning

However, for the craftsman, it is a struggle to grow up. His aversion to structure, his preference for personalized relationships and his reluctance to accept constructive criticism makes growth, with its implicit need for a more sophisticated infra and supra-structure and greater decentralization, increasingly difficult to handle. Hoarding of information, inconsistencies in the day-to-day interpretation of company policies, playing of favourites and refusal or reluctance to let people really know where they stand does not contribute to an efficient and effective organization. Mediocrity, thus, becomes an established norm. Many respondents who have set up their own small company or NGO entity have not proved to be great institution builders. Their effort to launch and set up independent organization has, of course, made an impact of varying degrees. Those who have great commercial acumen have left their focus on process-driven thematic thrust as part of their organization.

"Out of the total 35 respondents, it was felt that the majority felt they were confronting their own identity during their professional development journey. The search for identity was very deep that gave them clarity of goal and new life roles in their work relationship. The most significant outcome was that most wanted to be a free bird. Hence, accepting dominance of authority and redefinition of their relationship to traditional authority system provoked them to take a plunge. But taking a jump without proper planning and supportive mechanism put them in a real soup that they could not deal with inspite of their knowledge of behavioural skills and understanding of self. Therefore, being a successful entrepreneur so far away game plan than to have deep clarity of process skills as a T-group trainer. Many wrote, "I jumped to become what I wanted to be, but failed to stay as an entrepreneur so decided to look for another crutch and alternative jobs having resigned from my early position". Another wrote, "I thought that T-group competency was an added value to my HR skill. So, I jumped

into the consulting market. It was a foolish idea that I found corporate did not look for T-group training for their executive development. Having completed my professional development programme. I choose to delink myself from secured job. Market needed something else. That is, offering* "quick fix" *semi-structural HR intervention.

"I became a loner on my path. As things moved ahead I felt the heat of the run. At times I felt low and started loosing my courage. No sooner, I felt the fear of failure has adversely been impacting me to organize my business plan. Impact of process training helped me to plan and redefine my goal. I started my own firm that works both in social and corporate sector. Today I lead an organisation that has made a brand of its own in social sector with more than 350 employees. We keep testing our mode to make a difference to life and living of the community for whom we are committed. I feel I have to travel quite far and we have miles to go. I am afraid of loosing myself in pursuit of leadership role. Role seems to have taken over me and I am struggling to confront the dualities of me and my role."

Many lacked organizing skills and delicate crafting vision of the new role, but had taken a plunge to be what they wanted to do. Many decided to do only after they completed their other social and family obligations. Risk-taking orientation and its conflict with their values also came into conflict. While the craftsman tends to create a rigid enterprise, the opportunistic entrepreneur creates an adaptive organization. The more drastic type of change is, thus, needed for 'craftsmen' for continued growth and success of the enterprise. Process trainers have the blend of both craftsman and adaptive player. Some of them want to test their power and authority by being independent confronting their inner counter –dependence. Entrepreneur is placed in his rebel syndrome and lives in a relentless testing frame of others' authority. They make use of that for one's own success. Power equation, leveling authority becomes the desired skill for an entreprenuer to excel.

It was an interesting moment of working with Somesh Chadha[16] as a co-trainer who had decided to build his entrepreneurial identity during the late eighties. I was working with him in a lab setting. He shared his fear

[16] Somesh, who is currently a professional member of ISABS, had resigned from a full-time employment to self-employment after he started working with himself in his self-exploration and experimentation. There were many friends that I know had taken the same path, but few could confront so deep within. Prakash was the regional Head of ISABS at Delhi, who had undergone similar process quite early.

of being independent and jumping into an unknown territory of career where everyday is unknown, no fixed remuneration on a regular basis. An intense work with another person on his unfounded fear was being dealt with by Oriel in the group through Gestalt mode. I was co-training with Oriel in that group. The same evening, I found Somesh getting in to his nerves. He found things moving for him. He saw an answer for himself. Of course, it took time for him to branch out but both identity and fear of failure were crippling variables for him to have a breakthrough.

Today, he is one of the leading consultants in NLP, who moved out of any dependency syndrome that used to be his scape goat. I have known almost similar struggle for Pradeep Prakash who owned a manufacturing firm. He has recently decided to wind up the manufacturing unit and give into full pledged process consulting value.

Exhibit: 1. Dimension of process training impacting entrepreneurial skill (N=35)

1.	Gave a clarity of my goal setting.	9.5
2.	Tolerance to deal with uncertaintities and ambiguities.	8.6
3.	Enhanced my risk orientation.	8.4
4.	Enabled my sensitivity toward handling group dynamics as team leadership.	8.1
5.	Built my relations management skill.	6.1
6.	Learnt to synthesise and differentiate content and process issue.	5.9
7.	Added my training competencies.	5.7

Note: Mean rank score as perceived by respondents themselves.

Value addition to entrepreneurial being through process training.

The study revealed that various dimensions of process training attended by ISABS has enriched and added value to entrepreneurial skill. The entrepreneurial being demands higher ability of group handling and team leadership coping with unknown and uncertaintities in the greater tolerance to ambiguities sharpened the focus of entrepreneurial being.

The implication is the need for attainment of a sense of psychological maturity, a willingness to assess personal strengths and weaknesses to master conflict-ridden behaviour and overcome and surpass the problems of the past. Separation from the enterprise in one form or the other is perhaps one alternative for survival. While entrepreneurial spirit is one of the countervailing forces preventing decay, in the final analysis, the price he pays in an emotional sense is also the cause of his self-decline and reasons for a sense of ambivalence from society. Adaptation to the present-day reality and forgoing the legacies of his personal history coupled with self-awareness and insight will engender continued survival of the enterprise by overcoming rigid behaviour and bring greater flexibility in operating modes[17].

Notwithstanding the business idea chosen by potential entrepreneur, the value addition to evolving entrepreneurial being has been very conspicuous. Analysis as eminent for exhibit I reached that process insight helped in goal clarity and risk orientation of proportional. Tolerance to ambiguities and dealing with uncertainties became critical high to impact the new mindset and altitudinal reorientation towards future course of life.

Exhibit:2. Self Perceived Traits of Entrepreneurs and Free-lancers

Entrepreneur	Freelancer
Aggressive	Aggressive
Innovative	Unique & creative
Networking	Networking
Organization planner	Poor planner
Strategic & visionary	Focused and selective
Independent and collaborative	Competitive & independent
High Risk driven	Safe player
Expansive	Limited & choosy

[17] *Brockhaus. R.H.*- (1982) The Psychology of the Entrepreneur – Encyclopedia of Entrepreneurship, Englewood Cliffs – N.J: Prentice Hall *Carland, J.W., Hoy, F, and Carland, J* (1988) – Who is the Entrepreneur, is a question worth asking. American Journal of Small Businesses. *Smith, Norman R.* (1967) The Entrepreneur and His Firm: The Relationship between Type of Man and Type of Company, East Lansing: Michigan State University. *Schumpeter, Joseph A,* (1931) Economic Theory and Entrepreneurial History, Aufl, Munchen Und Leibzig. *Kets De Vries, M.F.R.* (1977), The Entrepreneurial Personality: A Person at Crossroads.

Entrepreneurial Types – Freelancers

Difference between the two is only of a thin line. However, the entrepreneur tries to expand its outreach, network and moves ahead to build organization identity. Freelancers operate within their limit with less ability to copy and deal with the uncertaintities. Study has not differentiated between entrepreneur and freelancers of course, conceptually it does differ. A large number of professionals have seemingly been entrepreneurial type. Their mindset and basic orientation has been to stand out with strong personal goal. Overall, sensitivity of professional members has been, visibly of a high order, so they operate very carefully with each other but in work life they are very often caught up with their own world and own entrepreneurial pursuit beyond ISABS. ISABS as an organization has taken a beating where most of them are busy working for their own, without paying attention to who gave them birth. 'I found it very painful to deal with moments while carrying both responsibilities on my shoulders as a key role holder of ISABS and running my own. Somewhere, it was clashing with my own interest. 'This was not my own view, but quite a few shared such an opinion at different points of time in EB as well. Hence, consulting function of ISABS was often questioned by many either as part-time action or full-time. However, the function has evolved its identity despite clash of interest with members own enterprising goal and organization's given thrust areas. Synergy between the two has not been very comforting experience till date. Entrepreneurial being is a crazy creature. The search for freedom on one hand and concern for economic security versus growth on the other.

An entrepreneur is the one who runs and manages an enterprise of his own; a freelancer never creates an enterprise or any structure. He is a floater and is free to take up any professional service as and when it comes to him. Freelancers do not like to tie their knots with structural entities and organizational responsibilities. They avoid getting caught into norms and boundaries of organizational umbrella. Freelancers have trained their mindset like a wage earner's self-employed consultant who may like to join with other members as a network associate. They also offer their substantial time to ISABS for consulting as and when it seems to them commercially lucrative. I guess idea of hiring full time Director for ISABS, agreed several times by the different Boards, has not seen the day, largely due to such as an unstated fear.

Exhibit: 3. Emergence of Freelancing Pattern over the Years

YEARS	Number of Professional Members	Freelancers%
Until 1980	30	12 FT, (40%) 16 Part-time
1985	45	20 FT 44.4% 18 Part-time
1990	60	27 FT 45% 28 Part-time
1995	87	35 FT 40.2 % 38 Part-time
2000	113	56 FT 44.5 % 41 Part time

Note: Freelancers are defined as those who are neither employed by anyone nor have their own firm. Part-timers are those who are employed, but have also been indulging in freelance consulting job frequently. A study by Srinath and Nagen could not furnish the clear picture of remaining members since many did not respond and we have no data of such a nature that describes the current occupational profile of each member, except their addresses. The current status (2006) of professional members describes more than 125 memberships in full standing. Trend of freelancing might have increased over the years. Of course present economy might discourage a few that has badly hit many training consultants.

Nature of Freelancers and Entrepreneurship:

Studies have shown that many freelancers have moved out of their organizational role boundary after they could work hard through process exposure in search of their identity and good clarity. Majority felt that they had already set their goal to be independent and their entry to ISABS professional journey was a source to strengthen their belief and goal setting process. Some of them confided that they had created a situation of no return with their employers. Employers had invested so much by nominating them to process training programme so many times over the years, but my craze 'to be a master of my own' had driven me to a point of testing my ability and confronting my fears. A senior professional member shared that his early days were full of challenge and creative options ahead of him. "I used to spend my freelancing actions for consulting mission on several grounds by taking leave. The frequent demands by the client and limited freedom available to me had forced me to choose an independent career. Of course, it was a great fun with varieties of jobs on hand. My specialization of T-group, clinic and process job had vast job opportunities. "It was difficult, at the outset, to look for my umbrella support. ISABS by itself gave me a bigger network platform to find avenues to serve my interest. However, as I grew my workplace, tentacles and developed my competency, demand of my services increased. Today, I am hardly available to ISABS National and regional event." A very senior professional member responded in anonymity. Shankar and Sushma appeared to be more adventurous in their journey and launched themselves with clear strategic move from freelancing to setting an enterprise of their own. New alliances and incredible networking relationship with strong professional impact has always made the process trainers to tick. Success of Udai and TV Rao has set a role model to in the current scenario[18]. I found many got inspired by Udai, Somnath and Manohar to step in to such role. However few could keep a balance between organizational secured role and their freelancing mode like late Dharni Sinha and Ishwar Dayal, until their fading stage of ISABS association.

Exhibit: 4. Entrepreneurial Being and their Source of Satisfaction

(N=30)	Variance in Sources of satisfaction	Rank order score
1.	Quest for Freedom	8.5
2.	Unable to cope with org. pressure and boundaries	7.1
3.	Establishing one's identity	6.4
4.	Exploring hidden goal and excellence drive	6.1
5.	Proving one's deviance	5.7
6.	Confronting fear of failure	5.6
7.	Urge to stretch one's limits & take risk	5.1
8.	Testing one's influence and professional power	4.5
9.	Capitalizing on network relation	4.2
10.	Grabing market potential	4.0

Above table indicates an interesting mix of findings. Quest for freedom and inability to cope with pressure and role boundaries in the current

[18] Excerpts from detailed interview, database of different ISABS' President from Viren Sisodia. Report on such an interview is still in a pre-synthesis stage (Nagendra Singh and Viren "walking unknown territory" occasional paper 2009)

organizational frame was found to be the top most rationale to align towards new entrepreneurial role. Supporting source of satisfaction was propelled by the search for achievement goal. Clarity of goal without adequate planning has also put many in the mud. Because achievement planning is closely associated with success of entrepreneurial path. Attainment of goal was possible in case a few of those who did master planning stroke with strategic move. Blend of process skill with content and other competencies made them prove to be different which they wanted to be. Sample size being very small, we may not draw compelling conclusions on the above hypothesis. However, general assumptions on high fear of failure, low business sensing had adverse impact on their entrepreneurial outreach.

Conclusion

The study on entrepreneurial being does not highlight the process of entrepreneurship. It shares the confidence of persons who ventured in search of their freedom to be. The quest for such a journey was a meaningful analysis to examine the underlying psychological assumptions of those who had undergone process training over the years.

A senior professional shared the view that "it was just my quest for freedom to take up freelancing venture in order to move into a process of my own enterprise creation. Some of the members began freelancing at the outset, but later created an enterprise of their own. Sushma Sharma is one of the latest such examples "To me, it was a dream come true the day I began my own venture in the early nineties by floating an organization of my own". She affirmed in an interface. Many think, if they are perceived as a part of the organizational role, it would also hasten the process of stepping into a free and economically recreating role of their choice. But this may prove to be a myth. The person's own inner faith to stand up at one's own is of critical importance. Many of us do not want to get into organizational identity since there are too many things to be handled. Recreating a new role relationship in economic pursuit may not be the area of one's career goal. Yet the concern in search of economic survival for many professional members cannot be ruled out. A growing number of freelancers amongst ISABS membership at an early age may be viewed, more as a quest for freedom than to assume an entrepreneurial role. In my opinion, it is 'not either or' a proposition. There are mixed signals in the current phase of growing passion of ISABS networking.

All of them have become what they wanted to be in their new ***avatar*** *as a so-called certified process trainer. But hopefully their journey is on in quest of their identity. It does not mean that they have, however, addressed all their concerns adequately. No one does it forever. Search for spiritual well being continues to be an ongoing process for those who seem to pursue the process learning goal as a means of their internal transformation and building a meaningful relationship with the environment. The entrepreneurial being has also been a contour for many that has broken the values of well being, ethos with an obsession to personal excellence goal and refrain from service to society beyond ISABS membership. Respectability to each others, equality and dignity of membership might acquire the back seat in order to pursue the individual mileage while using the organizational role. Race towards freelancing has increased, may be for the reasons stated above. What about organizational goal and its system to bring collective success?*

One may experience the eroding values with growing entrepreneurial passion in many organizations. If an organization has done little to contain such human need except encouraging token reward and incentive through consulting function it does not take it further management institute and corporate sector have encouraged intrapreneuring to contain growing needs of individuals. The issue of ISABS is quite different but this book does not intend to go in those details. Every organization keeps breeding entrepreneurial team in its own design. Organisations need to have well guided transparent reward system, guidelines and board must have proper policy frame to encourage the quest for freedom and identity that several stakeholders entertain in their mindset. The inner contradictions of individual and organization goal are generally addressed in a half hearted mode and confidential reward system breeds suspicions and distrust.

Chapter-III

Cognitive Mapping: Insight on Becoming a Person

Concept of cognitive mapping has originated from the analysis of conceptual relationship to emotive processes generated through self exploration. The inner awareness of feeling and attitudinal clarity is strongly rooted to one's values and beliefs. Self concept is appropriately blended by layers of self esteem, self image and attitude that a person has been carrying over for years. Thus cognitive mapping draws a picturesque of self exploration. The foundation of learning comes from inner experience not from external notes. Thus mapping process has been instrumental to picturise one's conceptual frame of growth journey at different points of time in one's life. "Drawing a cognitive map based on experiential learning of personal growth reflects emotional state of being that has roots in one's own conceptual overtones. While writing this, people take into account the feedback that they have received, and also the ideas, thoughts, insights developed on their own". During or after the group work. Present collection has integrated focus on Cognitive Map, Life Goal and Action Plan that has been described in the following frame

Therefore, a Cognitive Map has three elements:

- emotional state of being.
- past behaviour and feedback.
- learning and growth experience.
- resolutions and action defined.

A Cognitive map is how a person feels about himself deep down with a transparency of his own self-knowledge. There is no uniform pattern of developing a road map. Each person makes his own frame and thematic outline. Terms used that have thematic boundaries support the meaning of emotive processes and define underlying assumptions. Therefore each case of self analysis will be unique.

Some authors have termed it as a concept mapping. Concept **mapping** is a type of cognitive map, in this sense, representing a structured process, focused on a topic or construct of interest, involving input from one or more participants, that produces an interpretable pictorial view (concept map) of their ideas and concepts and how these are interrelated. Basically, a concept map is a graphical representation of the structure of knowledge. In the 1960s, Joseph D. Novak at Cornell University began to study the concept mapping technique. His work was based on the theories of David Ausubel who stressed the importance of prior knowledge in being able to learn about new concepts. However, we shall emphasize primarily on cognitive mapping alone in with illustrative insights of those who have gone through process centric professional development programme in their personal growth journey. *Names of the individuals have been changed to maintain the anonymity of the cases. Lessons learnt are clear to understand the cognitive mapping exercise taken by individuals. Review of such cases indicates that majority has taken up simple cognitive mapping technique with depth and understanding. Nobody has done alternative mode of analysis like semantic mapping, semantic networking and intrapsychic cognitive mapping method etc*[19]

Cognitive Domination: A Framework

Cognitive domination has emerged in order to understand an individual being. Emotion, cognition and action are distinct features of analysis. T–group takes special attention on emotive process but limited attention is paid on cognitive frame work. Assumption is that emotion being the

[19] Intrapsychic cognitive maps are defined as an effort to examine the introspective study. These maps provide intrapsychic space in a plural personality, one characterized by multiple principals or sub personalities, each presenting with an associated archetype. Relationships are multiplex in schemata of this sort; those relationships indicated in the map serve to generate deep-level insight that is better served in the absence of precise definition. These are "fuzzy" maps, in that sense, allowing greater freedom for interpretive association.

liquid ingredient appears as a plaster around the cognitive frame that binds the clarity of self towards action. It takes us to the minimum dissonance. Of course theory of cognitive dominance is about the `conscious effort on the part of the person who takes up the task to explain his or her behaviour on cognitive frame. Subhash(2006)[20] attempts to explain that such practice may be seen as a trainer's ability to have cognitive dominance *by theory of shabd*.

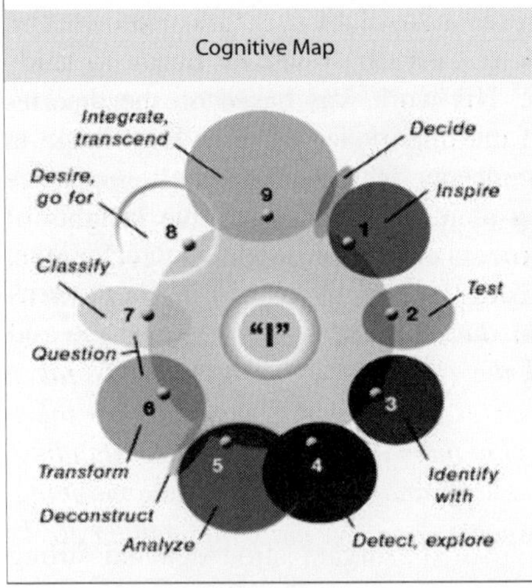

'I' stands for egocentric postion of individual. In process of self exploration towards understanding change and changing location intrapsychically one goes through various stages of analysis.

Inspiring,testing and locating one;s identity moves forward to series of self questioning with desire to change and transcend... The diagrammatic circle defines the multistage cycle of thematic sequence of cognitive mapping .

The above map represents the Gestalt of all nine principals and the "I" (central sphere), acting in unity through the relational self (upper sphere). These maps represent an inner landscape of continuously evolving factors. The representations are static, but the factors so portrayed are not. source:

[20] Subhas Sharma has elaborated the mystical overtone of cognitive frame which very often we in small group process learning prefer to examie ***"why we do what we do"*** ..Formal cognitive input is strongly discouraged, in a typical traditional process learning work that ISABS adopts in the pursuit of deep process work .Though NTL is opposed to such practice. They would like to blend cognitive input every alternative day on regular basis during formal day session along with T–group work carried. It used to be early days of NTL while marathon session of fifteen days lab work used to be the frame of design. Pulin, Garg and Somnath also kept this mode as one of the most sucking and absorbing mode of small group process work in India until late eighties.

"Words do acquire technical jargon to provide power over the learners to dominate. As the word view present the world view, it is necessary to demystify them and reveal the true intent of the jargon or words used" by trainers that is quite common in T–group learning process. Subhash[21] affirms that by constantly re-examining the true intent the nature of dominance can be understood. This may be true in self analysis process both for trainers and for the participants since they are learning concurrently in small group work.

Rationale of Mapping – Applicability and Methods

A Cognitive Map in simple words states ***'who am I' or 'where am I'***. The preference in this collection is on `where I am'; as it connotes. Journey as well as state of being where as ***'who am I'*** lacks journey aspect. The two logical steps to 'where I am' are `how I am here' that is journey up to this point and `where I am going' i.e. intent to travel in future. Each Cognitive Map is unique in its own way and has emotions, issues and growth as the person has experienced. There are some generalisations, which have been made after reading 10 Cognitive Maps. These patterns cover the areas of time, content, growth, emotions, event, space and relationship dimensions.

Usage In Organalysis

The diagnostic exercise taken up in the organization demand strong skills of cognitive sensing by the diagnosticians. These tools give clarity of issues and process impacting the organizational outcome. *As stated Cognitive* ***Mapping is a technique*** *which has been developed over a period of time and through its application has demonstrated its use for Operational Researchers working on a variety of different tasks. These tasks include; providing help with structuring messy or complex data for problem solving, assisting the interview process by increasing understanding and generating agendas, and managing large amounts of qualitative data from documents.*

Whilst Cognitive Mapping is often carried out with individuals on a one to one basis it can be used with groups to support them in problem

[21] Subhas Sharma, Management in New Age, Western Windows and Eastern doors" New age international publishers 2006

solving as well. Cognitive Mapping may be used for a variety of purposes although a "problem" of some sort usually forms the focus of the work. It is a technique used to structure, analyze and make sense of accounts of problems. These accounts can be verbal - for example, presented at an interview, or documentary. Cognitive mapping can be used as a note-taking method during an interview with the problem owner and provides a useful interviewing device if used in this way. Alternatively, it can be used to record transcripts of interviews or other documentary data in a way that promotes analysis, questioning and understanding of the data.

Usage In Self-Analysis

It is interesting to note that more the narrower **time** boundary during cognitive mapping task, higher is the indication of a person on 'here and now' frame. Nevertheless, large time boundary in terms of past & future is not necessarily to be understood otherwise all the time. The **details of volume do** indicate comprehensiveness but at times it may lack process understanding. A brief insight may be reflective of conceptual orientation but may lack visibility of the whole. An **emotional** description is a flow of water or a journey while a conceptual framework is an indicator of stability and clarity of thoughts. A stepwise development indicates a steady **growth** while jumping indicates strong achievement orientation. Significant points indicate presence of milestones and focus the presence or absence of inertia & situational insensitivity. Two models have been developed wherein impact of space occupied by a person has been studied. The space[22] here is defined as a struggle to locate one's moment of pause or speed in self-exploration. The study of space analysis is central to cognitive mapping process.

If we look at the thinking power of mind more scientifically, its layering of information stored over years and years is retrieved in our subconscious mind when body goes to rest during sleep. The desired

[22] The process of self examination does not stop at a level of diagnosis of thought-the mind alone. It goes beyond the emotion and action. But mind being the central one cognitive layer of self is the most powerful one. Physical science tells us that body cells perform duties of continuous segregations in their communion with nervous sytem.at different levels (e.g. kidney functioning, heart functioning etc). If mind is confused, depressed and disturbed information flows down the line to all cells of the body and heart thus our cognitive structure is adversely influenced...Giving space to yourself is giving moments to your mind to search for its data base and help retrieve agenda of your growth logically and intelligently (Swami Sivanada ,'Thought Power' Divine life society publication 2004)

practice of cognitive mapping for self-learning is purely an effort of chetnawastha (conscious stage) to tutor ourselves for being a rational thinker to understand our emotive and physical being.

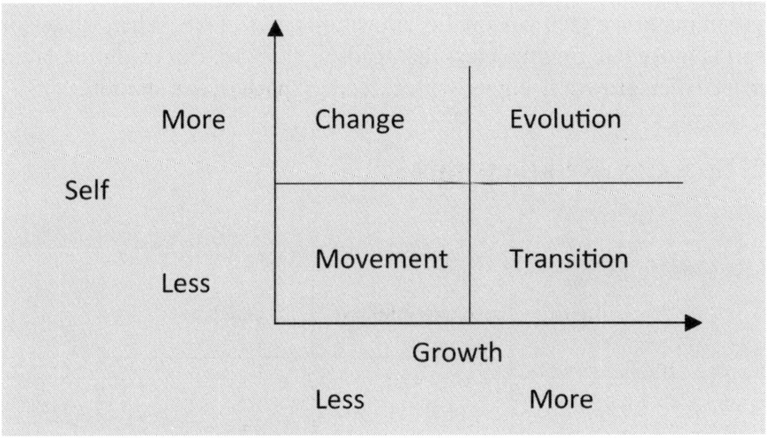

1. Self Space vs. Growth

Let us look at the dichotomy from different perspective of our self-growth.. The concept self-growth has been debated both from Jungian and model I following note with limited research base[23]. I have used the intuitive I bring here vedantic theory to support the analysis, which has strong convergence on self-learning. Space has been defined in the following context the pause and moments to stay with your being. The moments of getting in touch with your being during self discovery process has been coined as self space contrary to action orientation or growth.

1. **Self Space vs. Growth-** It is a process of giving pause to mind to look inwardly than to run for external or other growth avenue.

2. **Self Space vs. Space for Relationships-**It is a process where mind gets so hooked to inward journey than relationship that matters for

[23] Normal thinking consciousness is characterized by dependenance on hopefully provable and observable phenomenon. It holds the patterns of our perceptions and belief. It holds to be selective and information available in this form of consciousness is retrieved and reviewed from the source of its deep layer to describe and understand our manifest and latent behaviour in group life((Jagdish Parikh ,Intuition ,Blackball/IBH 1994) The subconscious mind is always active and has same level of reasoning collated data base but not available to conscious mind unless we build our cognitive competency that learns to connect within at much higher level. Vedantic theory has explained that such competencies are unavailable to common man unless he has deeply awakened spiritually.

social existence gets cracking.

When the space occupied by self is **less** and growth is **less** in that situation the person makes marginal movements but when space for self is **less** but growth is **more** then personality transition takes place. When space for self is **more** but growth is **less** that leads to changes. But evolution takes place when growth is higher with extended space of exploration.

2. Space vs. Relationships

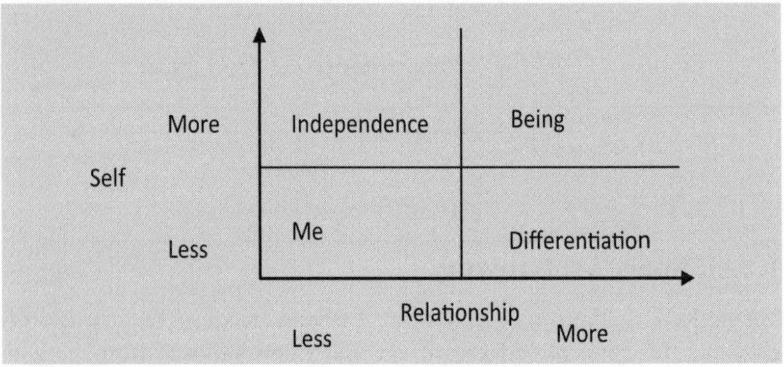

When The space[24] for self is **less** and relationships are **less** then there is search for 'Me'. When self-space is **more** but relationships are **less,** the person looks for independence. If self space is **less** and relationships space is **more** then person looks for differentiation and when both are **more-more** then a person is complete and whole and he lives with his *Whole Being.*

---

[24] The concept of space is very intriguing in the backdrop of self, role and relationship. Space may be viewed here synonym to universe and human's existence and its relationship with the world around him for the time being. As stated above human being does seek a space from his inner and outer universe of relating with the world and, giving space to oneself . Let us visualize our world of coexistence with self and others, where one might not have learnt to relate with the world around but has given enough space to his inner self. Self directed person being introvert gives more space to self but offers little to his relationship with others.

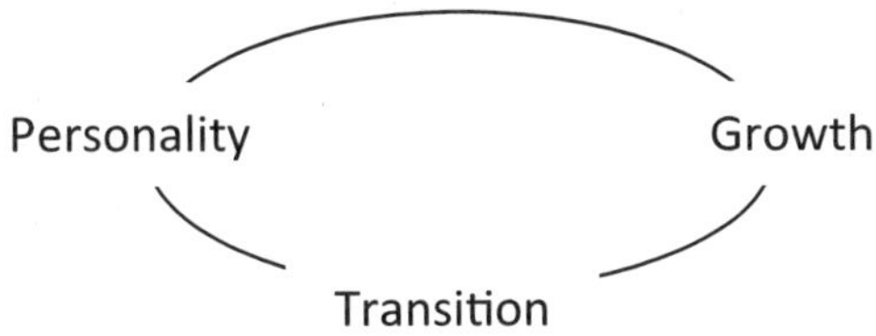

Speed to grow and catch up with the external world is almost synonym to joining the race against time. **A person becomes action and performance centric in order to seek a vertical growth. Psychological transition may not be smooth in spite of growing awareness of the new role expectations, workspace and growth opportunities.**

How can we identify a person's cognitive map?

The data we collect from subconscious self is on same mode like that of conscious one. For example, hearing and listening scans but registers only what it wants to hear rest of goes to deep subconscious like that of store house for no use of conscious mind. Attempt is made in cognitive mapping technique to stimulate the mind's thinking pattern to reorganize the logical understanding of inward journey purely at conscious level and explore its potential impact also on subconscious level on one's emotional self and actions.

"Cognitive mapping techniques aim to provide a tool for revealing peoples' subjective beliefs in a meaningful way so that they can be examined not only by the individual for whom the map is constructed, but also by other individuals and groups. The resultant cognitive map will not represent an entire belief system (this would be impossible) but hopes to portray those beliefs that are held to be most significant by the stakeholders concerned. In this way, valuable knowledge can be entered into the decision-making process that may otherwise remain hidden. Individual decision-makers might be encouraged to reflect on their own, perhaps rather narrow, understanding of a particular problem." Malika's case stated in the introductory frame touches the following as to how crossing the bridge of sorrow is painful but rewarding as well".

An illustrative cognitive description of self

Names of several process learners have been changed in many cases to maintain the privacy. Following persons have worked with me at some point of time or have presented their documents as part of their log work and documentation. Some of them are noted professional members and known process trainers. But few have decided to walk out of the race for joining the trainers's career. Therefore, it appears loosing connectivity from one to another case. Each write up or the case, may not be complete by itself but it does give new insight of one's clarity of cognitive frame with its own originality and freshness.

Case one: Individual's rebirth after death- case of Anie[25]

Anie refused to send the log writing note in spite of our repeated reminders. She was lost and had resigned from her journey to pursue the professional work within ISABS professional development mainstream. Multi stage counseling and mentoring gave a turning point with a gap of many years. I have taken out a piece from her write up that impressed me the most.

The passage below would give us clarity of different depth of a person who '*died*' psychologically and had a rebirth in a small group process work. It was a moment of trauma for a mother when her young daughter deserted her but she was alive, no sooner, than another little baby girl was born in the family. She wrote a couplet during her group process, very clear cognitive frame of person that evolved from her emotional trauma.

"I had lost her after she deserted. I was half dead. Though she came back halfway the midnight. I got up from my comma.I came to my life after she was there around. I seat her out on my laps with grace and dignity. Yet it was not fully alive. Limping and crawling inside the womb of the mother playing inside with food and water it could get from mother's body. Little one newly born was my hope. Though she is not my baby. New baby born in the family of 'sister' she come out from the grave. I was also coming out of the womb of my silence and loneliness obsessed in the world of my task. Malika had collapsed when she discovered after she heard that her daughter had eloped with a boy of a different religion. She

---

[25] *Name of the respondent changed to highlight the case analysis learning* insights sensing delicacy of issues involved.

lost her balance, left her home, and started staying with her only married younger sister. Time passed but she was not in her form. After a couple of months her sister was blessed with a baby girl. She played with her fondled her cajoled her and learnt to live with her joys and tears. A life that took a turn around. She became vibrant, alive and unhooked herself from the past, came out of the grave with a new lease of life

She smiled one day that was the rebirth of a person who was dead some time back lying in her grave", She wrote;

> ***'I am crossing the bridge of sorrow***
> ***Empty with yearning and full of tomorrow'***

This is something very exciting about ISABS an exhilarating experience. A few learn to derive new meaning to their lost life. Where many just do not since they float for many years before they learn to dive and swim across the river of sorrow.

I define my Death in strictest psychological sense as long as I had not come to terms with self. I came to terms with myself. That gave me laying foundation of my rebirth.. Psycho-analysis of *grief work*[26] is fascinating contribution to examine my clarity of process work**.** *It can only be managed by grieving that is what I used to assert. Many call it as a grief work. it is good to experience the pain of loss.* That is a concrete experience.

Analysis of new order: New Birth identity

It is a productive behaviour pretending to be happy and unruffled when your primary identity has suffered the death blow. It will only lengthen the sadness while allowing self to feel that it will dissipate as quickly as possible.. It has been seen in most of the cases selected for this study that catalytic event has given impetus to the turning point.

Catalytic events, as evident from case analysis, have given the new birth identity.

[26] Grief slows you down so you will need more time to do even mundane task. You will go to the period of denial whenever it will reappear. Identifying your losses, sharing your feelings and grieving over them though is absolutely desirable to for preparing you for new lease of life. I wish there was another way. But I have never found one. (Purnima Sinha counseling workshop during 1977 author made a count of lab proceeds with her in early ISABS encounters, Bricks of foundation, ISBAS 2002)

Cases are very intriguing and deep. I could sense that beginning of square of change and departure from death box is a painful but the most rewarding stage. It is worth locating one's catalytic event to enjoy the new lease of life. It is possible if one is alive in his death and be in touch while grieving. Catalytic shocks come from outer source. Say for example many who have been, if I am not disconnected while I am internally driven with my grieving.

I am the subject who is changing within or struggling to change. Catalytic shocks are not from within. In such a case the review and analysis of, Case one, two and case five are very deep and touching. Transitional events have caused more social disruption and blocks of growth. Authors in their log work during professional development struggle have not done justice to the task in many cases. However select cases reveal some meaningful analysis of their cognitive structure evolving out of their emotive process during group work over the years. Attempt to build cognitive mapping is rooted in the emotional count of individuals as they move further to comprehend and understand their process of emotional coping skills and maturity. Clarity of cognitive structure demands deep understanding of intra-personal process in addition to human process sensitivity of the person in small and large group setting.

Case Two: Case of Mohan

Mohan is the changed name of a person who did intense work to locate his own cognitive frame very systematically. However his struggle has posed series of questions in the making of his cognitive being.

"I have been serious, quite, unassuming, practical, matter-of-fact, realistic and a logical person. I like to take responsibility and accomplish my goal with steady focus regardless of difficulties and distractions. I am a dependable person. I am introverted, adaptable and tend to be introspective. The last few years of my life have been one of transition–transition in terms of settling in a new city, transition from a corporate job to being an independent consultant, transition from being dependent (on joint-family support) to becoming self-sufficient. Some of the significant aspects of personal growth over the last few years have been as follows:

1. **Self-confidence:** I have picked up on this quite a bit. When I quit the job and started off on my own, there was a security blanket of about a year's retainer-ship with the organisation. However, over the next

stage of 6-9 months time frame all the projects, which I thought would be the mainstay did not work out favourably. Consequently, I had to quickly adapt myself to the newer opportunities available, which fortunately I could, with support from fellow colleagues and others. Self-confidence is also linked to feeling of security, which in my case manifests in the form of financial security. In this connection, my wife taking up the job and a couple of high value assignments have given a boost to my feeling secure. However, I still do not say that I am totally confident. I look at a 6-month time frame for financial planning and like to have a detailed back up plan.

2. **Fear of Failure:** This has been working positively for me. It results in my working hard and not becoming complacent in activities. The flip side of it is that I do not plunge into high-risk high-return situations. I prefer very calculated risks, where I am clear about the likely damages. The fear of failure also manifests very strongly in the first time anxiety. I go through bouts of anxiety before doing anything for the first time. First few minutes in any inexperienced situation are uncomfortable for me.

3. **Emotions:** Though I am comfortable experiencing the entire spectrum of emotions, I express my anger much more easily than any other emotion. It is also very difficult for me to be demonstrable about my love and care for others, especially grown up people. Here analysing part takes over and I tend to hold back on expressing the same, especially orally and directly to the person concerned. I also hold back appreciation, especially for what I consider not very significant aspects.

4. **Appreciation & Compliments:** It has been difficult for me to receive appreciation and compliments from others, till recently. I tend to underplay my achievement if it is appreciated or undermine its significance rather than accept the appreciation from others as such. I appreciate others only for substantive issues and not just like that. I definitely would like to improve on this aspect since I realise that appreciation has impact on both/all the persons concerned and should not be rigidly seen from my perspective of whether it is worthy in my standards.

5. **Self-disclosure:** I am rather restrained in self-disclosure, especially with people with whom I do not interact frequently.

6. **Relationship:** I prefer few deep relationships than superficial relationship with a lot of people. My concept of relationship is one in which the people in relationship could be mutually complementing and helpful. I do not mind going out of my way to help people with whom I have deeper relationship. At the same time, I do not mind if the person with whom I have a deep relationship does not go out of his way to help me in certain situations. On a few occasions, I help others at my cost. I am not comfortable with this. However, I still tend to do that.
7. **Gratitude:** I sincerely express my gratitude to those who have helped me and my family, during crucial occasions. However, only of late I have started openly acknowledging my sense of gratitude and appreciation to such people. Otherwise my way of expressing gratitude is through actions, reciprocating help, courtesy visits, etc.

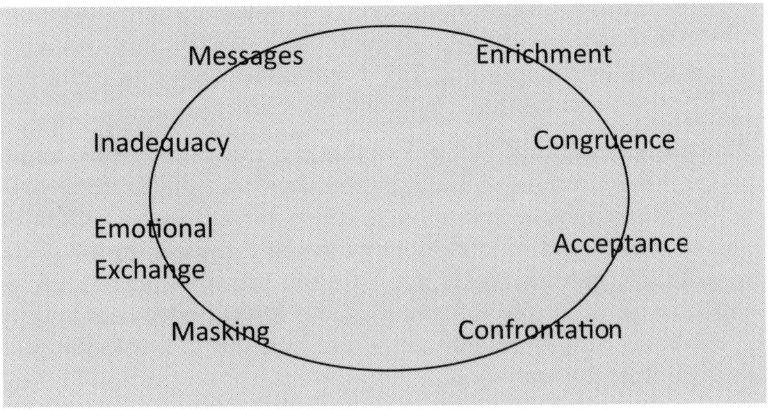

Case Three-Exploring growth process

During my pre-lab setting I had accumulated plenty of stuff from my '*authority sources'*. They were injunctions like 'dos and dont's. This case is quite similar to mine (during my twenties) I do not recall what I wrote on cognitive mapping exercise. But when I read this one I found it a close resemblance with my struggle.[27]. Following case is placed in an analytical mode to highlight as to where the author could have made a difference while placing his authentic understanding on a cognitive map.

[27] Author's (Nagendra Singh) case is presented in this chapter as a piece of structuring his own cognitive mapping.

Injunctions recorded during childhood

Let me jot down some of the significant injunctions of life that impacted my growth process.

- You need to work hard otherwise you would fail.
- Be perfect you need to be controlled at all the times to find the right path.
- You should never be wrong in order to succeed.
- Why you make mistakes again and again after so many instructions and prescriptions.
- You need to show to people–prove your point of view otherwise they will never understand.

If we look at the above it is obvious that self-denial was ingrained and strongly rooted in the person. These messages used to lead to non-acceptance of self in totality, low self-image, self-nagging, fears, and victim–persecutor roles. The dilemma was not of awareness of what has been blocking me, but issue was that of its non-acceptance. This led to self-denial.

Locating positions in the group work

I got in touch with my inadequacy and low self-image and from low self-image in relating with others, comparison, competition, need to prove, jealousy and judgmental behaviours. Value conflict, masking self and then try to be what I am not, anger on self and on others, fear of failure, fear of rejection, fear of unknown were also created. Performance anxieties, helplessness, setting standards, for others and self. Ability to receive love and give love unconditionally is very difficult for me, that's why most of the relations remain on affiliation, recognition or affection level (superficial) love and intimacy needs are not fulfilled which generates felling of loneliness, sadness and vacuum within which is painful.

I also realised how difficult it is for me to enjoy–relax–receive love, warmth and confront authority how nice to sulk and blame. In receiving love the message, was "You do not deserve" and that is why either I started returning immediately to be secure about flow of intimacy in future also, which leads to deprivation and search for people–affection–relations–appreciation and proving to others.

The positive aspects of self were my spontaneity–glow–purity–flow–value for self-growth hard working–disciplined ability to recreate self. In touch with self, my interventions were more corporate and even my anger was functional when I expressed it fully. I was able to confront authority and cope with my fears in touch with self and by acceptance of total being as I am today.

Confronting Authority

I used to experience lots of fear in confronting authority. Fear is that of rejection and failure it is also because of low trust in self-ability to stand without authority's support. Repeat message to be perfect. Out of this fear I do not confront which gives a feeling of being left out, rejected withdrawal so the authority is also not having any choice other than that to reject. As regards the choices, unwillingness to confronting is in any away seating on the fear of rejection only. At times, I also reject myself that needs to be seen as a process of self -rejection and self denial. I got a success experience in second week it also helped me to perceive softer emotions of authoritative figure and saw him as an person not as an authority symbol only. I experienced like receiving–giving affection–sharing–fun–joy appreciating etc. He was not an authority symbol alone. He was a full person.

Rejection and Acceptance-coping with task role

Rejection from other person is rejection of self for me mostly, and then look for acceptance through task was my behavioural pattern.

I got in touch with a small person and a big person within me and acceptance of self in totality with all weakness, doubt, confusions, dilemmas, and vulnerabilities darkness. Accepting is the only way I could help myself to come out of them. Acceptance of task role was a great coping mechanism that I adopted. It gave me a significant move in terms of my quest for self acceptance. Performance of task was giving me a new identity that I was devoid of. So I became a task manager, yet with so much of self doubt and confusion.. I discovered that my root was deeply placed that even task role did not give me self -acceptance that I wanted to have. I had miserable time both in basic and advance group process work. But clarity emerged as to what I have been looking for.

I learnt that looking into data through honest self- exploration and locating multiple choices is a better strategic growth option rather than

rejecting self. Author's shift of this kind has made significant impact in his learning graph. It must have been a painful journey since roots were deep seated.

Confronting self

Dealing with feeling of inadequacy and fear was a challenging agenda for my growth option. It was not enough. There were too many things to be done- all interconnected with each other. My effort to do something for one part used to bring me back to square one again and again. The plethora of issues that blocked my movement from one end to another.

I tried to deal with my feelings of inadequacy–jealousy–anger–need for affection–recognition–performance anxieties–masking self–persecutor–victim roles–authenticity in expressing affection–and receiving affection. To a great extent.

I could do this by loving self and receiving love from different sources and allowing self to be nurtured to improve poor self image and I experienced that a change in self image takes care of many negative feelings and bringing change from internal layers is faster that leads to more permanent change in behaviour.

The path I selected before was rough it used to consume lots of fuel and it was an uncomfortable journey. Now the journey is smooth–comfortable–faster and less fuel consuming.

Commentary[28]**:** ''Above cognitive analysis has been a very powerful way of self presentation on a different frame. ***The ambiguity of issues and confusion to set the priority of growth agenda has always been complex area of self struggle for the learners. Many learners have experienced this during their early human process lab until they reach stage of professional development mainstream. Author's confession of taking long and arduous journey of self growth is a glaring example of this hypothesis. However, it sounds very bookish and heavily loaded with logical bend of mind. The person has done however, solid work of theoretical connectivity with his thought process.''***

---

[28] Late Dharni sinha had sent his commentary on the log note submitted by Nagen (the author) as an editor of the ISABS journal during early eightees (Extracted from personal note of pre edited article)

Case Five: Goal Setting towards Self Growth

I got in touch with myself and used my positive strings, the strength to face life getting in to each struggle and blocks to work on my goal of self–spontaneity. My definition of self-spontaneity used to be grounded in fears and disbelief compared to what it is today. It has been difficult and stupendous task to fill in thoughts with positive vibes that has already stored so much dirt and filth over the years.

Agenda for new image

I used to think of poor me self-image filled in with *jealousy, fear and inadequacy. All toxic feelings were creation of my weak and dirty mind.* Evils collected were transferred to my emotions from the mind hence it was obvious in my action. I had lost my spontaneity. Withdrawal, passivity and tendency to stay in my cocoon was typical overt behaviour visible in me.

Resolutions

Making life more meaningful in each dimension of self enriching in all my roles making them more meaningful, and experiencing completeness of being here and now in each movement.

Disciplining the Thoughts and Sensing the feeling

Ability to see the situation in its completeness perceptual blocks I would like to list down.

My Action Plan

My action plan has been a loose congregation of low self will power as evident below:

1. Making time available by analyzing all the activities and stopping the activities, which are meaningless, and not giving any satisfaction.
2. Experimenting to be with spontaneity in all my roles.
3. Caring for self in all the ways, giving gift to self for which I feel deprived of.
4. Creating new meanings in all the relations and investing in all my roles.
5. I resolved to act firm on my inner change process step by step.

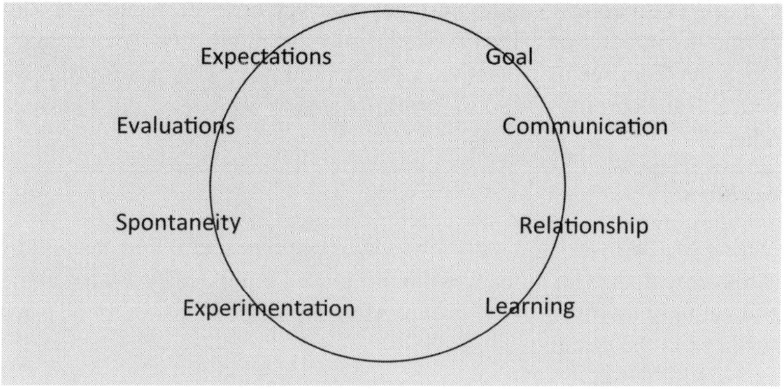

Looking Inside

I had come to Phase `A' with the following expectations: It was a stupendous task to redefine the meaning of role relationship in my growth journey.

1. To learn experientially about feeling and behaviour in intra & inter personal relationship in a group situation.
2. To conceptualise the experiential learning.
3. To link theory & proactive.
4. To attain process skills.

The above expectations have been fairly met during the two weeks lab. The cognitive mapping is indicated in the three areas viz. **Thinking, Feeling & Action**.

Thinking - examining 'self-spontaneity':

I had been working on the issue of "spontaneity versus analytical" and on the first session of the lab, the group was groping in "then & there". My intervention made the group move towards "here & now". All through the two weeks, I experimented with spontaneity & analytical to learn the method of striking a balance. The lab enriched my knowledge & had thrown open a good number of issues and concepts to ponder over. It also raised many pertinent questions in my mind.

The bulk of the feedback was appreciative of my cognitive skills and participation. I was also able to relate my experiences to concepts.

One of the members suggested that I was "certain" in whatever I said during the interactions. This evoked a query in mind "does my certainty block me from seeing others view/or uncertainty?" This is an `issue' on which I am currently working with to enable me to see the views of others.

Feelings:

During the two weeks, mostly I was happy and peaceful with a sense of achievement that learning was taking place. Emotionally I was stable and actively involved in the group. After my self-disclosure, two issues surfaced in the group:

- Anger against people breaking the basic values.
- Fear of losing relationship or something unknown.

As I examined the issues number of questions came up in my mind-.

"What right do I have to impose my value system on others?"
"How do I like/dislike when others impose their value system on me?"
"Can I accept people as they are?"

'Fear' appeared to be a dominant factor & particularly the "fear of losing". My tendency to avoid confrontation in the lab may be due to "fear of rejection" and the strong need for affiliation. I started experimenting with fear by confronting and facing the consequences. There was a definite movement in me and I was able to confront and face confrontation with ease and quick to join back the group with in minutes after an altercation.

Concerns and Journey:

During the two weeks of work within the group, I became close to two of the group members, who highlighted my strong, need for relationships. I also raised pertinent questions like.

Do I come to ISABS to pick up relationships?
Does this hinder my learning process?
Where is the source of my security?

When a member of the group was going thro' catharsis, I had a dilemma, whether to confront her with words or silently communicate my concern. I decided to experiment with silence and later checked with the member whether she picked up my concern. The answer was in the affirmative. It was a learning of communicating concern non-verbally.

During the feedback session, one of the members felt that he was not taken seriously by the group which made me think "can we give feedback and also continue to vibrate concern".

Action:

I sincerely followed the suggestion and systematically recorded the events, observations, experiences, and concepts/issues/learnings every day. I intended to continue this habit. I had the issue of procrastination, which I consciously overcame by writing the diary every evening without fail.

During the lab, I started acting on dealing with issues, like fear of rejection, Spontaneity Vs. Analytical by experimenting in the lab.

Strengths & Weaknesses:

I perceived myself to be a good observer. I also experimented in the lab to observe self, others and the group at the same time. Others perceived me as a caring person, helpful and friendly to others.

I was fairly good in processing and diagnosing the issues of the group. Interviewing and confronting were the areas where I had to concentrate for developing these skills.

Goal:

I shall continue the learning process and seek voluntary retirement from service and take up training activities for helping individuals to understand their feelings/behaviour, build up groups to initiate change in society for better harmonious living.

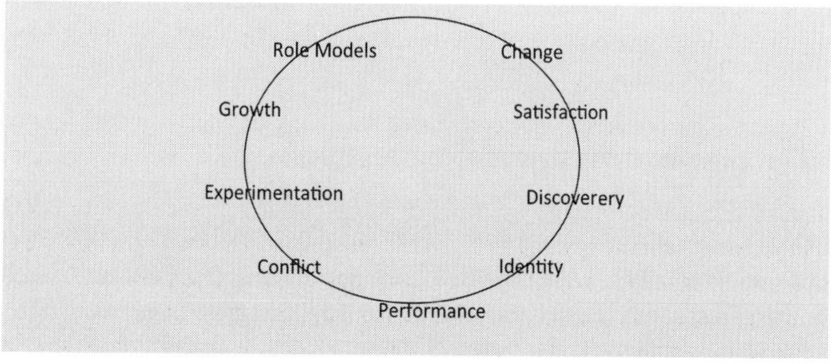

Changing Gears:

My parents moulded my initial growth. It is strongly influenced by my mother. She is an authority figure in my family. She has given me a lot of drive in my life to achieve high in every field.

My father had a strong struggle in his life. He was a self made man, and his fighting spirit had a great impact on me. I learnt a lot by listening to his early life story. My experience with self up to 11th class, is full of love and affection. No failure in life was my achievement of those days. I was a good student and a good sportsman at the same time.

My experience started when I went to college and faced the different world. I was somewhere lost in the crowd, which was not acceptable to me. I fought and made my space to perform. I was not good in studies but I was good in making friends and playing hockey, football, cricket and weight lifting. I could manage to get my identity established in college by getting "college Games Blue" and keeping 1st class in my Engg. Degree.

I started my career in a Steel Plant as Management Trainee (Tech.). I was of 22 years. Young and just completed Engineering Degree. After formal Induction Training I opted and was posted in "Blast Furnace Department" as Mechanical Engineer. I was working with new project *Blast Furnace Complex 7). After start of Blast Furnace–7, I worked in different areas of Blast Furnace Complex. I got two promotions in Blast Furnace department.

During this period, I worked hard. I earned good reputation and experience in both Technical & Administration field. Due to my 8 years of working in Blast Furnace, I experienced a lot of growth & at the same time I became very ambitious for my career. I was treating promotion as my right. During my next promotion, the Steel Plant Management took a policy decision, due to which I was not getting promotion that year.

First time in my career I got concerned about my career growth. I fought for my promotion and I got my promotion in time.

Then I decided to change my field of work. I got a chance to join HRD Department. In the year 1992, I was posted in HRD. I got my next promotion in 1994 in HRD only. I consider coming from Blast Furnace to HRD as a real radial movement for my career. I have seen three vertical movements in my career. But big radial movement I experienced after coming to HRD. If I look at my career, I am feeling satisfied within

2 years of my initial working. After starting in Blast Furnace–7 and running it successfully, I got more confidence in myself. I became much more independent in the next 4 years. This independence had created problems in my working. I had a lot of conflict with my bosses earlier and ultimately I changed my department and I joined HRD. After joining HRD, I am finding myself very much suitable person for this job. I became tutor for four Training Modules and I have discovered myself a different person, in the last three years. I have experienced real growth in my career in the last three years. I am now a very much respectable individual. I have proved myself in this new field.

Now I am able to devote more time to my family. I have two sons and I am finding myself much more satisfied in my family life. Now I am 35 years old and I am looking for some more inputs in HRD field. After getting more exposure in HRD, I will go back to Blast Furnace department and I will try to work differently.

Cycle of me

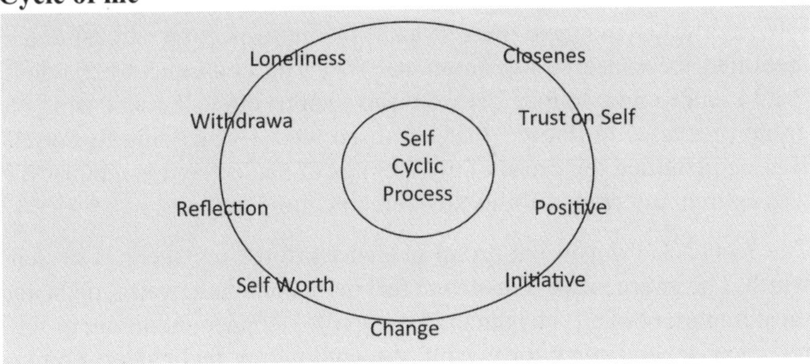

<u>Commentary</u>[29]: The self cycle is rooted on several assumptions and conclusions made with limited substance with internal self exploration. The authenticity of the author is quite high. However, content orientation of mapping is more than process stint." Cyclic process of activity orientation has been visible in the emerging cognitive structure of the case author. However the self descriptive mode of the author is quite similar to the earlier one.

[29] The comment from annoymous facilitator on log work is placed for reader's reflection on quality of cognitive mapping.

Case Five-Discovering Me

My emotional state at the time of attending Phase I was one of withdrawal, self-negation, loneliness, rebelliousness and self-pity which directly or indirectly affected my interpersonal relationships. Although consciously I did not want to be distant from people, I found in me a block, which prevented me from being close to people. I often wondered why people did not like me. I did not see anything seriously wrong with me. This question would haunt me. I would try to get close to others–feel inadequate–stay away–feel sorry for myself–blame others. This vicious circle had become a part of me and my vision had become limited that I did not see beyond.

After going through Phase-I, I realised the futility of feeling the way I did. I was shocked (Pleasantly though) when I realised my negative feelings towards self and feelings of inadequacy leading to lack of self-confidence were nothing more than `man made feelings'–a self fulfilling prophesy.

I have always indulged in self-analysis, introspection etc. and had identified the cause of my emotional state and consequent behaviour. But I seem to find no way out from this vicious circle. I was during the group processes in Phase I that I realised what I was doing to myself. Having identified the cause of my feelings of neglect and inadequacy, it was entirely my responsibility to overcome these feelings.

The feedback I got in the group helped reinforce my feelings of self-worth. The entire process made me feel more confidant, warm, open and most important of all, I began to like myself. I stopped indulging in self-rejection, feeling sorry for myself, discounting my feelings or jumping to conclusions about people.

When I reflect back I can visibly see the change I brought about in myself. Thereafter a new chapter of my life began and I made determined efforts not to allow myself to slip. I began taking more risks and initiative both professionally as well as in relating to others. I began to realise that these were negative autosuggestions, which had prevented me from building effective relationship with people. When I began looking at life, people and myself more positively, I found it very natural to come close to others. It did not require much effort. I began enjoying others and myself the way I had never done before. My family, friends, colleagues noticed a marked change in me–from an inhibited, rebellious, self-rejecting person to a more spontaneous, confident, open and authentic person.

Another characteristic change I found in myself was my dependence on structure, order, rehearsing etc. was gradually decreasing. I could face unexpected situations and improvise in the face of an emergency. In the work situation there was a marked change in relation to my taking lectures in our training programmes. While earlier I could leave no stone unturned to prepare my lecture really well, plan and rehearse it; I later began to trust myself and my abilities. Shortly after attending Phase-I, I was involved in a training programme in Goa. I recall feeling different in many ways. Predominately, my involvement was to a greater extent and there was no fear of failure. I enjoyed that programme. The fear and dread of not being accepted by others gradually gave way to accepting others and myself. Behaviorally, I found myself expressing my thoughts and feelings, for instance in meetings, discussions etc. now, I do no think-rethink and rephrase, before speaking.

It is amazing, but after I have begun accepting myself, I find I'm so much closer to my family and friends, I receive more positive feedback. When I received positive strokes earlier, my typical reaction was either to refute it outright and if not, I would debate in my mind/ask searching questions before accepting such feedback. I could never gracefully accept a compliment.

Being able to accept positive feedback now, reciprocating similar feelings requires little effort. At the same time I find it is very natural to be able to express negative feelings to people when I can express positive feelings.

Where Am I?

This is how I felt when I came to Phase II. But I was aware of many more emotional problems which I needed to sort out. My two major concerns were those of need for love and acceptance and secondly my high need to control.

I also realised in the group that I experience guilt feelings when I express anger. The genesis of this guilt is fear of losing a relationship. I express anger–imagine the other person is hurt, feel guilty about hurting him and try to make up/feel sorry. When this behaviour was analysed in the group I became aware of my need for acceptance, love and recognition. I also realised that my inability to live with my feelings of guilt, hurt etc. would make me swiftly change in pleasing the person, I believed I had hurt.

I have been concerned about another issue, which I did work on, in the group. I find a discrepancy between my intention and feeling, and my overt behaviour. This causes a lot of misunderstanding in relationships. For instance when I am not feeling sad or depressed, people perceive me as looking sad. The same goes for other feelings. When I have no intention of being nasty, the tone of my voice is perceived as indicating anger, aggression and so on.

I would like to recognize the gap between my intentions and behaviour. I think this aspect of mine is related to my being perceived as unpredictable. Even people who are close to me, at times fail to understand me and are not sure of my reactions. The life goal exercise gave me further insight into my state of being. I am predominately in the emotional state and relatively low on action and knowledge. I become dysfunctional because the positive and negative aspects in my emotions almost balance as a result of which my entire energy is utilised in moving from positive to negative aspects, leaving me little energy for `doing' or `knowing'.

I knew I was lazy, but the life goal exercise was a starting revelation to me. I have been using my energy in controlling others, being reactive, rebellious, aggressive, abrupt etc. I have decided or rather already begun to underplay these aspects of my personality and spend more energy and time in `doing' and `knowing'.

I have the competence, capacity and initiative to do many things and I have begun doing them, rather, than being pulled down by my laziness. I would like to improve in certain skills like processing and diagnostic skills. I am quite confident in skills like intervention, confrontation and caring.

As far as knowledge is concerned, my proficiency in theories regarding self is quite adequate, but I feel I need to do a lot more work in learning about large systems. I have begun reading on group and large system and plan increasing my span of reading. I am not too sure if I would call the above my life goal. To my mind goals keep changing. However, I am determined to continue looking within myself and analyze how my behaviour affects others, be more warm towards people and develop skills and increase my knowledge for becoming an effective trainer.

What I have mentioned above pertains largely to me vis-à-vis others. Although these are very crucial aspects for me to look at and change, I have not focused on the single most factor that is of immense importance and that is “ME”.

Here, I am working at myself as a person excluding relationships with others. How I would like to see myself or what I 'd like to become as a person? 'recognized this point repeatedly because what I am today is not because of 'me' but as a result of what I do. In other words, my feeling of self-worth or worthlessness is a direct result of what I do not that I am. While on one hand this makes me want to do things, to achieve and to recognize. When I am appreciated for something, I have done, it gives me a feeling of self worth. But I now recognize that I am beginning to be increasingly dependent on work or task to feel positive towards myself. To that extent I feel I would be nobody if I quit my job.

My work gives me a feeling of security, satisfies my need for recognition, and makes me feel worthwhile as a person. To the extent, that even in my personal life, I feel- it plays a recognized role. I believe that people respect me, love me, and show concern because of what I do.

If I trace the origin of this need, it started when as a child I did not get the recognition or strokes, I needed. The situation as I perceived it was that there were neither positive or negative strokes forthcoming, it was only when I did something, achieved something in terms of task that I got a lot of recognition. It became a patterned behaviour in me and I tried my utmost to be recognized in school, college etc. just to be stroked which to me at that time was synonymous to love and concern.

When I reflect on my behaviour I recognize that the recurrence of my shells of depression and dejection were when I felt I was not doing anything. It's not just keeping busy but doing something useful where I know I'll derive satisfaction. And my satisfaction would explain in terms of being recognized, accepted, and appreciated.

Forgetting self and enhanced dependence

I can see myself so clearly now. My whole being has been so dependent upon others. I have developed various mechanisms to be accepted by others that in the bargain. I forgot myself, that I am a person-an entity with needs and feelings. I discounted my own feelings just to gain acceptance. Or else I rebelled to achieve the same end. The need was always to get attention, I don't think I had a mind of my own (except when I was rebelling) I did not even buy my own clothes something that an adolescent enjoys doing. I believed what others told me would undoubtedly be better. I convinced myself that I was not really interested in deciding about such aspects as dress etc. and would rely on others suggestions. The fact is that I had no faith in myself.

I wanted to get out of my dependence on work. I knew it was a difficult task. I began at it and started accepting myself. It has been a long journey to be able to be oneself but not an insurmountable one.

Let us look at it from pure analytical form. The fact that one would like, at the outset, come to terms with oneself is the process of shedding past identity

Case Five—Flowing Again

My life I picturise as a river with bends, curves, calmness and ripples, turbulence… If I had to broadly place before the other what my life has been like in phases, it would be like I have drawn it.

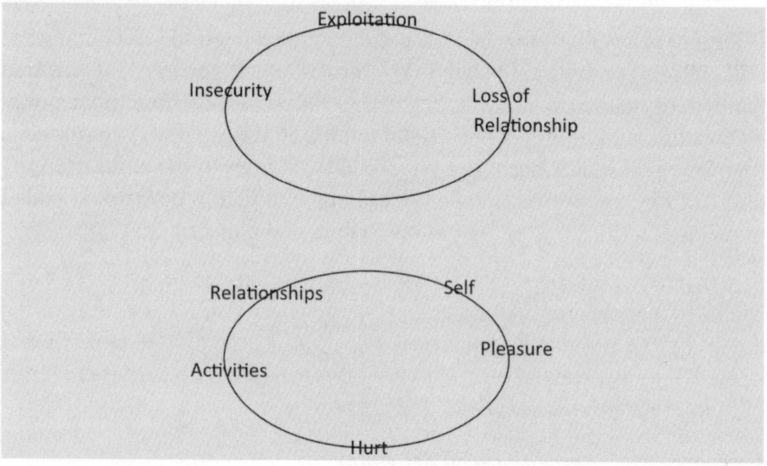

The first 10 years or so, I was discovering… I remember how beautiful and new everything looked to me. I was a curious child, very articulate, very talkative and interested in everything. I have drawn a bridge at the beginning.

"It's the bridge connecting two cities, where I spent the years of my childhood. I remember standing on that bridge early one evening glued to the side and watching the jellyfish float by in the water-beautiful, golden and translucent. I loved plants and trees (we had a lovely garden) and the open and I remember wandering around that side of the island near my house looking at the water and feeling the breeze and seeing the trees. That's how I have a tree in the picture. As our garden was full....

Full of flowers, there were lots of butterflies in the garden. My sister and I once caught many butterflies, some tens of them in different colours and sizes....we were fascinated with them. So we put them in a box. My sister and I promised that day that we would never again catch butterflies or hurt them. I have never since.

Discovering Nurturance and Control

Moments of Joy as a child

I remember discovering the pleasure of the letter A. some moments even today, I can fleetingly get back some of the excitement I felt while learning the alphabet but it is fleeting. My mother taught me to read and write even before I went to school. She taught me arithmetic with cast–off shuttlecocks from the nearby badminton court and the little squiggles next to the shuttlecock are worms… earthworms, big fat ones I remember seeing in our garden when we turned the earth. They look so awful and slimy and marvelous. The indistinct creature near the book is a frog. There were great big fellows of frogs in the garden. I remember once my father hitting one with a stick and the frog wasn't hurt….just hopped away. There is a picture of me and my sister with our plaits, small and shrimpy as we were as children (quite the opposite of how we look today at 41 and 40. It was a lovely companionship I had with her and one of the things in life that have hurt me the most when she stopped speaking to me after I broke up with my husband.. Seven years later, all the bitterness was gone, I called her up one day and she eagerly responded. We are friends again but that closeness of childhood was so special.

My river took a curve as I came to girlhood. That was a vibrant period. I drew, painted, did clay work, read, read a lot of the classics, Russian authors, plays. I even wrote some poetry which I remember, came so spontaneously. Besides the paint-box and brushes, you see on the other side of me, little clay figures of a Victorian maiden, a little horse and another girl and the little squiggles are pots, cups, that kind of thing. And the books. In fact I think I did more serious reading between the ages of 15-20 than I did later till I was 30. I lived and breathed <u>creativity.</u>

Fear of Insecurity

I see clearly the curve my life took after my father's death. I was shattered plagued by insecurity, largely emotional, which I am dealing with even today. I felt pushed rudely into a world that till that time was totally unfamiliar–bank accounts, pension correspondence, form–filling and more form–filling, post office, and dealing with mother's total helplessness to do any of the things because she too was in the same plight. I took up a job, took up another job 3 years later because the whole family depended on me and I just could not afford to be jobless.

The organization, which I joined, was my greatest security over the next 17 years. The financial insecurity also plagued me over 20 years until I had the courage to quit my job and venture into new work at the age of 40. So you see, this phase of my life I think I just existed. There was work, work and more work at the office and in the home. There came a husband whom I married out of this insecurity. The children I had- not one but two–to cement a marriage that had gone wrong in the first place, and financial commitments to the home, to my mother and brothers who were still financially and emotionally dependent on me. I was unhappy and depressed. I fractured an ankle, had urticaria, had sinusitis, tore a foot ligament, fell ill and what was thought to be malaria but wasn't (and with which I was down for a month because I had lost the will to live). Both the children were born by traumatic Caesarean section.

About the age of 30 I began questioning whether this all was life. I didn't know what I wanted but I was beginning to see that I didn't want a husband who lived off me but made me feel guilty in the process, a mother who was cold because I had married of my choice, two kid brothers one of whom got hooked onto drugs when he was 19 and who was a drain on finances and emotion. About this time, I got seriously involved with a younger man, 8 years my junior because he was kind and caring and had time for me when no one else had, accepted me as I was. While exploring my feelings, aim in life, I could no longer continue in the same fashion. My relationship with my husband was seeming intolerable with his constant sexual demands on the one hand and total indifference to me as a person on the other. I asked for a separation to see whether we could recapture some of the love and friendship that seemed to have been there earlier. But he didn't seem to believe in a process of rebuilding the relationship.

With the divorce at the age of 33 opened up a world of more uncertainties social ostracism from flat–owners in the building where I lived, strained and later broken relations with my mother, sister, brothers, who all felt it was such a 'nice man' I was leaving (though the first they got friendly with him was when we separated). I could not take my mother 'ganging' up with my husband and talking ill about me to the children. I took the decision to move out and took a transfer to another region. The cracks in the relationship with the young man began to show up when he also came to the same city and joined me and started being bossy, being exploitative (a pattern, I realise, I had set because of my insecurity, I felt so incapable of doing anything on my own (though) in fact, I was doing so all the years). I began getting attacks of bronchial asthma every year in an unconscious effort to get some love and caring and struggled through illness, the hostility of my children who must have experienced me as a self-centered uncaring person even while I cooked proper meals, cleaned house, earned a living and tried to tell myself that I was being a good mother. But I also experienced an awareness of myself, my thoughts, feelings, ideas, my body and its functions the awareness was painful and constant and exhausting, but I was also interested in myself and in Relationships…I discovered for the first time in my life the joy of friendships because I was always a shy and lonely and self-conscious person: until one day I discovered when I plucked up courage to talk to a girl at the bus stop who she was even more shy than I was and I realised, perhaps that is how it is with most people whom I have experienced as forbidding. (She, the girl, told me I looked haughty and forbidding)

I have rediscovered the joy I have in music and song once again. All problems haven't been solved, despite even acute awareness sometimes. But I have, along with illness, pain and problems, also experienced the joys of singing to myself and acknowledging that I have a lovely voice, for good and loving about myself, made many women friends and find it is so energizing and supportive, this sisterhood of women. I began to draw again 4 years ago, have now began drawing cartoons resumed going to plays (I love theatre.) with my daughters, visit friends, have a good male friend (an ex colleague) with whom the relationship is so delightful, reciprocal with myself and with my daughters, to quit my bank job and work with an NGO. I see my relationship with a man, my friend of the past 2 years, as not fundamental to my existence though I still am grappling with problems of relating to him as a person without loading the relationship with emotional baggage of the past. I feel again the desire to write, to read, to be creative. I see myself, as in the last curve of my river till now, as a lamp too, giving light and warmth to myself, my friends, my children and my home, and trying to keep space for myself without guilt or resentment.

Meaning of life and anguish

Along with these comes a great desire to work with people who like myself are struggling through life unaware or unthinking or uncaring–to work with them and learn with them that powerlessness is largely in the mind, that confrontation need not necessarily mean break- up, and that conflict is not necessarily a bad thing, and that there is more to life than just eating, drinking, holding a job, producing children… Feeling rootless, powerless and incapable of choice- making. I experience anguish at the meaning of life. Who am I where am I going ? What am I doing I would like to work in particular with women because so few women today have emotional support systems, particularly single women. Most women are conditioned to believe that their problems are only theirs. They do not see or experience the strength they can derive from the common and shared life- experiences of women…other women like them. Most are conditioned to think that their life goals end with the kitchen, childcare, service to the family and the acquisition of material goods in a desperate effort to fill up their lives and the fears, anxieties and questions that are the common human experience.

I resumed after 17 years my maiden name with a lot of trepidation fear and, anxiety. This has also been a way of reclaiming one of my disowned selves. The children have been agreeable to it and went along and assumed my maiden name in their names also.

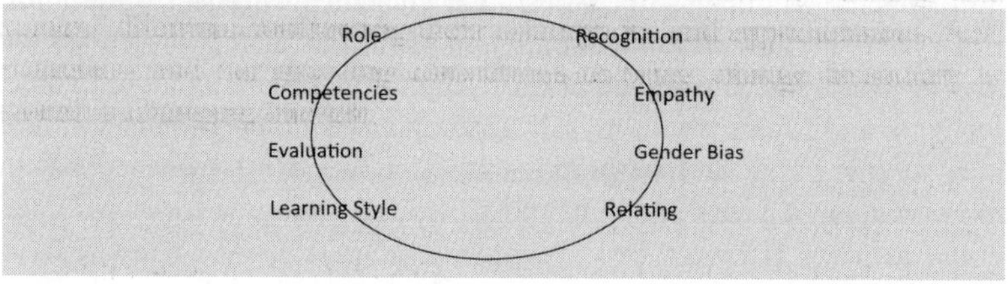

Case Six: Who am I?

And why am I what I am? I have deliberated deeply and intensely on these issues and I have dived deep into the ocean of my personality passing down the various layers, encountering various creatures on the way. Some harmless, some insensate that are dangerous. I am still searching and will but at times I feel I can see the clean spring-water of life, the natural original my self. Which I have been trying today to find and bring to the surface. It has been a long journey to the place where I am standing today. I have passed through a whole range of emotions, I have flown in the brilliant sun shines and have had my feet burnt by the hot sands of emotion but I have been traveling determinedly with my eyes set on my goal.

More of thus later, let us talk of the journey first. Though life accepts no boundaries and like gravity in the vicinity of a black hole, these boundaries coalesce and work around each other would divide this journey in three sections

a. Upto basic human process stage of training (BHP).

b. After BHP to Phase A(Professional development stage entry).

c. After Phase. A.

Basic Human Process (BHP)Lab and phase A naturally being the source spring of (b) and (c) they, form and yet do not form a part of the journey, because for me during these time stood still while I moved on made friends (made a shift to time- space dimension very different from our own)

Entry point of personal growth (Pre- BHP)

Anger and affection, these are the two emotions that shaped my first 33 years of life they pushed me, they pulled me, they created traps for me, they lifted me, whatever it was I was always immersed in them, pulled by them, lost in them and lived with them all the time.

My first major emotional experience of life was when I was 5 or 6. I had been denied some peanuts, which were being given, to my younger sister. I had a tremendous sense of rejection, hurt and consequently a huge typhoon of anger built up inside me. These feelings then stayed with me and eventually I got addicted to them so much so, that I used to create them where they were not available. I think I become an angry young man at the age of five. Since I perceived lack of affection, I began to overcompensate and like Oliver Twist of Charles Dickens began to ask for more and more. When these demands could not be fulfilled I would feel rejected, become full of self-pity and sulk in my very own corner. My attitudes invited negative attention both at school and at home and it became a catch 22 situation, the more I would sulk and not work the more punishment I got and so on and so forth.

Tracing the contours of change

- I felt rejected by my parents and my cousins, I began to reject those relationships.

- I felt a tremendous affection deprivation, became over affectionate to my peers; to the extent of becoming a martyr, in the sense of taking responsibilities for other peoples' mistakes, shielding them at all times. It was a search for affection.
- I was perpetually angry with the world and instead I lost my desire to live. This does not mean I developed a death wish–it just means I gave up all efforts to be involved in life I would eat, sleep and play, but that was it. Nothing more.

At around the age of twelve, two major events occurred in my life, which changed the train of events of my life these were:

a. I read my first book of Ayn Rand, who from then on become the dominating inference in my life.
b. A small incident occurred in the playground, where while playing a game players try to hit others with a ball. I came in first of a friend who had got rapped so that I got hit by the ball instead of him and got hurt in the process

But before going any further. Let me recount what I remember of Ayn Rands hero's (I have not read her for a number of years) they are courageous, competent, self motivated, tremendously self-confident and self contained. Successful with a clear vision of the future which they try to achieve even at the risk of annihilating themselves.

Since I identified so totally with Ayn Rand's heroine's, when the incident narrated above occurred it shook me into my sense and I asked my self for whom am I living my life, for others or for myself? I then decided firmly that I would hence forth live my life for myself and the vision of life that I constructed for myself, which was to have a very important bearing in my later years was "justice for all".

My life changed dramatically after that and I began to win honours in whatever field I entered, be it academics, extra curricular activities, or sports. Subsequently I was made a prefect at school. Being a prefect in a public school is a very heady experience, in the sense you become different from others even to the extent of wearing a separate tie and standing separately at assembly. From that point of my life I began to feel and think that I am unique destined for great things and perhaps superior to others. So by the time I left school some more traits had crystallized in me these were:

a. I am some body special, definitely superior to others around me.

b. I would have a love–hate relationship with any authority figure.

c. I had a compulsive need to seek affection/attention from people around me especially females.

d. I did not need any support from anybody, i.e. could win and fight against the world all alone. A rising out of my feelings of superiority.

e. I began to lose my sensitivity to other peoples' feelings. As is evident, attitudes (c) and (e) are contradictory. Since I could not or would not seek people my need for affection would not be fulfilled and because it would not be fulfilled so I would be miserable. To cover up this misery and self pity I took the help of anger and achievement orientation already present in me. The process probably was

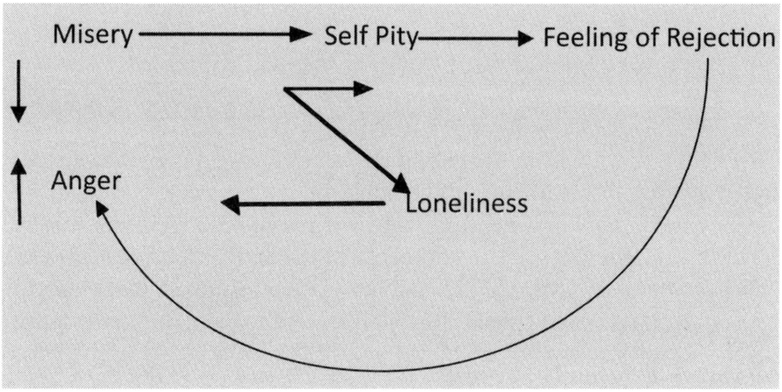

In University

I became an active in student politics taking a lead in agitations, becoming involved in various battles with authorities I became the lone crusader, hitting out at authority in any form. But the major plus point at this time was that my loneliness sparked of my creativity. I begin to write poetry no doubt it was the angry poetry, which was popular in that decade, a form which did not follow any meter or rhyme, but original work non the less. This gave me an enormous sense of satisfaction and purpose.

At this stage of life again two major events occurred which changed the course of my life. First, I discovered I was in love with a girl I knew from childhood unfortunately also I knew she was not from our caste and I knew my father would throw me out of the house if I married her.

Secondly, one day after I reached home, ***disheveled***, after a demonstration where we had severe clash with the police and my father took me apart and explained to me that his was the first generation out of poverty and if ' I did not make something out of myself "he would really not be able to support me.

My sense of anger and rejection boiled over and I decided to take the first job available. Subsequently I moved to a hostel where my sense of loneliness further increased this resolve. Fortunately or unfortunately I was selected in the first service I sat for and entered insurance however by this time I had begun to associate affection with power and hence developed a strong need for power.

After joining service, again to my misery, I discovered that I was not cut out for it. This may have been for the following reasons:

a. I was just another cog in the wheel, which went against my feeling of being special.

b. There was no power associated with the job.

c. As per my perception, there was no intellectual content in the job.

This belief, that I was in the wrong job, combined with the fact that my father artfully threw me out of the house on my marriage and made me create a time–bubble around me where I existed along in my misery, bitterness, anger low self esteem (because I no longer felt I was special) and may be an impotence. This bubble was so exclusive that I did not even let my wife enter it; and my loneliness, began to eat into my guts.

Moving to next level of growth

Time passed and I rose in hierarchy and one day found myself handling HRD for a region in our company. Since by design, no power was associated with the job the contents confused me and made me restless then I was nominated for BHP.*

BHP for me was a unique events I was part of a group inter close relationships and the best thing at that I was feeling affection from the group without anyone expressing it. I almost began to feel that I had returned to the warmth of my mothers' womb. Naturally my innate leadership qualities come to the fore and I at times began to lead the

* BHP or BLHP (Basic lab for human process) is used interchangeably in this book.

group, but the major change was, that, I was doing it with affection a few major events which made a deep impression on my psyche have to be recounted here.

We had two facilitators in our group I perceived that one of them leand towards me and gave me some extra affection, I think subtly I began to play off one against the other until finally one of then asked me why I was playing games with him. That statement shocked me; me playing games? The honest straightforward lone ranger playing games? And to my horror I realized that I was manipulating for the sake of gaining affection.

Secondly, after hearing of my problems, my group suggested a role-play with one of them playing my father. In this, it struck me clearly that I had never expressed affection in any form to me father. The group then suggested that I take a gift to my father, which I did, around the end the facilitators asked each participant to describe the others in one word. One of the members of my group called me'slime'. He may have very well shot me I was against, how could nice, gentle, just, me, be perceived as slime? That made me realise that there were facets in my personality of which I was not really aware of.

Even though in BHP, only one of my major issues the authority issue was partially dealt with, it triggered of there a major search in myself for myself. I began to examine myself and began to try to get in touch with my emotion what precipitated those actions. For example a few months after coming I visited one of my divisions and viciously discussed with the Branch Managers gathered there. But after it was over, I examined the whole issue and discovered that in the guise of giving feedback I was satisfying my need for power. And on that day I understood my anger, I am not saying that I lost my anger, but learnt that I was myself creating it; in the process most of the times I stopped getting angry I also discovered that I was rebelling against authority just for the sake of rebelling ; that while masquerading as a rebel I was actually a conformist at heart ; these discoveries probably resolved my authority issue considerably. Improvement of my relations with my boss and my father probably is a result of that I also began to feel some elements of peace within me, or probably, I began to understand what the meaning of being at peace with myself, could be:

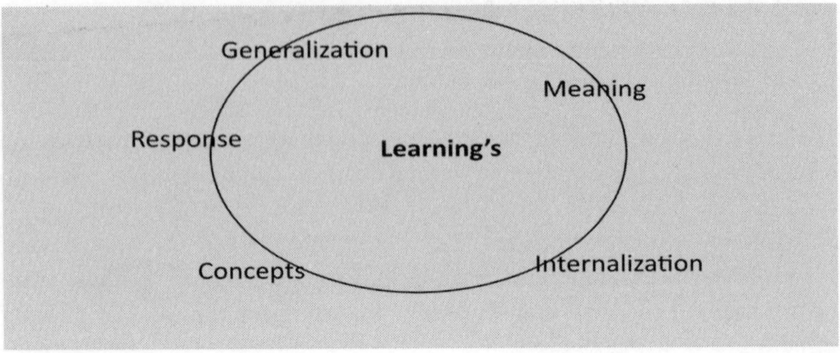

Struggling Ahead

My understanding of my experiences in T-Groups and in real–life situation are generalized by me as my concepts (theories). My knowledge from observation, experience and published theories helps me to generalize (theories) my personal learnings. This conceptualization (generalization), I call as my cognitive map. The changes in the effectiveness and strength of the different components of my cognitive map is indicative of my self-growth or regression.

I understand my life as a series of my experiences. Experience is not what happens to me. It is my response to that environmental stimuli (what happens to me) that impact (penetrate) on me at a given point of time. I also originate stimuli towards others. My creating stimulus comes out in the form of my behaviours (experiences). My stimuli seems to flow from my repertoire of past experiences, my conditioned responses. My responses become stimuli for others. Stimuli are what other people and I speak, express or do and what happens at a point of time in the environment. These stimuli and responses, inter alia, create new experience that sometime confirm me and at some other time confront me, when I am confirmed I feel comfortable and I absorb it. When I am confronted, either I ignore (don't perceive at all- cognitive dissonance) or become uncomfortable. When I become uncomfortable I decide at my cognitive level (thought) either to continue with the 'status quo' (past) or to change, my behaviour (my stimuli and my responses) become different to the aspects of change.

My "self" (the person "I"), in my understanding, has five dimensions.

1. My self- concept, (2) Body, (3) Mind exterior, (4) Mind-Interior, and (5) Spirituality.

2. The core of myself lies in my self-concept, which is the seat of my self-confidence, the source of my energy. This is the center of what do I believe myself of be: whether a significant and an important person–whether a capable-competent and lovable person–whether I have the strength for actions and the potential for growth. These can be positive or negative in any or all of these aspects of self–concept.

3. My "body" comprises my reflexes, senses (seeing, hearing, smelling, tasting, touching, balancing, kinesthetic). It is my appearances; charm (or otherwise), bearing. It is conditioned by my mental (brain) and physical health.

4. My "mind-exterior" does the function of perception and cognitive learning. It identifies my needs, goals and cognitive learning. It identifies my needs, goals my expectations for my satisfaction. It generates motivation, thought processes and feelings. It is reflective of my roles, moods, beliefs and character. I may call it as my psychology in a loose sense.

5. My "mind-interior" is the seat of my memory, knowledge, intelligence, logic intuition and creativity. It generates insights and action-plans. The reinforced learning that takes place here has a futuristic orientation (helps or hinders in future).

6. My "spirituality" refers to my life-goals, meaning of life, values, ethics, wisdom ideas and eternity (unending pursuit of my existence and soul).It is also the seat of my unconscious, "Maya and fantasies." It gives me sometimes myself experiences. My biological clock gives a time dimension to my life.

The model of my cognitive map as conceptualized how do I live viz; the process of my living, my living, my existence. To be existential (to be here and now), I should become aware of the processes of integration going on in these five dimension, among these aspects of my living.

The external stimuli acts on my "body" all the time. My reflexes respond to them and protect me from dangerous (threatening) stimuli. Many of my thoroughly learnt responses also become my reflexes. My senses perceive the stimuli and send them to my "mind-exterior". Selective perception takes place in my mind depending on; the strength (urgency) of my need or past learnings. I immediately create expectations and goals (wants) to satisfy such need. I get motivated to behave in a way that is appropriate to me to achieve the goals or fulfill my expectations. When my needs are satisfied through the behaviour (action), I repeat the behaviour and it becomes my learning. My learnings when repeated become my habit. My habits become my character and belief. If I get satisfaction of my needs I get a positive feeling (joy). If I am unable to satisfy my needs, motivations are frustrated and I get negative feelings (anger, sadness). In both the cases learning takes place. After selective perception, my thought processes create this learning. My mood is decided by my state of feelings depending upon satisfaction of my successive needs. My expectations are regulated by my role. The need is the same but my role decides my expectations. Also, some needs surface and become strong (drive) depending on my roles. All these influence my "body" to respond to the stimuli through my behaviour. My behaviour is always goal–oriented.

The second level of my internal processes is the interaction between my" mind exterior" (M.E.) and "mind interior". (M.E.) ME learnings and feelings go into my M.I from M.E. and processed by intelligence and logical thinking. They are recorded in my memory in two tracks viz; contents and feelings, a part of which becomes my knowledge. Response flows from M.I to M.E. either to accept the learning or reject it when it is accepted it becomes my habit and belief. My thought process in M.E is related to my habits and roles. I will call this as a function delegated to M.E. by M.I for preliminary dealing with the current happenings. My intuition and intelligence create stimuli based on past experiences (learnings). All these stimuli flow into M.E. to regulate my behaviour.

My spiritual frame is the result of the processes that have taken place in the past. The components of this box are almost permanent (long-term) and perpetuating unless I make a conscious decision to intervene and change them by processing back. Spiritual frame determines and perpetuates my self - concepts, which influences body and mind incessantly. My self–concept seldom directly influences my spirituality frame. It takes a long route of resistance and struggling processes through body and mind (which very rarely occurs once in a blue moon).

My self-concept is fairly permanent (long term). To change my negative self-concept into a positive self-concept I have to struggle through and wait for getting the necessary permission or injunction by convincing appropriate ingredients of the Spirituality frame. For the purpose, intense processing is to be done in box 3 and 4 and continuous communications have to take place 'inter alia' through internal stimuli and responses. Sometimes my self-concept does not supply sufficient energy and I get into a vicious circle.

The process of professional journey helps me to make appropriate interventions into my sensoric system and activates the cycle of change though also influence my personal meanings, values, wisdom etc. to activate my self concept to release energy for change. The struggle for change and continuous learning for growth also directly interacts with self– concept that generates energy. Energy is generated and released, the changes in my mind-interior by becoming aware of the prerogative for change and taking a decision. I call it is "resolution or resolve". The resolve has to be sieved through my life-goals, life meaning, values etc to secure my acceptance and action for change. Then my self-concept changes to become positive and energetic. Then the cycle works for making me of more effective organism to actualize. Then life becomes a bliss.

Hence the processes of my professional journey are my effective interventions for exploring the meanings of my existence in joy, tranquility and peace of my soul. My self-concept and spirituality.

Case Seven—Trainer Me[30]

I have initiated to explore, experiment, and conceptualize thereof with data of my own." Who am I" traces the root of the self with the present states of being, where as the emergence of the trainer role amplifies the process of convergence of the identity with the task and the role. The conceptual; aspects of this study appear to be the hypothesis of self-experience which is yet in the process of testing and pre-testing.

As I Grew

I grew as a child largely under the influence of my father. "My father has been powerful as a symbol of authority all throughout my life. His control threatened me and used to reinforce my fear against authority. He has been a teacher by profession at the school level. I learnt to emulate copy and imitate many of those behaviours that teachers used to have. I recall my early child hood rehearsing teacher's mimic and role-plays at home with my younger sisters. Teacher's role-play used to be my pastime during primary school days.

---

[30] Nagendra Singh's own case has been retouched and edited after extracting it from Bricks of foundation Published from ISABS 2003 Delhi. This was originally written during early eighties as a part of his internship stage. It has also been published in a Book by Indian society for Training and Development (edited by CM Srivastava) 2005

At emotional plane, feelings were intense and strong; the fear of insecurity and deep desire for love and acceptance taught me to manipulate myself. Love to me was a commodity of bargain that was centered on search for acceptance. Thus performance syndrome took over my sense of being.

I kept doing things that I assumed the authorities liked. I also did things that I knew I like. I also learnt of my father's script and the kind of sacrifices he had made for us. I also discovered his love for me when I was seriously ill at the age of 10. I could see his concern. Love and acceptance used to be a reward for any standard performance set by parents or by teachers. I needed to perform the best to draw the attention/ acceptance of the authority. Following hypothesis emerged as foundation of growth process.

- ***Better performance would give me acceptance and identity in what I am and what I would like to be.***
- ***Teaching and telling others need to make impact if others pay attention to what I say.***

"Believe me not" became the predominant aspect of my product scripts. I disliked authority in my father from within but accepted from outside. My rebel child was weaker than the scared child whose apprehensions, fears and distrust was rooted in the family and social acceptance. My fear overpowered my rebel child. I kept quiet and continued doing things that I even disliked.

My options were rewarded "posthumously" as an "obedient, sincere, industrious, record performer child". I started deriving pleasure in an illusion of my so-called sacrifice.

I saw my father living with the same script suffering and punishing himself as loner. I disliked and hated to live like that, at unconscious level, but at conscious and awareness level. I kept doing on and mortgaging myself to the values and beliefs of that of martyr's. However, I realized the implications of my life and price of living when I was 25.

Teacher and My Child

Somehow I knew as a young child that I am going to be a teacher. It was not due to my hidden goal but a silent search for identity in order to influence and impact through being.

My attraction to debating, poetry and dramatics were rooted in my father's manifest skills as a teacher. I was not so physically strong to get in to any other career in my own self- assessment.

Teachers were lovable and whose influences during my childhood were immense. Their unconditional love and acceptance to the little child in me was a message of doing more, learning faster to receive the same continuously. My initial attraction towards a particular subject was largely based on the nature of teachers handling those subjects. I was little weak in mathematics form early childhood and I see the genesis in the following incident:

"I *was assigned to complete homework of tables. I examined it thoroughly but failed to reproduce the same before him correctly. I was told that I do not know mathematics; I am weak in that, I was punished for that. I always disliked that teacher; I never wanted to learn his subject even at home with involvement. To unlearn that belief I hardly did anything nor I aspired to be a mathematician.*

Teacher's control through punishment used to scare me. However, I started accepting (not so strong a dislike) even though the teachers at later stage of my growth when I saw a value or justification in their concern to help the student. Quite often I used to have a complimentary relationship despite my discomfort of working with them. This was noted in my apprehension about the teacher authority.

I never liked teachers who used to enter the class with a stick. But I still admired them for their competence, if they had any. I liked those who were free and extempore, never relied on any books or notes during teaching. I liked those who made the group lively with their wits and stories in the class. I hated those teachers about whom I heard and understood they are biased and prejudiced. I see today the sources of my likes and dislikes for a trainer in my little child teacher relationship too.

On the impact of teacher's judgment on the conduct and performance of the student. I stared questioning the right of the teacher to conclude about the taught on his merit.

- As I was a rebel child who challenged a few teachers (of course non- confrontative and at inner level) to disapprove their hypothesis about me. I also realized my sense of worth at an early stage. Teachers who contributed to this are still held in my high esteem.

- I also discovered a corollary of my overall life script as stated in the period of my teacher taught relationship till the age of 20. I see its impact in my values about trainer in me.

Creativity and Idea-centric trainer

My creativity, a part of my being, always fulfilled my need of acceptance and influence, when I realized that my creative strength had become the manipulative strength, I was running fast without looking at where I have reached. I was more concentrating to receive visible rewards on a very high price of self. The significant event in my life gave a break to my speed.

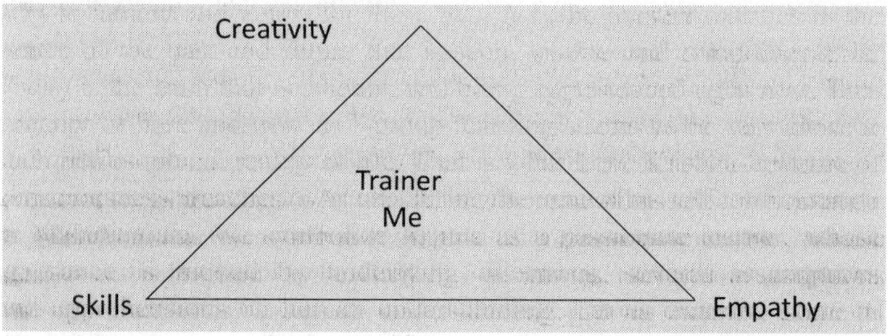

I changed the gear, looked at my self for the first time. I thought I was popular in the campus. I lost an election of the students' union where as I had firm belief of success. It was non-availability of formal social acceptance form others of which I was very much certain. It was to my dismay, I realized that I have been using my creative strength to gain acceptance form others, as if my being could not be accepted as such by the people. I was shocked to discover[31];

- That performance alone does not really give the acceptance from others untill I accept my being of whatever I am.
- Process learning profession suited me the best since I could connect the depth within and beyond
- Empathy with strong sense of listening supported my creative and idea centric skills to shape my trainer being

[31] C M Srivastava "Memorable Experience In Training" (ed) the above article of Nagendra Singh has also been published in its modified form by Indian Society for Training and Development Delhi 2006

I realized that I can energize my creativity even in my professional field of training and research. I am aware of my creative self. I enjoy being creative. Dramatics and stage performance gave incredible insight of my duality of being.

It is the treasure of joy that I draw from within whenever I want. Creativity to me, today, is a source of self-expression that gives a new meaning to my life and adds to its quality. It is a strength that raises hopes of my life and makes me fully alive.

Working with the groups:

It was an exciting moment to go for training session entrusted to me for senior officers at the age of just twenty eight. I mugged up the entire forenoon lecture to perform better and satisfy the perceived expectation of my boss and guru in training field for whom I had great respect. Even today, he retains his place in my heart. It was Sujit Bhattacharjee, a known process trainer of his times.

I was sinking and swimming in the class to perform better. The group grilled me until few participants were generous to bail me out of my pathetic moment.

- I learnt what does it means to fail in a class due to acute anxiety to perform.
- Avoidance of failure was strategic mode in search for efficacy as a trainer.

I examined myself for the first time when I attended the first lab at Bangalore in 1975. I was terribly reactive in relating to the world around me. For me performance had never been a failure till then. The task of working with myself in-group was dominant; I hardly realized the need of others and led implication therewith. The distrust rooted in me never allowed me to remain in my natural form. Thus the values and beliefs as I grew, had taken their seats deep within me. While I ponder back, the following hypothesis about myself seemed to have influenced my behaviour:

I wanted to lead the group at conscious level. I wanted to project, myself also as a leader, adviser and so on and so forth, whereas I kept disowning my role whenever I was being pointed out by the group. The group rejected me. I look back in my history sheet and developed a behavioral justification of today in my past leadership's failure. "My need was to draw attention of the trainer authority" through my over dominant concern to talk more about myself than to go along with the group. A very strong sense of fear of rejection by the authority always remained at the bottom of my heart. I was not aware of it not owned up when I became aware of it. I remained with the group as a performer of a task. A basic disbelief has been about my own existence as a person of the group.

Mythical assumptions:

That kept my being in illusive sense of powerful and impacting young trainer. My game plan used to be high dependence on tools and instruments with high doze of slides and aids.

- Excellence in task influences authority and power.
- self-manipulation is the only way to influence the people.
- Inclusion and acceptance is possible through reducing myself.

Deep insight of process learning gave me the ability to confront myself and own my dark spots as I was busy in conducting one after another-training programmes in my work life. Participants were the greatest source of learning and self-growth. I owe to them for whatever I am in my role effectiveness

I recall how difficult it used to be the long three hours sessions with stuff in my *bag* unless I had some jokes and story to support my innings. I was looking for my survival on many occasions in the class. But journey of process insight and struggle to look at my own sense of inadequacy and search for inner acceptance taught me to be a trainer of great worth today. The experience of the group work as process learning was painful. As I started unfolding, the hypothesis became "hyper-thesis". It was thwarted. Pillars of the self-image broke into pieces; it took six months to gain strength to stand up and collect the pebbles of my self-image. I looked around at the reality of my existence.

Experimentation Phase

Unfreezing process: Trainer Self

In my first group, I had a traumatic experience. It was a sense of failure on finding myself not being accepted by the group. I saw myself manipulating and controlling others at my various stages of encounter with my work group. I quote precisely an experience of this significant event of my group life as under:

When I look back, between my first group experiences as narrated, and today, I find that I have traveled far from my place where I started. I feel excited, envy at the same time, thrilled to experience the perceptible sense of growth on various facets of my life that I have ever experienced over the years. The options were many. Each namely, research, training, etc, had its own attractions for me. The dilemma continued whether to be a trainer of diversified professional interests or to be a trainer working in small groups. I moved to the latter, and while working with small groups I had varying experience of pain and pleasure.

While I relate my part and see through my gestalt the concept of trainer training and learning seems to have undergone changes. I trace my dilemma in choosing a trainer career or of university teacher, researcher or administrator. I debated for sometimes and still could not resolve it. I realized a sense of growth within myself working as a trainer, working in the group with people. Every new group used to influence my unfreezing process. Looking back, I find a dichotomy of growth precedes within me-my unlearnings and learnings over years. In the process of experimenting with myself, learning new behaviour and unlearning the old ones, I disclosed 'dyodic' TTS model of learning and unlearning.

Failures Vs. Success

Failure:

Failures, to me, were very largely negation of others towards me. I would normally have avoided plunging into the things where the probability of failures was high. "What others will think of me if I fail"? As if I need not fail. I never used to forget the pains of even my small failures. In fact, I never wanted to fail in a task situation. Task in a small group, was to me, relating with the group, influencing them and influencing the trainer. My concept of group life then was entirely different from what I see today.

Success, to me, was a source of satisfaction derived from others; recognition of my attainment. Success in training has largely been in the form of the impact made on the group. Initially I was working in the training group to produce the expected consequences, as stated above.

No sooner this I realized I was more concerned with attaining the result rather than sharpen and clarify the training objective.

Fears

I liked the trainer in me; my first entry as a trainer as early as in 1974 was a thrilling experience to begin with. The glamour of the training world, the superficial recognition, prestige and wide contact reinforced by adherence to the career of training attracted me more towards my trainer self. I liked to be with the participants and enjoy their company. Their acceptance of me as a person was more important for me. I remember how uncomfortable I used to be in the class in the early days. However, I had maneuvered myself to look comfortable through deliberate jokes and spending time on lighter issues. Initially, I disliked the co trainers sitting in my class, as I was not confident of myself in the new role. I realized very soon my fears in the class as trainer and I started working on them.

Need and Anxiety

It started fulfilling my need to influence the people around me. I remained dissatisfied with what I was doing. I always wanted to perform something new, even in the class as a trainer. I think I still continue to operate on the same predominant need. In my need to do a very good job, I experienced dealing with my own anxiety of excelling.

While working with my anxiety, I also saw a pattern. Whenever I remained anxious to help or reach the other person, to my dismay, it was rejected by the person. It was turning out to be unhelpful and unwarranted intervention. At times my intentions and concerns were also doubted. I started accusing the group that it is not a good group but very soon I realized that I was not sure of myself in the class. I used to keep my own fences so that none in the class reached me, unless I was sure that I was able to respond to them. My fences were heavily loaded with concepts, leaning towards multiple themes at a time and allowing no time for discussion.

My learning has largely been more from the participants as well as from my initial flops in the training. I recall an incident where I went to the class for the first time as a trainer. The trainees were officers of the state government. I prepared the background paper. I had covered a number of aspects in the stipulated time. I was all the time concerned to do an excellent job but hardly gave an opportunity to the group to raise issues.

I made it a sheer lecture session though it was not intended or expected by the course coordinator. I was dissatisfied from within on the coolness of the group's response.

- While working on anxiety, I also discovered the process I used to pass though. I used to find myself very uncomfortable and make others uncomfortable too while I was unaware of my anxiety during a particular situation.
- Immediately after the incident, I started feeling sad about myself and of the things being done. I realized that I seemed to have been operating from my need to protect myself, artificially decorate myself essentially to fit in my new role as trainer. I realized the pain of my frozenness that I experienced after that.
- *In my recent lab experience* ***I also discovered a perceptible sense of mobility in my state of immobility. I also saw my delusion of being immobile and again getting lost into the anxiety. It was a moment of growth when I traced the locus of control in*** **me.**

Conceptualisation Phase

Trainer me:

Till late 1976, I realized that the new role as trainer was satisfying my need to influence people and seek acceptance form others. I also experienced myself that I have been running fast and always looking for a shortcut because of my need to do better and excel. While this realization came to me I started looking at myself as a trainer in person and resources within. I am listing certain ***assumptions and apprehensions***, which I had during those days:

- Participants may not accept me as such.
- I may fail to influence them unless I prepare myself thoroughly.
- I may not be effective unless the visual aids are there to help me in the class.
- Others (co-trainers) might know and criticize my ability and competence as a trainer.

I was painfully happy when I realized for the first time, in 1979, that I needed to raise my articulative ability, my clarity of thought and devote more time on acquiring knowledge (which I had been doing otherwise too). New task and the working climate gave ample opportunity to work with myself; it was challenging, exciting at the same time and painful. I had the payoff in terms of my growing acceptance in the various groups and also through the organizational rewards. I realize the significance of group climate in trainer's growth.

Training and Trainer's Role:

Trainer's role to me has been a situation where I detach my being from the self. I realized that it was an illusion to be a non-being in the task situation but the dilemma continued for years till the recent past.

1. Whether I am performing a role or am I there with the group as a full person?
2. Whether the trainer is there to learn or to provide learning opportunity for others?

Kurt Lewin's theory of unfreezing, freezing and refreezing seems to have direct relevance to the process of exploration, experimentation and conceptualization. On various accounts of myself, I am still at freezing process and sometimes at unfreezing stage. Whereas on many other counts, refreezing has already started taking place. Training, to me earlier, was something performing and evaluating the trainees for reward and punishment. Training, to me, is now a process of inculcating and reinforcing knowledge, skill and attitude in the person. It is a process of knowing oneself exploring and experimenting with oneself. It is essentially a situation of change, awareness, study of change, and ultimately changing the person.

The function of the trainer is basically to inculcate the process of learning within the participants. As learning takes place within the individual at its own as a result of confluence of diverse, inter-twining, and occasionally opposing influences, irrespective of the field of specialization, the competence of the trainer seems to assume a greater significance in influencing the learning process. It is admitted that the subject matter is no substitute for the training skill and vice-versa. The trainer has to acquire skills so that he affect the learner at his best pace. Circumspect timing of inputs of new data and of different kinds of activities and concerns are one of the trainer's most delicate task. What matters most is not the event or the act but the meaning that the participants attach to it and this meaning has a lot to do with the social process through which the particular training group develops its distinctive character and reaction. For me it is important to create a training climate where the participants feel free to express their views and feelings. A group climate develops when the trainer moves close to the participants as a person.

"Please.. I am Human[32]"- case eight

A colleague of mine with strong insight on role and sense of being has set a new paradigm for the quest of being. He does not believe in detailed cognitive mapping exercise like many other illustrations give in this chapter. However the idea of placing his note has been to appreciate that arrival is not the goal, journey is the quest and struggle in search of being.

I knew Sankar for many years since we worked together in the small groups in our early days. His shift to understand the duality of the role and the self and glimpse of a new identity affirms that trainers after having spent several years of work continue to move forward if they wish to.

"one of my first experiences of struggle to identify myself and differentiate it from my role was when I was five years old. It was when my would-have-been sister died in the womb of my mother. I felt happy that I have no one to compete for my mother's love though I lost the chance to play the elder brother's role. My 'self' won and my role needs were kept aside. Then I said to myself…."I'm only human"

Most of the next 25 years of my life were spent to create a role for myself in this world. This was through the process of "proving" my self worth to myself–through good marks, success in quiz, elocution, essay and other competitions as well as attractiveness to the fairer sex.

Exploring with ISABS….

Then ISABS came into my life and my outlook on my identity and my role changed forever…In June 1993, when I became a Professional member of ISABS, I got my license to be a T-Group Trainer but then it

[32] R Sankarasubramanyan one of significant role holders of ISABS has been President of the Board has shared his sense of touch and inner connectedness .It gives an insight of his journey where role and me has been dissected . It is so tacit and visible to understand that ***role perse*** has all potentials to underplay quality of being if a person is not in search of that.

also meant that I have lost my license to be a human being. Maintaining boundaries, not using group's time to deal with my issues, contriving happiness during happy hours, not smiling too much at the participants of my lab during the breaks and so on….

In the lab also, I used to squirm like a worm when people used me as a tool for their learning process, show concern and affection for other members while leaving me alone. I felt empty when the group did a round robin and just skiped me as if I did not exist. I felt like a low level animal when on the 3rd or 4th day the group appreciated me for my humanness to a fellow participant. I touched, and felt myself to be sure that I have flesh and blood."

"Please……..I'm also human". *A powerful reconnect that one has yet to work hard to be that he wants to be. It is a restatement by the author that gives us a signal of sustained self acceptance. He further adds;*

"I used to be role bounded in the first 3 days of a lab and then slowly bring in my being. These two were integrated by the fourth or fifth day. Now I found myself fairly integrated with the process from day one itself. May be as per David Bradford's model, I'm moving from "Trainer as a Role" to "Trainer as a Being" and towards "Trainer as a process".

But I don't rush in for help when my heart bleeds for a participant in the lab, I trust the person and the group to handle it. I still feel bad when I sometimes "conveniently forget" my role and let my personal needs of affection take over me.

But then, I say to myself….Please, I'm also human.

I feel good seeing this change within myself. But how will the others experience this process? There is a tendency among participants to believe (it is also perhaps to mock at us) that we as facilitators have "arrived" and we should "role model" appropriate behaviours for others. I think it is easy to get into that trap!

I left my well paying job in the Caribbean, came back to India and started on my own as a Consultant at the end of the last millennium. The need to take an entrepreneurial role came in to satisfy my personal need for freedom. I took the risk of leaving the job of being a Head of HR in a multinational organization in the USA to carve my own personal path since that role demanded of me to subjugate my personal identity to meet organizational demands.

My being is more important to me than the roles I play. This is the characteristic of my humanness. But I do pay a price for the same.

This is the price for being human. The biggest learning in my life is the realization that there is no "arrival" but a constant "journey". My sense of identity has transformed through my experiences and the various roles that I have played. But I have managed to retain the core of my being without getting corrupted by the roles that I had to play. Wherever the roles have enriched me and brought the best of my being to the fore, I have enjoyed and succeeded in those roles. Else, I wilted.

I can only say this….Please, I'm human. Quoting this is not an excuse from accepting ownership and accountability for my actions. Saying this is to remind myself and all of you that in my differentiating my "self" to become the "role" and "being", I do not wish to lose the "human" in me. That "human" in me is the most precious me.

Please, I'm only human….

Case Nine: Making a paradigm shift

It was a co- training moment that I had with a seasoned T group trainer Sujit Bhatacharjee during my internship process. Some of the veterans of today were going through their final phase B during early 90's.Members like Nagbrahma, Rajan Gupta and C M Srivastva etc had been giving a grilling time to me. I was seen a copy cat to add to the fuel of frustration in the group process. Total silence and lullness in the group was making life very boring, apathetic and alienated to each other. However, individuals were in their inward journey inspite of their disconnect.

Meera (name changed) *was fully wrapped up in herself. She was completely cut off for many days from the group..Many felt she was a loner and just did not bother to relate to anyone.Group had ignored her. Dynamics of the group was to avoid confronting her as she was unwilling to do so herself. The underlying gender issue was also a taboo for the group. Only lady in the group had been sitting on her issues for quite some time. Almost every body shared their agonies and acute frustration to trainers–myself and Sujit. In fact Nagbrahma*[33] *was quite vocal about*

[33] Nagbrahma is currently Director of a nationally well known Pai B–School at Manglore ,Rajan Gupta is professor with premier management institute in Delhi where as Srivastav has also been teaching in a reputed B school at Mumbai. They are known process trainers who have made strong application of process insight in the their insti-

redundancy of the group life and others too joined the chorus taking me as a soft target. Our unrelenting silence and visible indifference to their anger was driving little impact on Meera. She was quiet but sobbing inside. She never joined the chorus with men folk of the group. Group was feeling agitated on her stance yet none wanted to take on her, I broke the silence and asked her," Every body in the group seems to be annoyed with me but I have not heard from you so far.Where are you? What is happening to you?"

I did not want to tag Sujit in my confrontation process I knew he was with me. Yet I could not dare saying that group is also angry with Sujit since most of them preferred to attack me than to Sujit. I was also aware of Sujit's unpredictability. Meera got choked and broke down. None could understand what was the intense feeling she had been going through. She did not articulate except her tears rolled down on her cheeks and these conveyed her anguish and grief. Like many other small group dynamics- a few moved forward to express their warmth and caring to her with a glass of water and tissue paper.. I discouraged it and I awaited for her verbal response. She could reconnect and organize her thoughts after Sujit's supportive intervention followed. ".What are these tears all about?,he joined me with a deep lump in his throat echoing his feelings.

She was dumbstruck and began mumbling."I was never a task obsessed yet my husband and only son felt that I was too strong on task relation. I had little emotional connect to understand their need of love and affection. I have been slogging to do so many things in my life. A career woman who did cooking, cleaning and handled several house chores while upbringing the son and addressing routine domestic responsibility while caring an old ailing mother in law No body appreciated me for what I did. My mother in law hardly considered it a significant task. I do not know if I had become a robot.....who thinks you are a robotic in your role? I quiped to her respose. She was prompt to say. "All of them including my husband felt that I was too much role driven and do not provide caring that they need. Here also in the group I was branded to be a task master. I decided to be just an observer after three days. I got fed up. Why people see me the way they see? I am not that person. May be if I look like that I do not want to be. "

---

tution building role. **Their small encounter in one group life impacted me the most in addressing my own authority issue. I was shattered inside but kept holding iron rod of Sujit my mentor and senior co trainer.** (Nagendra Singh "learners'diary'ISBAS panaroma"newsletter 1991)

"So you are angry "here and there". All that you do to deal with your anger is to sulk, react withdraw and let yourself slogg inside" Sujit my colleague spoke. She nodded and broke again but wanted to wipe out her tears to avoid getting in to cathersis.

"Let flow the tides of tears. You have stopped it enough in the past" I told her. She continued. I never had occasion to share my grief to any one. In fact I felt that I need to be busy to prove my worth. My activities overtook me. I got busy in my action without any joy. I ever realized it was my body in motion not my heart and emotion."

The self disclosure of Meera was deeply moving to most in the group. The learning climate changed the contours of group process. The anger to authority and self-exclusion of one turned in to a melting pot of closeness, caring and love that the group had been seeking and looking for. The dynamics of group process also built the edifice of resolutions that may be seen from the extract of her learning journal later submitted to me. I became her mentor in subsequent years. She was clear and firm as she moved ahead in her journey of life. Let me place a cognitive frame that evolved an interesting insight to me in my own encounter to unlearn the fear of failure ingrained in me as a budding social entrepreneur later during early nineties.

Dissonance and Conceit

Incongruance in thought and action is rooted in one's inability to be his own self. There is a constant desire to be the other person. I want to be that. I had the role model in me to be my mother who did so many things for others and became a sacrificial goat her self. She accepted endured and never felt the agonies of having stepped in to the mould that she was not. Inside her heart she felt cheated and robbed. But to others she collected the stamps of reward and nice role holders of traditions and obedience. On the contrary, she resisted it internally." I kept asking myself why do I carry such burden and do not resist. But my response was otherwise. Eventually I felt myself in same trap. I did not like it. I argued within myself but met with despair. I learnt after paying the price of my agonies and deep pain. Resolutions that I made about myself at some point of time during the intense group work. It was interesting to examine the process of building hopes and optimism within me that I had completely lost. I had become a pessimist by nature, and did not know how to move forward.

Disputations with self Accusations

It is quite an interesting mode to argue with oneself internally. Theoretically speaking there could be four ways to dispute and argue with yourself.. I did it over the years and saw a radical change impacting within.

Searching evidence I found there were many worse cases happening around me.. I got to argue that I must not be carrying the belief that I cannot change. I started asking why I cannot change? What is the evidence that I cannot make a difference? Of course, my ghost mother role model -I had embraced and yet disliked was deeply ingrained within. The best way to argue was I can and I will instead asking negative– why can't I change.? Very often I used to argue by negative questioning process.I discovered that;

Learnt optimism never works through an unjustifiable positivity about the world but through power of non negative thinking.[34] The lesson I learnt was 'how to dispute my own unfounded accusations about myself. No sooner I learnt that my dormant skills would kick to propel new insights for action. Because negative beliefs that follow adversity are generally inaccurate. One of our most effective technique in disputation would be to search for evidence pointing to the distortions in disastrous explanations. The question that I kept asking to myself, what is evidence of cynicism within me? Why did I think that I can not assert and change my stance ? I kept telling myself, ***every day and everyway I am getting better.*** It gave me power. But I was having psychological education background. I new theory more than others–I thought so. On the contrary, I hardly accepted cognitive frame of my own belief due to my skepticism. It demanded more evidence, factual proof to tell me that if others have done it why not I.?

Generating Alternative to disrupt the despair:

I kept on searching the roots of my problems in my past. That gave me a way of latching onto the worst of all those possible causes–the permanent, pervasive and predictive one "I told myself I am too old to start afresh." I had stopped looking at several options, I had in my life space. I began exploring alternatives. I saw that it was not so much of reasoning and

[34] Learnt optimism has been pioneered by Martin Seligman during early 90s that surveyed several fundamental studies on clinical psychology and therapy of handling deep depressions. (Learnt optimism published by Simon and Schuster USA 1991)

causal factors but largely due to strong desire I got so deeply grounded in my fear. In order to dispute my own belief and fear I picked up the destructive habit and thereby became skillful and generating alternatives. The resolutions by its self did not help me until I discovered how to break the ground rules of staying negative and pessimist.

Locating skills in developing alternatives:

"I attended some problem solving workshops arranged up by my organizations. It was of course a clear structure and content loaded learning opportunity. Surprisingly my input and presentations during several group works on task related issues turned out to be an impacting moment since my inner dilemma and conflict emerged on the surface. The element of process issues like fear of failure, and undefined blocks sought attention to help me drive on building my skills.I began asking not the logic of my belief that appeared to be my hidden blocks. Belief was factually correct. I was dark and not so beautiful. Physically I was not able to attract my male colleagues. Before they reject me I used to reject myself"

The fear of rejection is strongly associated to pessimist syndrome. Until one builds the counter strategy to face the life the agony of self pity, self exclusion dominates the life space. Resoultion with acquired skills builds competencies. May be keeping notes and diaries might have helped Meera to a great deal in relaying bricks of her foundation. The implications of so what if I am weak, dark and small? So what if I am not accepted by boys? So what If I am not attractive? The series of questions drove Meera towards self confrontation process.

Self confrontation and self acceptance:

*"I knew that the belief was true and factually correct, the implications examined by me raised my inner strength and built my self esteem. I began confronting myself leading to a process of coming to terms with myself."*It may not be an easy going. A painful journey to question oneself and examine the usefulness of **being the person you were meant to be**. A deep seated sense of inadequacy if not confronted by the person himself the process of self acceptance would become a remote possibility. T group learning design does encourage a mode of self driven learning process but the laboratory experience is not adequate enough to help you resolve everything you want to. There has to be an ongoing quest to accept what you kept denying all the time. But it does

not happen so. How can we accept that we deny all the time? Ironically speaking, process of denial is at a manifest level whereas acceptance has to originate from a deeper level. For example, a physically unattractive aging lady tries to use heavy make up and cosmetics all the time to look beautiful. She denies the fact that no amount of cover up and cosmetics will make her look impressive at all. However, endless effort continues on her part to be what she is not. The moment she gets in touch with her inner awareness, the process of self acceptance begins impacting her. Over a period of time she does not need to go for any artificial cover up. Her inner charm and simplicity would make her look more appealing and gracious person than what she tries to be. ***The growing urge towards inner self- acceptance propels a person for coming to terms with oneself. Self denial therefore is an invisible block towards self acceptance in becoming what we want to be..***

T-group–a process of relearning mode:

Several *cases discussed above have presented an account of the accumulation of knowledge, skills and wisdom in relation to T-Group training, The resources of developing the T-Group methodology have been generated from experimentation by using the action-research model of changing. In a T-Group, the objective is to mobilise group force to support the growth of members as unique individuals simultaneously with their growth as collaborators. The members have learnt to help the facilitator as he assists in the development of individual and group learnings. A training laboratory is a community dedicated to the stimulation and support of experimental learning and changes. The experience in T-Groups helps members to plan change efforts in association with life outside the laboratory. Cognitive analysis of learners has touched the hard core of their being and new insight on T-Group training theory. It may be important to underline that I have used process training or process work synonymous to t group work in this book.*

As a member of the T-Group[35], some recollections are meaningful statements of a facilitator. I collect data about my behaviors; I analyze the data with the experience, which generates the behaviours. My learnings are tested and generalized for continuing use. I learn about my motives, feelings, and strategies in dealing with other persons. I learn of the reactions I produce in others as I interact with them.

---

[35] **T-Group theory and Laboratory Method by L P Bradford, J R Gibb & K D Benne**

Form the confrontation of intentions and effects; I locate barriers to the autonomous functioning in my relations with others. I develop new images of potentiality in myself and seek help from others in converting potentialities in actualities. I increase my abilities to respond, interactively and adaptively to situations. I achieve concurrent growth in personal autonomy and in social effectiveness.

- Increasing awareness of an sensitivity to emotional reactions and expressions in oneself and in others.
- Improving ability to perceive and to learn from the consequences of one's actions through attention to feelings of his own and others.
- Stimulating the classification and development of personal values and goals consonant with democratic and scientific approach to problem-solving in personal/social decision and action.
- Developing concepts and theoretical insights which will serve as tools in linking personal values, goals and intentions to actions consistent with inner self and requirement of the situation.
- Developing behavioral skills to support better integrations of intentions and actions- Achieving behavioral effectiveness in transactions with one's environment.
- Helping to transfer new learnings to back-home situations:- applying the new ways of behaving with typical ways of behaving in home settings.
- Learning how to learn;- Analysing one's own process of learning.

The facilitator needs to be continuously aware of that he is working with group members towards re-education. Everyday in a laboratory he is full of episodes of relearning, of reorganization of precious learnings. I confront my old patterns with new possibilities. The above 7 objectives of T-Group involve examination of the relation-ships between old and new experiences, between old and new learnings, and the arduous process of achieving some viable choice or synthesis between the old and the new.. I have seen many facilitators growing and changing their nature and quality of interventions with passage of time but research based documents have been wanting in the Indian scene. Many professional organizations that are professing the T group centric training intervention are nothing but a training body. We lead to actions and actions without thinking and serious research support.

In place of summary:

Many case studies have touched the core of the quest for 'being' the constant journey of a learner. An endless, untiring demand of a learner to be what one wants to be - the human. We have noted that unfreezing process can be very painful but rewarding. It does reveal that personal growth as a succession of three stages flows in a continuum. Unfreezing is necessary, because the participants carry at the back of one's organization, family and locality. They come with ingrained habits of feeling, thought and action. In order to produce an impact one's normal habit has to be disturbed or unfrozen and it is at this stage where new idea of experimentation process is initiated to create a new movement. If the experiment provides a sense of growth and learning in the changing needs of the trainee as well as of the trainer, the growth is really experienced.

It is established by studies that the state of readiness at the individual (trainee or trainer) level leads to exploration. The process of initiating new acts and experimenting with varieties of intervention with oneself follows subsequently. While choosing options at group or at organizational level, the trainer explores the needs of the receiver, his own skills and competence and resources. The organization provides a culture and environment to enable the trainer and trainee to interact and encounter with each other. The degree and nature of impact or visible change will largely depend on the trial stated above.

- *The trainers with academic and content bias would focus more on structured session preferably lecture-cum-discussion. They may like different kind of sitting arrangement even in the classroom.*
- *It appears from the above analysis that trainers own life goal, his self image, and the personal attributes have some bearing on the kind of methodology he chooses for training and also on the impact he makes on the trainees.*

I have felt the impact of change in me while handling different small group process work, over the years. The propensity of learning process examined my own model of being that I was not aware of, until I tested my failure at existential and group level. Change that takes place in a trainer as a process of his group is influenced by intervening variables of the organization. Majority of the trainers' experiment with the groups have the bearing of their respective training organizations and varying group climate. I see the change in my persona-my styles, my fears and belief that has impacted my values set towards training profession in general. ***Training has taught me to be the person that I meant to be.*** An interesting shift has been witnessed in some cases by people who shared their transition in self concept. It may be noted that self-concept is fairly permanent (long term). To change one's negative self-concept into a positive self-concept the person may have to struggle through and wait for getting the necessary permission or injunction by convincing appropriate ingredients of the Spirituality frame. Sometimes self-concept does not supply sufficient energy and a person may get into a vicious circle. ***Self -awareness, therefore may not be adequate enough to drive a person to the desire for change. In fact, it may resettle to superficial inner clarity by getting in to inner cyclic process setting an unwillingness to explore an evolving meaning 'me and my relationship*** *" Case six and five stated earlier have highlighted similar frame of unknown blockage in the 'emotive artery' that system has yet to discover by revisiting the self diagnostic process. The paradox of self nurturance and control followed with to be or not to be always propels to unkown inner conflict that a person may not be aware of.*

The process of professional journey has helped many to undertake appropriate interventions into their sensoric system and activated the cycle of change through influence of personal meanings, values, wisdom etc. to activate my self concept to release energy for change. The struggle for change and continuous learning for growth also directly interacts with self–concept that generates energy is generated and released, the changes in interior mindset by becoming aware of the prerogative for change and taking a decision as "resolution or resolve". The resolve has to be sieved through life-goals, life meaning, values etc to secure one's acceptance and action for change. That would take process of self-concept moving to a change process into positive and energetic shade of wellbeing. Then the meaning of life cycle works for making me of more effective organism to actualize. Then life becomes a bliss that I am, instead struggling to project what I am not. Some of the cases have strong insight of conceptual frame with unique identity. Each person has stated his cognitive mapping as an original piece of analysis.

SECTION – II

What Makes Me A Group Facilitator Or Trainer?

Desire to become a group facilitator and my experience to work with several small groups over the years has taken me to a deep experience towards my power of being, my own authority issues getting projected through many more unresolved issues

Chapter IV

Group Process–Facilitation Identity, Authority and Power of Being

If we look at the entire range of human behaviour in a small group work as a trainer and a facilitator, an interesting paradigm seems to operate at different levels. We continue to deal with relentless search of our own identity, unsettled power and authority issues as a trainer while stimulating and encouraging the participants to deal with their authority issue. Facilitators' role is not only critical but the most significant one. It occupies seemingly an undisputed powerful location in the group dynamics to make or mar the capacity of learners. The confronting role of a facilitator has been to deal with underlying issue of identity, authority and power of being as a person in a given role

Role and Person

Let us examine and explore the meaning of the dual concept in the backdrop of T-group learning process. Trainer's behaviour and their style has been discussed in subsequent chapter. It speaks of multi-skilled trainers with different spcialisation. Role has been defined as a bundle of expectations with a set of functions that a person is expected to perform around a position at a given point of time. Person is very important to the role that he or she is performing. Let us introduce you to a clipping of T-group faculty meeting before starting the community session and small group work.

Entry Behaviour

Entry behaviour of a trainer and the group is very intriguing and an absorbing process to understand. Content analysis may be viewed from different perspectives, however, the processgraphic description ***of the content is the most meaningful part of T-group learning. I shall place some clippings to have deeper insights.***

Inclusion process *Inclusion is not an easy and simple process in group work. Trainers may have different styles for different levels of the group.* If it is just basic human process where none knows the clear frame of the programme and participants have a very confused notion of the design at the outset, entry behaviour may be quite jerking and would produce a strange a feeling. Very few participants would enjoy the romance of early lubrication. Entry of the trainer may be hurting due to very strange behaviour. No sooner a few set up themselves to have the fun of knocking each other.

If giving need of participants are high their entry orientation would be building social cohesiveness strong networking to search friendly mismatch. If it is low giving need, they would be quiet, remain watchful, observant, and be a passive learner. If receiving need is high they would be responding to any request made by other group members in order to make social networking. They may need some one to stand by. They feel good if supported but will ask for it openly. High need in expressed inclusive orientation would support, endorse and enhance friend circle in the group.

Low inclusion on receiving mode would put a member on a lonely position as stated. *He will feel aloof and avoid being included. He will have several explanations for his distant and quiet behaviour.*

Let us examine the trainer's inclusion process. Some knock at the door bang bang. Some peep through the window before knocking. Some stay aloof for the door to open.

Some trainers, while making an entry process start by saying, *"I am in a role but I am also a member of this small group. I am here to facilitate the group work towards the common learning agenda. As a group you are free to start work in order to understand the basic human process and explore the impact of your behaviour on the group and vice versa "*

Trainers' level	Group level
Assumptions: Statement on role clarification at the outset helps the group to take up clear position and set their learning agenda and begin interactive process. Trainer assumes that group will act and move into sorting in to ambiguity of task given the freedom of choice. *Behaviour:* Trainer will further reinforce his proposed role or maintain the silence to convey the message to the group "that the group is autonomous and has to carve out its learning goal without trainer's support" He negates their requests to pitch in.	*Assumption:* Trainer will come to lead them and direct after some time. We need to begin our performance, he will guide us very soon. Let us test our approaches, hopefully, it would get approved by the trainer *Behaviour:* "Group starts intro-game. Vocal members take the lead to speak out their name tag and seek others to follow suit. Cycle gets completed very soon. Air is out and baloon is fused. Silence and waiting for the trainer to pitch in becomes obvious. A few speak out asking trainer if some directions and support can be extended.

The role that gives us power to be what we want to be does make incredible impact on group behaviour. Trainers go on demolishing the design and structure that is built by the group member or any one in the group after having acquired the pseudo autonomy **announced by the trainer role related statement. Some one puts up seeking similar introduction from the trainer' why you do not introduce something about yourself***?*

"Trainer chooses to remain silent and speaks out precisely" Am I here to read out my resume to establish relationship with the group? Does it matter so much in abridging relationship? I do not know what the group is doing by collecting bio-data of each member?

Another trainer may come back with clear restatement and state "I have said what I had to. I have nothing to add now. Let the group decide what it wants to. But I do not know why the name tag is so important to the group to understand each other?" There was a silence. Group looked at each other with a sudden note of wonder and sense of mild regret and discomfort.

Trainer's level	Group Level
Behaviour: Refuses to share his resume, and raises the question on the value of collecting general profile thus demolishes the early design created by the group	*Bahaviour:* Group feels unsure if the process is adequate enough to go ahead. It continues seeking signals from the trainer that task taken up is on right track. A few of them take inititive to set the directionative to seek direct intervention
Assumptions: Participants need not look for approval and validation from authority after having defined their autonomy. Participants will make and remake their agenda of the day with trial and error while chaotic process leads to blankness or confusion. Greater frustration and confusion in the group evokes deep emotions to build connectivity.	*Assumptions:* Participants think that trainer alone can give the right directions to help achieve the learning goal. Group may correct its focus of learning provided trainer makes intermittent intervention and redefines it's human process objectives.

The limited nature of their perceptual ability, coloured by the strength of emotional investment in it, drives group members "see" boundaries of role. A portion of the unmanifest universe thus becomes manifest through human imagination. In the "end" every perceived entity once again becomes the cosmic continuum.

Gauranga Chattopdhaya writes[36] that *Vedantik* and *Tantrik* view, developed through experiential learning several thousand years ago in the Indian subcontinent, is currently supported by the experiment based theories of quantum mechanics, which also hypothesis a boundaryless cosmos. What all this adds up to for me is that the individual's identity is an illusion since, like all other things perceived as bounded entities, the individual is also identical with the cosmic continuum. The issue is that of how one deals with one's personal authority. Since "personal" authority immediately links it with one's identity, logically it is also illusory. Should it, therefore, be linked to trainers' role and his or her persona. Trainers's style and his own self image, therefore, has been one of the most significant factor to understand latent dynamics of group process. Very often process trainers pay little attention to participants' unsettled and unresolved authority issue

Ironically most of them fail to examine their own unresolved authority

[36] Gauranga Chattopdhaya wrote in his article in "Here and Now "journal of ISBAS (extracted from Bricks of foundation published by ISABS 2004 ed. Nagendra Singh)

and power issue. They expect others' authority issue to be resolved in the group dynamic process.. A very interesting case of a process trainer came to the surface who happened to work with us as a co trainer in the field of group dynamics on a semi-structured training design. Another senior trainer had no exposure of process insight but he was very good in conceptual frame. Of course the programme was heavily content centric. The young process trainer was definitely very confident and articulative person but had tough time to deal with rigid and fixated stance of the senior trainer. I asked young process trainer," *How did you find working with your new colleague on a structured training design.* Her spontaneous response was *"I need to work with my residual authority issues. I guess there is something deep down on assumptions and belief that I have been nurturing. To me it was my senior colleague's authority and rigid stance that gave me a challenge to examine my inability in handling my inner power issues"* Such a profound statement came as a touching remark of authenticity.

Process trainer assumptions (with adequate T group exposure and comfortable with unstructured learning setting)	**Non process trainer's assumptions** (content-centric person with structured mindset)
• Participants need to have adequate space to express themselves. • Participants learn at their own since, they want to learn not because trainer's teach. • Participants need to test their doubts and fears on several inputs before they are asked to experiment new behaviour. • Participants need to confront each other and also the trainer to experience freedom and autonomy. • Process is the most critical element in any training to generate high learning. • Coverage, time plan, strict adherence to schedule is not so critical to learning, it is the method, climate, and process that contributes to long lasting learning.	• Trainers must deliver everything and have absolute freedom to give whatever they have prepared to deliver. • Participants learn because trainers offer the most. • Trainers must guide and direct every move to determine effective and efficient learning. • Participants must not confront the trainers who have the highest authority in the group learning process. • Content coverage is the most important element in training than any other aspects.

While examining the, the group dynamics as one of the key objectives to deal with trainers' personal authority issues of comparing review of several trainers profile may offer interesting foundation of process learning. Trainers self-image with strong authority orientation is closely related to freedom of space extended to learners. Rigidity of learning space determines the learning orientation and preferences of the participants on mode or style of learning. In order to understand shadows of power and authority of trainers we may go through the dichotomy of personal and social face of power. Power is of course inner but authority is acquired and legitimately bestowed by the external mode.

Task centric Power: It defines *the center of gravity of inner energy to influence others and take charge of the situation and one's own self. However, the source of satisfaction lies in seeking one's own dignity and elevated self esteem. It accounts for seeking self-gratification by one's own self as the most powerful self righteous role holder. If he is confronted by any one in the group trainers takes it as an offence, however, the anxiety to ensure that group must work on visible interpersonal or intrapersonal issues remain on surface. The trainer gets deeply hurt if he does not ensure the task completion and keeps exploring various modes of driving the group to perform. In fact the trainer prefers to design a task where content becomes significant.*

In a semi-structured learning mode one can find out large number of trainers who adhere to such biases of strict time boundary, course calendar etc. But in T-group setting adherence of strict time plan, coverage of deeper issues, long marathon sessions may have special symptoms of high task obsession. Symptoms of self indulging beahviour is also an expression of task centric power that gets elongated to egocentric manifestation as discussed below.

Belief and normative behaviour

Participants learn by action, speaking and keeping direct focus on the content.

Participants learn by indulging in activities assigned by the trainer.

Learning is maximum by showing performance in the group, therefore, something or the other needs to be done.

Participants continue their job work by raising agenda,breaking silence,hooking with someone as an easy escape goat. Trainers feel good by encouraging such a process of ' hit and run'and spreading its volume of attention by the group on interpersonal level intervention.

Following task related normative behavior is commonly observed in the group.

Members take active part in giving and receiving process.

- One may initiate an idea of soliciting feedback from others or offering feedback to others as a task of the group.
- Silence of the group is normally broken by some activities proposed either to take up some game and repeat sharing etc.
- High energy is shown by the group the moment any activity is assigned by the facilitator.
- Members show high performance orientation during the group to seek validation or approval from the facilitator.
- Disapproval from facilitator puts off the group on a low ebb.

Source of satisfaction: *The source of satisfaction for the trainer lies in quest of inner power of making people dance to his tune..If the group does not, he feels nothing is happening. He creates a task structure asking participants to move in. At times trainer will design an intervention, create a task to break the silence of the group. Generally speaking,, participants also derive satisfaction by taking lead to prove their presence by being talkative, vocal, supportive or coercive while taking up a task and proving their worth.*

***Ego-centric Power:* It centers around learners dire need to prove themself, establish and reestablish their identity as one up. Their anxiety of winning at all costs and in all situations is visible.Tit for tat and settling score is common behaviour of participants. Trainers with deep need of this kind become very destructive to self and others. They would always like to add their strength to prove their point "as to what they said was something very meanigful but the group did not take note of it"**

They assume that they are witty, sharp and intelligent and thereby cut on edge over others through needless sarcasm. While making observational statement in the group trainer would rub on their wrong side and derive pleasure in catching the 'tail of the monkey 'than hitting it on the nose'

"Ravi a trainer had picked up an issue with Joseph (participant) who refused to yield to his advice to carry on an exercise to offer a negative feedback to each member in the group. The participant 'smelt the rat' and refused to perform. Ravi in his role of authority felt belittled. His design to create a task to help group move did not work.. Ravi went on asking as to why he did not do what was asked to.

"I am not obliged to respond if I don't" participant said in a cut and dry mode. "I know what you are up to", he added.

"You seem to be knowing every bit of what I intend to do well in advance; have you been a palmist by profession "Ravi's sarcasm made him pale coupled by thunder laughter in the group.

Joseph remained quiet, withdrawn and silent. Nothing shook Joseph. Ravi did not leave him easily. He pounced on him by asking the group to share what is that Joseph had been doing to the group and himself. The group joined the trainer's army and found an escape goat until some one, after a while, came to Joseph's rescue. Ravi did not like any one's rescuing Joseph. He saw a pairing process and confronted again, "What is the need of your pair up"?

"I think you are being unfair to him" Sunil jumped with gun.

"Are you his rescuer if so why?" Ravi asked again.

"If does not help him to open up, I think the group needs to give him space" Sunil spoke.

The Group had a point to note.. It did sense what was going on yet there was none to resent and disagree. Trainer Ravi registered the feeling but reacted,"Have you been authorized by Joseph to protect him or you are playing an angel?" "Neither I am playing an angel nor I have a desire to do so. I do not need to be authorised to unblock him".

"So You want to displace me;I do not approve of such behaviour" trainer said.

"Do I have to play my role with your approval and disapproval.? I have been myself. I can not take people dominating and bulldozing others just because they are in power and position.. Knowing that you gave us the autonomy to be, I did what I felt like doing…" Such a strong statement by a participant put Ravi off.

Ravi lost his cool. His face was red with anger and he spoke, " I cannot accept whatever you do. I am upset and angry." It was the second day of group movemet. Group was blocked. Nobody spoke thereafter for almost the entire afternoon. The group lost its guts to confront the authority.. Ego centric need of a trainer. Does not allow the group to charge the trainer's position and authority. In fact it was a one to one encounter between Ravi and Sunil. Tactically speaking rest of the members were not part of the exploration to help understand the overall group process.

Belief and normative behaviour

The trainer believes that he or she is the only responsible person in the group to drive the learning outcome. Participants are expected to learn according to the tune of his intervention.

Trainer must control the process and impact the participants learning goal. Trainer must give everything that he has in command of his knowledge and insight. Participants need to learn, synthesize and develop their learning journal emanating from the wisdom of the trainer. The participants need not show their wisdom and knowledge by competing with the trainer..

Following normative behaviour is observed in the group.

- There is a sharp reaction by the member on any strong feedback that is brushed aside.
- Members tend to block the trainers intervention by rejecting., disagreeing. or questioning the process, at times members confront directly.
- Facilitators discourage the interactive process what he or she believes is not functional.
- Facilitator does not encourage the experimentation by the group and prefers to take the strings in his control.
- Facilitators tend to retaliate and settle their score with members if they resent and show high counter dependency.

<u>Source of satisfaction</u>: *The source of satisfaction of the trainer is to search his innate strong need to prove that he has the ultimate power to impact the learning process. It could be wanting, invisible need to gain acceptance or have absolute control of other's behaviour.. No body should touch me and point a finger on my style and approach.. On the* *contrary trainers' need to remain in the center and have the full freedom to express his control to ensure group learning design remains the prime source of satisfaction.*

Maintenance Centric (MC) Power

Trainers do take maintenance centric power in order to build harmony with the group to avoid any conflict and coercion with them. It builds an avoidance centric mode of trainers survival and keeping the group existence without any rupture and break. It is a power to manipulate others and protect oneself to keep off the potential confrontation. Jokes, humours and stories are generally introduced to seek general acceptance and inclusion in the group. Thus trainers do not have to go through their stress and strain nor any minor encounters. The group moves very smoothly –all fun, while participants learn and generate social harmony with each other. It is a hidden influence over the group to drive them for a common goal through a non-confronting path.

Any small breach in harmony of group relationship is addressed by repair and maintenance mission promptly. Many trainers in search of their own self acceptance jump into the fray of the mission of repair by different stance. Of course participants prefer this mode since they do have to go through the acute pain and' hurt' at all. They would avoid offering critical feedbacks to their group members. They would not like to say the truth directly to the trainers, however, they do display several clues of self protectiveness. The stance of self protectiveness in a group behaviour is displayed by protecting others and thereby developing pairs and triads within the group. The need to help the so called weak does not originate from receivers' real need. It is givers' anxiety of helping in order to acquire the power of 'being the giver and saviour' whether one needs it or not. Participants tend to protect others and hence themselves from receiving critical feedback process.

I recall a group insight where (in house team) participants had gone through a long silence after I had asked them to share feedback to each other. Group did not offer a single negative or critical remark to their team mates. On the contrary, they felt it was too unfair to give a critical remark to a friend. I have experienced a very senior trainer with whom I worked as co- trainer on several occasions., It was Dileep Lahiri, a noted T group trainer of his times. Of late he is not so visibly active.. To quote the experience, let me present another dimension of something that I had noted in my own learning journal during late seventies, as below:

It was a group of young interns who had gone through several group dynamics labs earlier. Sharma (name changed) had great impact on quality of their mutual feedback process. I saw the group playing safe game to each other. I asked the group to locate one negative quality of every member and thereby offer a mirror to them. After a few minutes of silence one of them spoke.

"Nagen, how can we do that task. After all we are all friends. We do not want to hurt anybody."

"What kind of friendship you have if you are not honest to each other and hide yourself to avoid hurting your friend" I put it loud and clear.

"Another participant came in defence," we hardly know each other. "It is just three days of sitting and speaking something about our profile."

"To be honest and true to other you do not need to wait for so many days. Find out from your friends if your honest observation is going to hurt them. I do not think, it will," I said.

My colleague Sharma allowed me to take the lead without any intruption.. He looked at me with a silent endorsement. Suggesting that I was pushing them to do what I thought will work. "In fact you could have let them experience the hollowness of friendship and superficiality of relationship", he said. I disagreed there and then. Later, I did see a meaning in what he said. The matter came up in the faculty review session. Late Sujit Bhattacharjee the vetran guru of many process trainers of today, confronted me with his piercing question. "What was your compelling need to design that intervention thereby asking group to offer critical feedback to each other.? Did you feel negated? How did you deal with that? Eventually no one responded to your task and you had to justify and explain the merit of it."

I sensed I was on the wrong side of the trainer. I felt I could have let them go.

Most of T-group trainers make mistake in designing their planned intervention..The merit of trainers lies in their recognition of their dysfunctional move and recognize their unstated fear.

Tendencies to ride the conceptual ladder during the emotional encounter has been the pattern of many a soft paddlers in T group setting. Why the group is not left by the facilitator to draw its own course of action during catharsis and confrontation instead driving them to conceptual lessons?

Belief and normative behaviour

Trainers' with high affiliative orientation and strong maintenance syndrome do show their supportive and protective behaviour. They believe that one should not hurt others as it spoils and breaks relationship. It is better to say nothing than to say strong and harsh feedback. Most often, they argue, negative feedback has to be packaged very carefully... Everyone may not cope with the strong and critical feedback ;hence it becomes dysfunctional. Relationship handling is crucial in order to become a good trainer. One must, therefore, pay adequate attention on helping and supportive orientation. The belief that I am very supportive and caring, therefore should I confront the group while they are learning. Some believe it does not matter whether the group is dependent or independent to the trainer. In fact, they are drawing learning lessons.,that is more important. Enabling and supportive feedback becomes the pattern of such trainers to participants. Let us view the normative behaviour on this aspects.

- Facilitators tend to be more appreciative to ensure love and warmth from the group; there by step in to nurturing mode.
- Members tend to support and rescue a sinking person in crisis or in a difficult time.
- Members also show general anxiety on breaking cohesiveness of the group.
- Facilitators tend to repair the underlying conflicts and differences in the group before they fade out from the group work.

<u>Source of Satisfaction</u>: *The source of satisfaction of trainers lies in their deep seated need to build intimacy and warmth with the participants at the core of seeking relationship..By giving positive feedback trainers ensure similar pattern of response from the group. Love, caring and warmth flows out of their statement to ensure deeper connect with each other. There is a possibility of shallow connect when trainer operates at inclusion and friendliness level thereby he tends to avoid confrontative intervention. Enabling, supporting and counselling may turn in to a mode of deriving various sources of satisfaction. That might become dysfunctional for some people who need strong jolt to work with themselves...*

Illusive Identity and contradictions

Psycho-social aspects of trainer's persona are an intriguing concept with full of inner contradictions..What they preach and advice, they, necessarily, do not practice. What they question in the group behaviour it may be visible in their own conduct. If we examine trainers ' *quest of being* one finds inherent contradictions between their manifest and non-manifest expressions. Social behaviour while building networking relationship and handling task related functions appear poles apart. Process being very significant for T-group trainers' conduct, goal, responsibility and accountability at times become secondary to them. Authority issues are critical and they test it in pursuit of their individuality and may become insensitive on the impact of their behaviour in the society. They might operate on assumption that they know themselves better than what others think of them.

Ironically speaking, the image of what others think of their conduct is least significant for their being *"I do not care what others think of me..I am aware of my values and beliefs that guides my behaviour*". You may find many trainers making such statements. Others would receive it and infer meaning the way it suits them? Is it acute arrogance of knowledge competencies or attitude issue that has bugged their psyche, one may debate over it?

It may sound an. arrogance of awareness of being what one wants to be. As stated earlier, it is the quest of testing one's power, authority on the contrary, questioning others' power need and stance of control over others. *I recall an incident of a participant who made a strong observation in a group work to a trainer, "Why you do not you let us work the way we want to go ahead.?At one level you pronounce of giving us freedom to be ourselves and experience our spontaneity, on the bother hand, you disapprove our group behaviour. What is this contradiction of giving and taking it away ?" Trainer's firm and authoratative response was loud and clear.", I have the role and responsibilities to ensure that group attains the learning goal. I would condemn and disapprove what I think is against the learning objective."*

"Why do not you set the objectives again. Many of us are not clear," one of the participants quipped in anguish.

"I am sure some of you already know the answer. I do not have to respond time again.

We have debated it a number of times. I do not need to repeat it now. Some of you do know the answer " Trainer's firm voice and clarity of role snubbed the group. There was total silence for almost 20 minutes.

Above examples do tend to support my hypothesis that psychological identity seems to be an illusion while role identity assumes critical significance. Role that is governed under both socio-psychological milieu of the group over takes the facilitators' identity. While the multi-faceted social identity is an essential but complex tool for engaging such an intense influencing tasks to generate emotive processes for a cognitive mapping. One may note either within the group setting or beyond T-group work boundaries many facilitators indulge in reprocessing the 'processed stuff ' in the name of clinic session in order to consolidate their learning. But truly speaking such a clinic session of post lab situation tends to convert in to an intense experience of trainers' inter-personal authority relationship. Of course, it turns out to be a rewarding moment but to many it may also turn out to be seductive moment of settling their score. The fact remain that the process and the person in a role, revolves around one's authority and power dynamics.

Knowledge and Role Power

Knowledge power and role power may be separated here to understand the finer difference.. Of course role has always been defined as a bundle of functions at a given point of time and positions around a person with multiple expectations that one needs to address..Thus the power and authority vested with the facilitator draws an intriguing mix to impact the group behaviour. Facilitator uses his positional authority whenever he or she chooses to be. The comfort level of the trainer is more important than the comfort level of the group. Paradoxically, he does not own that stance at conscious level. However, facilitator may find it difficult to stay in his own comfort zone since the role associated with responsibilities demand attention. Philosophically speaking, the facilitator can not and need not do whatever he wants to carry on to enjoy his comfort level. The fact is that it does not happen so... One notices many trainers operating on their set pattern with little reorientation to meet the group response. Trainer with vested role power may like to use his diagnostic knowledge and skill power, thereby gain a commanding impact in the group. It depends, 'how and when' he chooses to intervene.

Role, Me and Organisation

As stated earlier, role is a bundle of expectations around a person and position at a given point of time with set of functions. It is heartening to note that most professional leaders in the organisations have been looking for a role thereby seek a space for themselves as if one does not matter without a role. Let us take example of ISABS where many professional members who founded the organization have moved beyond the gravitational force of the role holding. They matter today for their substance of giving than holding space through role in the board or committee. There is a growing tendency amongst many social leaders to seek space in order to influence the organizational process. Of course organisational reality does offer authority to role holders to enable them perform effectively. But the fact is that inner power matters a great deal Yet many process trainers strongly feel that they matter if they have role in the board to bring impact around them. Essence of impacting lies with the person as a powerful being not through an authority vested in him through a role in a system. Of course, it is true with many formal organisations where people do not think of their power without authority. No sooner they feel powerless and feel vindicated without an adequate authority. Role overload might take or arrest a person to delude him as a being. It may happen that a person would find difficult to step beyond the role whatever may be the location of his being. I have come across several examples of several managers, admistrative officers, army and police officers who have spent several years in service, found themselves arrested in their role identity and lost their being. Let me narrate an interesting experience of my group work for school teachers. *It was an in house lab.*

***Arti** was working as a team leader and chief Mentor of a play school leading a team of a group of about nine or ten teachers(mentors).. She was very articulative and protective of her team. No mentor was willing to share any critical part of her behavior and its impact on the team. They were unwilling to speak about their chief mentor whereas it was known to the facilitator that undercurrents were being dealt behind the scene. In fact facilitators repeated intervention toward seeking sincere feedback from each other was strongly resented by every one.*

Arti chief mentor raised serious objection to the very purpose of the process. She declined to offer any critical feedback to her team members. Eventually she defended them during the feedback process whenever critical feedback was offered to her colleagues during the group work. It was strange to note that she was so soft on one hand and so confrontative on the other on the issue of group value of creating openness. She questioned the intent of the process. At one stage she reacted and said, "I feel I am being evaluated, and do not like to be prosecuted in the presence of my team. I suspect your intention as the open human process feedback culture..The session was meaningful. Many decided not to share with others - particularly any disapproved behavior. I confronted her "why do you suspect my intention ? Does it take us forward to work together if you doubt my purpose of openness on self disclosure and receptivity on feedback./"Atri was unyielding and said she was in a role of team leaders. Any open feedback would demolish her self image, therefore, She was never in favour of that.

Astonished facilitator asked if she was in a right place to attend the lab. She could choose to take action if she thought otherwise. She said, no it was fine to be there as a routine."

It was a clear issue of authority being addressed where many decided to pass time and remain indifferent to the task.

Group learning experience with unclear structure has been a big blow to their being. Many government officers, teachers, managers and 'big bosses', therefore, have shown strong reluctance to such a laboratory training after one or two such big blows in their system as a learner. Indian Police Academy (IPA) was a classical example of our success to intensive process exposure for young probationers for several batches over the years.. Most of the learners with high authority orientation would prefer to opt for structured intervention in formal organisations where role seem to have overtaken top leaders and senior officers of the system.

Conclusion

The role poses certain challenges that drives facilitator to perform what is expected of him as a trained and effective T group facilitator. His vested authority and inherent power with multitude of skills does create an identity. He is aware of his potential impact of his stance and styles. Many professional members in the making who work as interns in the early stage prefer to act as co- trainers by choosing their senior partner based on image that such facilitators have. Let us recall and visualize how many of us abuse and use our authority as a group work not because we intend to, but we are used to.. Conversely, one abuses one's personal authority when one chooses to engage in tasks that are primarily oriented towards self-indulgence.

The contents of the above anecdotes and examples bring a complete full circle and reflects to one's connectedness between authority and identity. As long as a trainer is able to utilize one's identity as a tool, it is difficult to guess if he is using or abusing his authority. The question is am I a pawn or a tool of my identity either in my conscious or subconscious being. ***However, the moment one becomes, as it were, the tool of one's identity, i.e. when either of the pictures of identity held in the conscious and the unconscious, or a combination of both the pictures, drives one to irrationality, even momentarily, one's actions are more likely to be based on others' authority or abuse of authority rather than on the use of one's personal authority*** [37] Our choice, therefore, becomes coloured by our conscious and unconscious identity related agenda.. Therefore, the more we examine the process of one's identity formation and it's evolution greater is the probability of testing one's personal authority. On an existential level let us learn to accept that 'identity and authority' seem to co-exist on a concurrent mode that defines facilitators self indulging styles seeking satisfactions of different kind. Trainers behaviour is thus guided by his self-opinionated identity, untested resolve to be or not to be. He, however attempts to work on participants' authority issue to explore their dependency or counter dependency issue. Eventually the trainer may seduce himself to work on his own unresolved authority image. It may happen that the trainer might not be in touch with his subconscious to connect within.. On the contrary his entire struggle would center around issues beyond him. Group level interventions are, therefore, determined on what trainer senses to be the seemingly significant authority issues of the group.. Seasoned trainers are likely to become more insensitive to subconscious than the new one. Since new professionals tend to manifest their adoptability in pursuit of the learning propensity.

The dichotomy of 'sensing and responding' in order to learn the depth of power dynamics between trainers and participants appears like a jigsaw puzzle. It depends who is more powerful at a given time to influence and control the learning environment.

The cycle of search, research while establishing identity of a facilitator has been a matter of growing area of interest for many learners. Yet the choice

[37] Gaurango Chattopadhaya *op. cit.*

of selecting or rejecting a comfortable co-trainer by a young professional member has been influenced by an image that has been created by the facilitator over the years. Many trainers prefer to live with the image of their own but some of them decide to experiment with themselves and choose to learn what they want to. I have seen them operating on the belief that I must give them all that I know of the subject. It has nothing to do with the learner's need to learn. Facilitators may be found obsessed in order to deal with his or her anxiety to vomit everything. It may be to prove his own knowledge power. Learning to learn assumes one of the most critical process dimension for facilitators to examine their styles and beliefs. –an area that has yet not been adequately researched till date, in my opinion.. Assumptions and beliefs of trainers, therefore, matter a great deal in their styles and approaches. Third section of the book takes us to trainers profiles, their styles and relational approaches reflecting their clarity on group dynamics and manifest behaviour.

Chapter V

Learning to Learn–A blend of Eastern and Western paradigm

It was a wonderful moment of my life that led me to set the foundation of my willingness to learn. I was learning, nevertheless, without knowing I am so curious to learn. Why should I learn at all? I asked this question to many professional members in their journey of PDP. Answers came very vague from many of them but few of them were quite focused and seamlessly tacit and clear. Learners do learn not because trainers train them or teachers motivate them to learn. Learners learn because they want to learn. They learn by themselves.

Answers do reveal that something that touched the core of my heart I felt like pursuing it as an agenda of my learning. Why do I learn or pursue specific agenda as my goal, assume greater importance than what I decide to learn. We choose different areas of our interest specialization in pursuit of our career goal. ***Agenda to pursue T group training and learn process facilitation skill has been arising out of a drive that sucks a person likes an addiction to work with oneself. The passion to pursue an inner search could be a driving force, yet all those who have completed the journey or are in the middle of the process have not stopped their quest of learning.***

The learning theory of the west has established a credible frame of cyclic framework. However, the vedantic mode also resembles a similar frame that the earlier chapter has also touched with a right cord..Lord Krishna's discourse to Arjuna has impacted many readers a great deal in rediscovering their oriental learning mode. Let me illustrate what happened in a workshop of sunrise session led by me. ***On Learning to Learn*** *held during one of the national event of ISABS. The following questions were given to the buzz group to examine and respond;*

Why do we learn at all? Why should we learn at all? When do we learn ? How do we learn *?*

The in depth meaning of the questions was debated at length. It was collectively felt that learners learn to address the quest of their learning. If the learner wants to learn nothing will stop the process. Though human being has instinctively been programmed to learn yet the person may choose not to do so. Learning demands that unlearning need to happen. If a person does not have the quest and hunger for learning, one ceases to learn. Therefore, they do not want to learn at all. Series of experiences of different nature do not enable them to learn. Because, they do not want to. The supportive theoretical frame, of course, added value to the deliberation process. Let us examine varities of learning frame that describes the foundation of human learning principles connected to oriental learning orientation.

Summary of Pedagogical model

<table>
<tr><td>Learning that</td><td rowspan="2">Knowledge is imparted (context independent…)</td></tr>
<tr><td>Knowing that</td></tr>
<tr><td>Learning how</td><td rowspan="2">Knowledge achieved through participation & experience (context dependent…)</td></tr>
<tr><td>Knowing how</td></tr>
</table>

Source: Karim Aly Kassam, "Development in Practice" vol 20(2) April 2010

In the pursuit of development research it has been revealed that a subtle difference exists between contextual dependence versus independence while knowledge is achieved through practice. Learning by doing has been a set theory in this regard for quite sometime, however, meaning to establish relationship between theory and practice is an outcome of our learnt behaviour. "Learning in the class room is abstracted from the context where the knowledge was generated. While this form of knowledge is necessary, it is different from knowing how. *Knowing how* considers how to achieve something."'Learning by doing' is an example of knowledge generation through knowing how.In situation learning, experience is the impetus of reflective thinking, which in turn impels requiring **Knowing How is** manifested in the performance of an act. A person who is bodily active is also mentally active. Learning is involved with each act, activity is tantamount to the movement of the person through the work.In order to achieve knowing how particular type of competence is required. Thus intelligent person performs and acts critically and also observes critically. We may examine a coherent mode of *learning how and knowing that* in a typical vedantic mode as we move further to determine the classic relational network between learning and knowing process of a person.. Development rcsearches have done extensive work in this regard in recent days which appears to be a more convincing model to affirm that a learner learns faster only after he has answered the why and how questions at a deeper level.

Learning theory and Neuro-Linguistic Pattern:

Every one learns and processes information in different ways. Traditionally speaking many of us probably do not realize that our pattern of learning has been quite structured. We attended schools where teachers delivered instructions and we did what was asked by them. Teachers talked to us, and we answered their questions. We indulged in pencil- and paper-based tests. Thus trainers and teachers did not encourage us to discover our multi -dimensional learning styles.

Psychologists have defined many different ways to classify learning styles. These fall into three general categories: **perceptual modality**, **information processing**, and **personality patterns**. These categories represent following ways to focus on the learner [38].

Perceptual modalities *define biologically based reactions to our physical environment and represent the way we most efficiently adopt data. We should learn our perception style so we can seek out information in the format that we process most directly. Educators should pay attention to modalities to ensure programs cover all physiologic levels.*

Information processing *distinguishes between the way we sense, think, solve problems, and remember information. Each of us has a preferred, consistent, distinct way of perceiving, organizing, and retaining information.*

Personality patterns *focus on attention, emotion, and values. Studying these differences allows us to predict the way we will react and feel about different situations.*

---

[38] Howard Gardner (1993). Frames of mind: The theory of multiple intellegences (10th anneversary edition). New York: Basic Books.

Education psychology has discussed several modes of human learning that can be defined from personality and perceptual modalities. If we revisit Neuro Linguistic Perceptual modality, we would find an interesting depth that refers to the fundamental way our bodies accept information. Researchers in NLP field identify ***auditory, visual, kinesthetic, and tactile styles.*** The field of accelerated learning has therefore been relying on evidence that explains how learners could process information faster.

Eminent psychologist Gardner suggested that humans can be ***(1) verbal-linguistic (sensitive to the meaning and order of words), (2) musical (sensitive to pitch, melody, rhythm, and tone), (3) logical-mathematical (able to handle chains of reasoning and recognize patterns and order), (4) spatial (perceive the world accurately and try to re-create or transform aspects of that world), (5) bodily-kinesthetic (able to use the body skillfully and handle objects adroitly), (6) interpersonal (understand people and relationships), or (7) intrapersonal (possess access to one's emotional life as a means to understand oneself and others).***

Scientists strongly-feel that we generally retain a dominant and an auxiliary learning modality. We pick up from our dominant mode at conscious level to process at primary level but at an unconscious level we access through all senses. It is something like the hard disc of a computer, data does get stored in our neuro- psycho system at unconscious level. In order to search what is stored in our learners directory of hard disc several techniques like brain mapping etc have come in to practice.

Visual learners *prefer seeing what they are learning. Pictures and images help them understand ideas and information better than explanations. A drawing may help more than a discussion about the same. When someone explains something to a visual learner, he or she may create a mental picture of what the person talking describes.*

Senses ‹----------› **Intuition**

If we understand psycho compass of our learning antennae they are viz. senses and intuition, we find that there are five senses seeing, hearing, touching, tasting and smelling. But intuition is imagination and picturing.

If you are a ***visual learner***, you may learn faster by seeing the person speaking. You may watch a speaker talk, as well as listen to what he or she says. It is quite interesting to observe that human's sensory organs have been placed by the God visibly in close proximity to human brain-the neurosystem. Thus NLP school of thought sounds very logical to define our perceptual modalities and understanding of behaviour. Imagine if sensory organs were placed on the body not where they are in the present form. So we call it deformed and handicapped physical structure. Let us assume if eyes were divided like one on the back of the forehead and another on frontalside. Similarly if nose was placed near naval position of the belly. Such dislocations would upset the entire neuro-system of the human body. There is so much similarity in terms of physical structure of human on the planet earth compared to other life and homosapiens on different planets. However we are intricately different to each other on many counts. Diversity is enormous and abundant. Even twins born do differ in many ways. Learning orientation and individual's propensity to learn always differ with each other.

Many people assume reading is a visual action. Though we see the words, most of us process the information by hearing ourselves say the words. Many scientist would say they are "Print-oriented people" who depend more on words or numbers in their images".

Auditory learners also fall into two categories. Auditory learners prefer spoken messages. The less understood auditory learners need to hear their own voice to process the information. The more prevalent type, '*Listeners,*' tend to do better than others. The listening acquires strong learning mode because of interactive pattern. Good listeners are good communicators therefore understanding and comprehension of such learners are of a very high order. They listen to what is being told at conscious level. But more often than not they may not listen to their inner noise unless their quest of being and sense of spiritually awakening through inner connect of subconscious and unconscious is a live process. Therefore, we encourage interactive process for effective learning. *While some auditory learners prefer to listen to both themselves and others, mounting evidence suggests the two types are distinct and separate. Hearing is not listening, former demands only one set of sensory organs ie ears. Listening demands synergy of all sensory organs including intuitive process of individuals.*

Kinesthetic learners want to sense the position and movement of what they are working on. Tactile learners want to touch. We use interchangeably both terms but in essence they do differ. *Their similarity is that both types perceive information through nerve ends in the skin, as well as organs through muscles, tandones, and joints. Let us see the example of different modes of learners as below. A few examples given below make it amply clear.*

Visual learner *would say, "I see your point."* ***Auditory learner*** *would say, "I hear what you're saying."* ***Kinesthetic learner*** *would say, "I feel we're moving in the right direction."*

Therefore, a mixed mode of learning climate is always better to impact learners' different instincts. "*Likewise, learners can compensate when the instructional medium doesn't match individual style. Kinesthetic learners may benefit from reading and auditory learners can improve their understanding by touching what they are working on. Possessing various compensating strategies allows us to benefit under all circumstances.*[39]" In process learning mode it is important to examine cyclic orientation of one's learning style. It has nothing to do so much with NLP relationship yet one may discover the association.

Learning Styles

Learners from school of process learning have always detached themselves from structured mode of analysis that NLP advocates. Of course, there is a beautiful blend of process and NLP dimension of self learning provided one prefers to examine the interdependence. Somesh Chadhha, professional member of ISABS has made a significant breakthrough in experimenting such blend in his small group experience.

It is interesting to explore cyclic process of learning styles that many of us link as universal pattern of adult the way they tend to learn. It is of course, a broad .classification with wide ramifications. Kolb (1984) provides one of the most useful descriptive models of the adult learning process available, inspired by the work of Kurt Lewin. He set the foundation of adult learning process as intrapsychic process viz. *unfreezing, freezing and refreezing as mentioned earlier in this book*

"This suggests that there are four stages which follow from each other: ***Concrete Experience*** *is followed by* ***Reflection*** *on that experience on a personal basis. This may then be followed by the derivation of general rules describing the experience, or the application of known theories to it (****Abstract Conceptualisation****), and hence to the construction of ways of modifying the next occurrence of the experience (****Active Experimentation****), leading in turn to the next* ***Concrete Experience****. All*

---

[39] Leslie Shelton, Joan Sheldon Conan, and Holly Fulghum-Nutters (1992). Honoring diversity: A Multidimensional Learning Model for Adults. Sacramento, CA: California State Library Foundation

this may happen in a flash, or over days, weeks or months, depending on the topic, and there may be a "wheels within wheels" process at the same time.

The emotive learning process is characterized by concrete experience of the learner. Let the person sink with his or her experience of the process before he steps in to cognitive mapping process of his emotional interconnect. One can find people saying " I learn the most when I feel with issues, agenda and process". Feeling driven learning is a very powerful mode to begin with. One gets connected emotionally before comprehending it at conceptual or cognitive level. The most direct application of the model is to use it to ensure that (pace the reservations above) teaching and tutoring activities give full value to each stage of the process. This may mean that for the facilitator or mentor, a major task is to encourage the learner to move round the cycle, asking questions which encourage Reflection, Conceptualisation, and ways of testing the ideas. (The Concrete Experience itself may occur outside the tutorial/mentoring session)". On the other hand one may find out where people keep stating,"I learn the most by getting in to logic and rationale of the issue; unless I analyse the facts in depth I do not take to my heart. "Some one says " It does not get registered unless I do it myself." That is typically action learning renamed as experimentation.

Following instrument of kolb clarifies it in a very simple way

The learning Style Inventory describes the way you learn and how you deal with the ideas and day-to-day situations in your life. We all have a sense that people learn in different ways, but this inventory will help you to understand what learning style can mean to you. It will help you understand better, :

- How you make career choices?
- How you set goals?
- How you manage others?
- How you deal with new situations?

Instruments—guidelines

Kolb developed learning style inventory that is so handy as a self rating instrument. Please read the following and respond to it as it describes your own self understanding of spontaneous learning.

Example of a completed sentence:

When I learn ……………I am happy ………..I am fast

……………..I am logical ………..I am careful

Remember: 4 = Most like you,

3 = Second most like you

2 = Third most like you

1 = Least like you

And: You are ranking across, not down.

LEARNING STYLES INVENTORY

		One	Two	Three	Four
1.	When I learn:	…I like to deal with my feelings	…I like to watch and listen	…I like to think about ideas	…I like to be doing things
2.	I learn best when:	…I trust my hunches and my feelings	…I listen and watch carefully	…I rely on logical thinking	…I work hard to get things done
3.	When I am learning:	…I have strong feelings and reactions	…I am quite and reserved	…I tend to reason things out	…I am responsible about things
4.	I learn by:	…feeling	…Watching	…Thinking	…Doing
5.	When I learn:	…I am open to new experiences	…I look at all sides of issues	…I like to analyse things, break them down into their parts	…I like to try things out.
6.	When I am learning:	…I am an intuitive person	…I am an observing person	…I am a logical person	…I am an active person
7.	I learn best from:	…Personal relationships	…observation	…Relational theories	…A chance to try out and practice
8.	When I learn:	…I feel personally involved in things	…I take my time before acting	…I like ideas and theories	…I like to see results from my work

9.	I learn best when	...I rely on my feelings	...I rely on my observations	...I rely on my ideas	...I can try things out for myself
10.	When I am learning:	...I am an accepting person	...I am a reserved person	...I am a rational person	...I am a responsible person
11.	When I learn:	...I get involved	...I like to observe	...I evaluate things	...I like to be active
12.	I learn best when:	...I am receptive and open-minded	...I am careful	...I analyse ideas	...I am practical
	TOTAL the scores from each column	Column 1 (Emotional)	Column 2 (Reflective)	Column 3 Aanalytical	Column 4 (Action)

Following Learning Styles have been conceived to define the inter relationship of cyclic process

Style one: Emotional and Experiential Style:

This style describes personal indulgence and emotional involvement with people in everyday situations. Here learners tend to rely more on feelings than issues. In a learning situation, one would rely more on one's ability to be open minded and letting oneself go to have the experience of the process. Learners always state, 'let us have a feel of the things before forming an opinion. It is called emotionally connecting to the process and learn the most. Learning from unfreezing sessions are considered to be very powerful. It is emotionally enriching and involving with an open mind.

Style Two: Observational and Reflective style

In this stage of the learning cycle, people understand ideas and situations from different points of view. Learners tend to observe, reflect and draw meaning from the context. In a learning situation you would rely on patience, objectivity, and careful judgement but would not necessarily take any action, You would rely on your own thoughts and feelings to form opinions.

Style Three: Analytical and Deductive style

In this stage, learning involves using logic and ideas, rather than feelings, to understand problems or situations. Typically you would rely on systematic planing and develop theories and ideas to solve problems.

Style Three: Action and Experimentation

Learning in this stage takes an active form experimenting with influencing or changing situations. You would have a practical approach and a concern with what really works, as opposed to watching the situation. You value getting things done and seeing the results of your influence and ingenuity.

Knowing versus Learning: Exploring through Vedantic Mode

If we draw parallel with Kolb model of learning cycle we may draw interesting similarities of process and its qualitative mix with that of vedantic theory which Krishna employed in learning frame to facilitate the learning of his disciple Arjuna. 'Knowing that 'process through class room preaching in Guru-shishya model in early days has no meaning unless the disciple-the Shishya does not take it forward it to the practice and experience. Knowledge of Abhimnayu[40] in Mahabharat on technology of battle field interception was of no consequence unless he moved to the real battle field. Absence of practice and real experience made him succumb to the enemies in the battlefield. The practice takes us to 'learning how'. Knowledge of shastra by Yudhister the eldest of all Pandava brothers did not offer knowledge of foul play and cheating by his cusions Duryodhan in the game of chess at the house of Pandavas.

Extensive dialogue of Krishna and Arjuna has been one of the most enlightening process of self analysis and self discovery while questioning the human learning foundation. Krishna spoke of a cyclic learning mode viz."Bhakti, Dhyana, Gyana and Karma". He found that each mode has its own significance while enabling a learner learn the ultimate truth.

[40] Abhimanyu, the son of Arjuna and nephew of Krishna had known that ***intercepting the chakrabyuh"the complex"*** **center of enemy domain was well taught by his father while he was in his mother's womb. But he had know it fully well that he had yet to learn since that was never practiced by him. He failed to succeed since he never' learnt how' part but had 'known that part'.**

Bhakti,form of learning orientation, according to him was the simplest but the purest of the pure. Because it takes one to experience the truth without any screening. Knowledge or Gyana enables to question and block one's emotional drive to understand the process. Let us illucidate how it makes a meaning to correlate the established western model of David Kolb with Krishna's philoshophical frame to help learn Arjuna mode of learning in Mahabharata in a great Indian epic. It might be interesting to examine the contemporary theories of learning and knowing before we dwell in to vedantic model that might sound too simplistic on its face value.

Phronesis—the Vedantic Comparison

The science of ***Phronesis*** is defined as Practice of Knowing. Very little has been done by school of David Kolb and modern organization psychologists in this regard. Nor management researchers have gone beyond process driven - experiential learning mode to a level of oriental understanding that Vedanta has taught over thousand years. I found some of the current literature with philosophical bend that seems to connect what I would like to offer postulates learning versus knowing. It might be seemingly a hypothesis that needs further tests and examination to collate deeper review of literature of our vedantic period of Gurukul traditions. Philosopher Gilbert Ryle during mid nineties has discussed in detail in his book ***Concept of Mind*** the subtle difference between knowing and learning. Karim's analysis in his recent work may find an interesting glimpse to locate the relation between vedantic learning learnt by Arjuna in the battle field. While he was in the battle field meaning of life, values, its existence was discussed to an incredible depth of clarity and conviction.

Pedagogical cycle:

Learning by Doing is the acquisition of experience that one is deprived by knowing alone through text books or class room teaching offers. Most of the structured learning mode offers 'knowing that' was taught. One could never know how to transfer it to the life.

Learning That In the absence of context – far away from reality of experience. Yet the person learnt that was taught. High capability driven learner do learn fast and better. But it may not be as realistic as it ought to be in the absence of context.	Knowledge imparted by Krishna Outside the battle field.. had Arjuna raised the doubt before stepping in the battle field. Experiencing the degree and nature of ambiguities and crisis of confidence might not have been visibly felt by the teacher (Krishna) and taught (Arjuna). The context could have been kept aside. Very intelligent learner like Abhimanyu, Arjun might visualize and imagine the context yet the real experience would be missing.
Learning How Context is dependent on quality and varities of learning. The learner is fully in the actual doing mode with the grip of experiential learning. It has greater risk for the facilitator as well for the learner. Lab setting offers the contextual reality though little away from real life yet the small group dynamics depict all that real life context like learning swimming in a swming pool with coach around.	Presence of Krishna and Arjuna in the battle field while directly addressing the confusion and disbelief on likely glory and fame with disillusioned mind of Arjuna must have given challenge to facilitator Krishna. He took eighteen days to dwell on the issue unless Arjuna was completely satisfied with clear sense of purpose.
Knowing that Context and real life experience is not felt but concept is imparted. Only few intelligent one might pick up the point. Rest of the learners would stay as laggard since they can not visualize the emerging real issues. Indian students joining the higher degree like MBAs and technical qualification like engineering etc without any work experience hardly learn the how part. They know that was taught.	Arjuna could have learnt much better than Duryodhan,because of his higher capabilities. Dronacharya teaching to Pandavas and Kauravas in Gurukul might have imparted knowledge with full sincerety. However, Arjuna's competencies made the difference.
Knowing how It defines how to gain something. Say for example learning by doing teaches how part. The quest of knowing how drives us to move to contextual reality.It is visible in the performance of an act. If a person is bodily in action he gets faster insight and does it more critically.	Knowing how drives to learning how and vice versa. It is coexistence of context, reality and learner. On the contrary imparting knowledge is a close to real life experience for Arjuna while and facilitator. Krishna's discourse to enable Arjuna in order to clarify his doubts.

Bhakti is characterized by devotion and complete sublimation to what one believes to be. Bhakti leads to trust that is beyond one's belief. It drives to faith eventually to ultimate trust in a process or a person. One undergoes concreate experiential learning of the process where learner dwels in to the inner connectedness with self. A Bhakti mode learner does not question the experiences that he goes through. He believes from the core of the heart, therefore, and moves beyond the scope of any doubt. There is a difference between belief and trust. A person who has not fully undergone concrete experience may not move to bhakti therefore how can he step in to trusting relationship. Trust is born out of love. If you find you can not because of loaded past experiences. Computer drive (CD) has to be rewritten. I need to clean it and work hard to create a new one[41]. Experiencing the present or here and now gives total synergy with ultimate truth.

> *Ye yatha maam prapdynate tamas thathaiva bhajamawaham*
> *Mam Vartmanvartante manushya parth sarvasha.*

Krishna says that "if one dwells fully with Him without any question or doubt in any form I am with him. I am there with a person who worships me in whatever form he wants me to bestow." While longing for success we worship and trust the God.

Bhakti learning styles

If we let our selves be with feeling and trust, Bhakti would drive us to deepest learning. Let us go to early days of Gurukul learning system, where Bhakti mode and complete trust in Guru was the strategic design for creating strong supportive learning environment. Shishya's full faith in the competencies and intent of guru was the driving force to bring them together.Degeneration of bhakti ie trust in the intent has eroded the quality and value of learning outcome.

I learn since I trust and fully sublimate to Him.

I learn the truth since truth has bestowed into me without any screening or filter.

I learn the most when I fully experience.

[41] Bhagavad Gita chapter iv lord Krishna says whatever way you worship I am available to you..I fulfill desires of the devotee's and walk through their path that worshipers want me to.

If we examine the questionnaire stated above few points resemble so close to what we have discussed. It is so connecting to drive a meaning of emotional and experiencing learning style with that of Bhakti mode of learning style.

Dhyana[42] is characterized as a mode of reflective and internal exploration of self. The reflective process is synonymous to inner observation. It is something like watching the mind where does it go. Therefore, most religious doctrines have suggested that there is "one behind many. 'The infinite, the absolute must form the background to the forms of the God we meditate on. Most people prefer to meditate on the holy forms of God. One need to understand that such forms are manifestations of invisible absolute the supreme. Therefore, why not mediate to something infinite like the sky or ocean or the sun for everlasting energy. Our personality is a combination of true and false self. If one is drowned in "the infinite ocean of consciousness, the person will feel that personality is subtle that has become gross[43]."

The mediation on anthropomorphic symbol of the divine, like ocean or sky may be construed as monism hence keeping the mind on holy symbol leads to dualism. The choice is entirely that of the learner as to what form he wants to proceed for dhyana.

- *With form and with attributes* ***(sakara).***
- *Without form but with attributes* ***(nirakara).***
- *Without form and without attributes* ***(nirakara and nirguna).***

Dhyana Learning style

In the course of dhyana mode of learning observation and reflective meaning of experience undergone has direct bearing to subsequent analytical and concept formation. How do we think of self that is identified as body and process within and beyond.

- I like to watch and listen to my inner noise.
- I like to observe and reflect uneasiness within self.

---

[42] 'Mystery of mind" has been discussed by Swami Shivanand deeply to highlight that Dhyana is a higher mode of learning in quest of superconscious.The power of kundalini awakening lies in meditation process that is popularly known as Dhyana. ISABS has recently experienced the meditation in a series of Sunrise session led by diffrent professionals.

[43] Swami Yatishwarnanda, 'Meditation and Spiritual life' op cit p419.

- I like to observe and wait to derive meaning of the interpersonal dynamics around people and process.

The observational learning mode is quite similar to that of reading mind, people and processes. It is higher than just emotionally like that of Bhakti experiencing. It is the process of calming and cooling to watch and read instead of getting hooked to feeling. One may move towards Bhakti to Dhyana or directly to dhyana state. David Kolb has also hypothesized that experiencing state is quite independent of observing and reflective states of being.

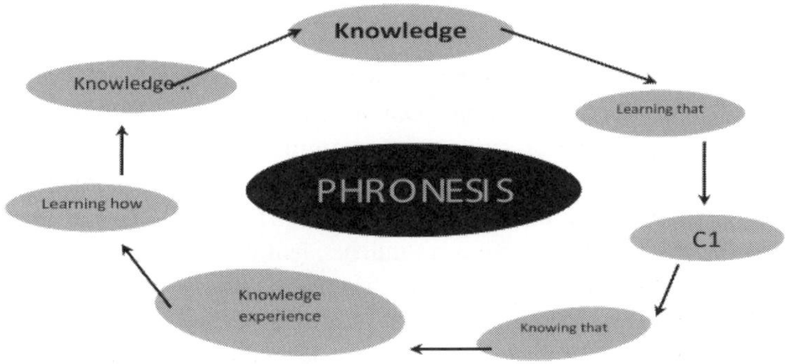

Intelligent performer acts critically and observes the process to follow critically.

Competencies Required

Subjects	Character	Competencies
Bhakti mode learner	Dedication Devotion Faith & Commitment Trust	Listening Involvement Focused to the goal Endurance
Dhyna mode learner	Concentration Neutrality Undeterred Detached Dispassion mode	Introspection Observant Meticulous Tolerance To antiquity Intuition

Learning System	Characteristics	Competencies
Gyana Learning System	Inquisitive Curious Investigation Confrontation Quest of Knowing	Logical and Rational Analytical Data gathering
Karma Learning System	Hardworking Persistence Perseverence .... Selflessness Sacrificing	Problem Solving Conflict Resultant Persuasions Result Imitation Executing and setting standard

Paradoxically the four learning systems have closely been debated in modern education psychology. David Kolb and his associates have stretched it further the supportive quantities and competences like that of above viz. diverge Assimilator, Adapter and Accomodator. But Vedanta does not talk of the four competences in discrete mode, nor the four systems can be viewed as an independent to one and other. One is studying connected to the other with the core of purpose as ultimate Goal in the centre. It gives modern meaningful them drawn for has not paid attention to gravitation force of learning. I would call it why learning? Why to learn?

Which part is the most crucial for being and becoming a person. Most learners do not know as to why they are learning what they have decided to Learn. Therefore action learning (or Karma Mode) has taken many of young aspirants with bright career in modern competitive world. Large number of young and brilliant young boys and girls after schooling opted to go for job in BPOs. They kept working in morning and night shifts endlessly. They learnt to join several language courses in early years of their career struggle. I had a chance of speaking to many of them during their pre-joining counseling session. Following excerpts of their interface with me might give us a clue as to how unclear most of them are?

"Common response on my questions as to why they wanted to learn so many languanges."

"It is job opportunities, most of them used to respond."

"Why to step into a job profile that is so sickening and disturbing to your body balance of working entire night hours."

"Good money with no string of higher education" used to be common response.

Money making with limited educational qualification, glamorous life with permissive work culture where boys and girl had chance to evolve their own friendly relationship in the garb of social skills."

"Are you going to take it up as a career?" I used to ask them.

"No never; it is just a stop gap arrangement" many responded. But I found that majority of them got sucked to it and got used to it. Of course many hated yet they had limited options to move after having burnt their cream part of formative career building age.

Short term goal

Absence of purpose in life with myopic vision of career, young people have lost their direction.

'Meaning of purpose' in life is closely associated to our visioning of learning goal. 'Learning why' is never examined by many. Most often we tend to move forward towards "learning that and learning how" with debating on the why part. Clarity of purpose and central goal of learning is the ultimate happiness and bliss. The vedantic model has already addressed long long ago which modern psychology and global literature of management have not touched a fraction of it.

Vedantic mode of human learning cycle

Krishna's untiring attempt to convince Arjuna was to help him understand the ultimate purpose of his victory in the battlefield. Arjuna's myopic vision of winning or loosing a battle did not ground him on the '***learning why'*** frame of Krishna.

He questioned his assumptions of underlying fear of loosing self acceptance and self esteem that he had earned by learning the art and science of weaponary from Dronacharya, the great guru of his time.

Krishna motivated him to self examine. Did he learn for self glory? Did he learn to win or loose a battle of great magnitude? Or did he learn to demolish the 'Adharma' (devils) and help replace Dharma on the earth? The ultimate purpose to learn was "to seek bliss, the greatest joy by destroying the evils from the earth".

The four component model is central to easy learning theory that Vedanta had advocated. It has impacted the learning stance of human beings in a natural mode. The cycle that has been established in modern management theory of adult learning frame [44] is close to western school of modern learning.

Arjuna was considered to be the greatest warrior (Dhanudharr) trained by Dromocharya amongst all his students, has been dismissed as is evident from several epics of Hindu Scriptures of Gita and Ramayana.

Rama's Voyage for fourteen years away from the luxury of kingship was closely linked to his ultimate purpose of his Avatar (incarnation). Entire family of Rama objected to his decision (except his step mother Kaikai). But he was awakened to his supreme goal. Therefore, he thanked his step mother and complied with her wish. Love bondage, logic and reflection by his father and other key ministers did not stop him in pursuance of his unstated mission of his life. To a common reader Rama's action appeared more as an obedient and compliant son of a step mother to fulfill the old promise of his father. But the deeper meaning of his Avatar (incarnation) was elimination of the evils from the earth. Gita has strongly spoken about Krishna's conversation with Arjuna on four vedantic learning models. At one stage Arjuna pleads to Krishna that dhyana may drive to deep attachment to lust and greed if the same is not neutral and focused to higher purpose.

---

[44] David Kolb theory of learning as stated above in this chapter has described four learning styles that draws a corollary with vedantic model. One can not affirm if David has read and acknowledged the vedantic model of Krishna .Nevertheless it is very similar to our oriental philoshphy as discerned .

"Dhyanat Vishyan punsham sangetpshu pajayete
Sangetpeshu jayate kama kamatkrodhat upjayete"

If the focus is too short sighted as mode of Dhyana it might drive the learner to lust and greed towards the goal; failure to that would drive to anger and loss of memory destructing the wisdom of the human mind.

Gyana learning style

Yearning to know and quest of knowing may be powerful modes to reach the ultimate destination. However, Gayna or depth of knowledge might be a serious impediment and obstacles in pursuit of discovering ultimate truth and self exploration. Gayna mode is a quest towards analytical orientation of self and the world where we live in. Learner who questions and poses serious doubts in order to understand the process and system he seems to be quite critical to accept things as they are. We have found in small group process work that those with psychological education background or with higher logical background of educational degree like technology and system. and Ph.D etc have serious emotional block to move towards process insight. Learner has a great difficulty in self acceptance and understanding unless he or she has come to clarity of thought and sound analysis.It is believed from philosophical origin that:

- Quest for information may or may not lead to knowledge.
- Quest for knowledge may or may not lead to gayna(wisdom).
- Quest for wisdom would eventually lead to wealth of ultimate bliss that stays for ever.

Ironically, those in contemporary world are striving to convert their knowledge in to wealth do raise their concerns as below." How long shall we remain poor with so many educated people exported to the rest of the world. The 'k' is not being converted in to wealth, should we not generate wealth by inviting the world to acquire knowledge through our innovation. Gayana the fulcrum of knowledge has always been center of learning syndrome of human beings. If we learn without gaining wisdom at the end of the day, the learning is a futile exercise.

Karma learning style

The karma yogi's classical example has been that of Krishna's entire life and living. The purpose of karma mode of learning is to become central to doing.

Therefore, Krishna advocated Arjuna to learn by karma mode than by emotion and analysis alone. "Having reached a point of karma why do you indulge in analysis and attachment due to emotive factors. It is your act without getting hooked to expectations and fruits.?"

"Nasti bhdhhirukatsya nachyauklsya bhawana". 'The steadfast wisdom comes when one is fully engrossed in karma without dwelling oneself in any other mode of the learning ladder. Karma or the doing mode of the learning, always encourages people to learn while doing not by brooding and reflection. Most technocrats, engineers in public sector organization have been found caught up in doing syndrome. Doing syndrome does drive people to target orientation, result orientation and action priority. Paradoxically speaking his poetry on karma the "play is done" reveals an interesting pattern of learning while living.

> *"Ever rising, ever falling with the waves of time,*
> *still rolling on I go*
> *From fleeting scene to scene ephemeral,*
> *with life's currents' ebb and flow.*
> *Oh! I am sick of this unending force;*
> *these shows they please no more"*

The flow of action drives me to learn with no yearning of outcome and fruits of efforts..Action learning syndrome of learners might dissuade him to swing towards emotional and analytical mode. However, it is the combination of style that makes him divergent or assimilator. It is the pattern of duality that determines the nature and emphasis of learning orientation of learner.

Conclusions

The learners learn by themselves. The learning process is self directed because we learn only when we want to learn. However it is strongly believed that twenty first century organization is driven by regular and rigorous learning, particularly through open and critical review and debate. This has to be addressed at all levels of the organization, as part of the normal work. Continuous learning is about sensing and responding to the changes in the external and internal worlds of the organization. If we take in to account at self level learning, the matter is highly psychological and self introspective. Above analysis and review defines the personal learning theories from different perspectives. Western school of thought seemingly reconnect our oriental and mystical belief. But most of such studies have hardly acknowledged their moorings to eastern origin. Nevertheless, it is better to find the unity and convergence in the process. Let us draw the implication of learning cycle at organization level in order to facilitate the organization learning The loop of policy learning followed with strategic and operational learning have been adequately discussed.[45]

We may draw corollary on related matter of self learning as against organization learning but principles of interconnectivity between self and organization are a complex task to comprehend. Individual orientation to learn and organizational process to build the capacity to learn is synergetic and complimentary to each other. However the focus of the above chapter was purely on learning to learn as a person not so much as an organization. I have addressed several workshops on building organization learning laboratory through human process mode. I found eventually that people's willingness, approach and ability to learn has influenced the outcome.

---

[45] Bob Garrat, "The learning Organisation" Developing democracy at work, Harper Collins, UK 200.

Chapter VI

Me and My Religion–A journey beyond sensitivity

I never knew what religion I belonged to until my parents told me during my early childhood.. I used to join morning prayers and weakly satsang with my parents to join the chorus. I had crammed the *shlokas* of Panchtantra and Nitipudesh of Sanskrit that did not speak of any religion but values of building sound character and human relationship. I comprehended the meaning of 'religion' as an italic origin word that conveys" binding together" Those tiolcversatile trainers who have gone through mills of training on applied behavioral science over the years have been very skeptical to speak on their religious beliefs and virtues in order to bring their grounded insight on process learning. Of course there are veterans who are noted process trainers, they have dealt with such intricacies incredibly well. Contributions of Somnath and Late Pulin Garg have always been a matter of significance in this regard with several modules. However, we do learn from the daily chores of life? Journey to pay homage to some one proceeding on pilgrimage has been a unique experience of its own kind.. Ganesh Chella[46] wrote a beautiful piece sharing insights of his personal journey. Very few people tend to reflect on such insights of life. This work speaks of lessons drawn of deeper level from such occasions of life.-

[46] Ganesh Chella a professional member of ISABS has touched an account of journey to a pilgrimage that he took up quite sometime back(Here and Now journal of ISABS published)

On Being Religious: And Faith

Religion has always been a bliss to the society at large but has also been a bane to divide one or the other to dwell in their cocoon and get rooted too deep to see beyond. Process trainers reflective journey can make a difference and build a common bridge to work for a much wider religion of humanity. Love, care, bondage, togetherness and service to the deprived and disadvantaged become crucial to all pervasive religions of humanity. As a born Hindu, I did carry a lot of my moorings to define the world of my growth through those symbols and virtues around my upbringing. As a child I used to sit with my father to join his prayers who had strong influence of Gandhian philoshphy. I strongly believe that all religions drive us to same God, but directions, rituals and symbols are different. However, we do hold on to our roots and beliefs and become too sticky.

Every great religion has placed mystic insight of all in their own.Regions like Christianity, Islam, Judaism have placed main emphasis on morality and faith as means of salvation.

Ganesh Chella[47] wrote quite sometime back "I recently undertook a pilgrimage to Sabarimala, which is the abode of **Lord Ayyappa**. The preparation for this pilgrimage, the journey and the darshan of the Lord was a very joyous and touching experience. While the pilgrimage has over the years grown into a very popular movement, not many have perhaps seen the potential it offers as an instrument for experiential learning. On the other hand, we seem to be attracted by the so-called Outward Bound Training Programs (OBTs) also called 'Wilderness Labs', 'Adventure learning', 'Leadership Experiential Adventure Programme', offered in the West". These programs use outdoor experiences to bring home learnings in human behaviour.

We also have our own homegrown Indian versions already existing, which can be made contextual. Do we learn from such experience where we join with family members to our pilgrimage? The following extract of Ganesh Chella is a touching episode of drawing lessons of new meaning of faith transcending to our consciousness.

[47] Ibid

Values and Virtues

There is a mythological and historical account about the existence of Lord Ayyappa. Historically, Ayyappa was the son of a priest, a brave and valorous young man, who led an army through the treacherous jungles in Kerala, across mountains and rivers, to free a temple which was haunted by dacoits.

The annual pilgrimage to Sabarimala in Kerala that people make is a symbolic recreation of the army's march to the same temple to worship the Lord.

In the process of building the army, Lord Ayyappa nurtured among people values of equality, unity and brotherhood through various symbols. He brought religious harmony to the extent that Muslims visit this temple to worship the lord and all pilgrims visit a 'dargah' as part of the tradition and offer prayers before going to the temple. Collaboration, courage, determination and networking is a continuous theme of this 'Hero Story'.

The Penance and Faith

Ganesh adds that "that preparation for the pilgrimage includes giving up footwear, adorning a dark colored doti, eating vegetarian food, addressing others respectfully as 'Swami' (the Divine in you!) and chanting God's hymns every day." Is it not tuning one's antennae to the divinity in a person and divinity in others who claims to be religious?. Being religious and ritualistic may appear contradictory but most of religious beliefs do have an intriguing blend.

This invites the challenge to help people understand the common value of humanity and faith for a psychological war in one sense. It also symbolizes a period of self-purification and selfless living. To me, it meant making commitments to myself and standing up to them. I met a Haazi returning from his religious trip back to India. He said with all humility, "I meant the trip was experimenting with a life of utter simplicity. I began to realize that what I thought was 'my need' was not really needed, and I could do without it. I felt every one was divine. Of course there were so many rituals that I had to experience. Rituals are desirable to fill in the girth of religious belief that adds value to it's faith that one persues."

The piece of such experience is process of transcending the faith in to a new consciousness and wisdom. Let us explore how such insight and energy may be shaped into wisdom. The fact is that there is no difference between the observer and the observed.

Ganesh wrote further that the "Journey is normally undertaken as a group, under the guidance of a leader called 'Guruswamy'. The leader plans the journey, makes all the arrangements and 'commands' the army. For me it was a good experience being a follower, being disciplined and not asking why. Each pilgrim carries on his head an 'Erumudi' which is a linen bag containing pooja material and also rice and provisions needed to cook food on the journey. This symbolizes each person carrying the load and sharing responsibility. Pilgrims normally travel light since the journey involves walking a distance of over 50 kms. barefoot, the terrain being rocky and mountainous and hard to the feet.

Bhakti is a manifestation of deep faith. That is not a mere feeling, but conviction consequent on the knowledge of relationship with the bondage of love to the supreme.

The group consisted of people from very diverse backgrounds and professions with people from all age groups. But all this diversity and differences and the fact that many were strangers to each other did not affect the ability of the group to mobilize resources, share responsibility, co-operate and yet respect boundaries. This was truly amazing.

With the faith I would believe that if they all could, I could too. I had made the choice to come and I had to keep going on. I finally made it, it was a moment of truth and discovery for me. When we all sat together and shared our experiences, I shared this experience of mine. Faith has been so powerful force to ignite my energy within.

Multiplicity of Rituals and Faith

Similarly, in Orissa, Bihar and eastern Uttar Pradesh the 'Sun lord' is worshipped with great sense of purity by the worshippers. Surya (Sun) is the Lord and honest ruler of astral plane. He is the bestower of intelligence, self illuminating, electricity, Vedas, truth and energy. He creates energy in the form of food and water and symbolizes the power, fame, courage and kinship Festival is known as Chhat which falls six days after Deepawali. Last year I decided to offer my prayers where complete sanitation around with strict vegetarian diet is observed while praying lord Sun. Devotees go for 48 hours of complete fast without water and food in a rare sacred mode of cleanliness in and around.

Entire family members and neighbours join the festival with great sense of unity and collective endevour. I never realized that I could do with so much ease. It was total faith unto God while mediating and praying throughout the fasting period. My actions were directed to a process of penance and faith by which that such prayers in Hindu practices are adopted. It was painful moment until I stepped in. The very task of choosing for the prayer along with family members made me feel different. Surya being innate source of life offers photosynthesis to vegetation of the earth and perhaps only visible and directly felt God in Hindu scripture. I discovered new meaning of inner energy, purity and was self - rejunvated.

Energy of the sun has been boundless and almost infinite much before humans existed on the earth planet. Different religions and civilizations worshipped the Sun in different symbols and modes. In Egypt people worshipped in the name of Ra. In Greece 48there were two sun deities Appolo and Hellios. The influence of the sun was on several religions.

I learnt with certainty that feeling of pain was purely psychological and existed only in the mind. It was the mind that was not giving me permission to try and move forward with faith and devotion. Large number of such devotees who have been visiting Amarnath, amidst snowy mountains and difficult terrain and have been taking walk up to height of Vaishno devi temple in Jammu & Kashmir in northern India. Himalya foothills have given permission to people who marched to offer their prayer with a tinge of penance and faith.

A visitor to Amarnath yatra shared "I was so scared at the outset but I was able to look at my own fear (especially physical fear), a feeling that I have been struggling to deal with for many years. I also became more aware of 'Faith'. The Faith in God and Nature that reassured me that nothing adverse would happen." The devotee adds further, "The water I drank from the river was not filtered, the river I bathed in was not purified, the food I ate was not quality tested and the places I slept in were not cemented or cleaned. Yet, nothing at all happened to me. These are things I would shudder to try out in normal life back home. I believe

---

[48] Editorial note of development milestone-journal of development leadership: Vol 3:2 2008, New Delhi.

that the difference lies in faith and belief. The strength of this faith and belief is what empowered me to do things that I fear and hesitate to do. As the journey progressed, I increasingly got in touch with this spring of power. I was also able to test out the depth and conviction of my espoused value of simplicity and feel proud that I lived up to it. My greatest discovery was seeing the power of teamwork on display in our group." Another haji friend of mine,very religious and pious person, who had returned from Mecca pilgrimage sometime back. He was a changed person. He used to drink casually though Islam religion does not sanction such practices at all. "I made a commitment to myself that I must stop drinking for ever. I did so next day and for the last ten years I have not touched alchohal"It was a memorable event for him to have sankalpa after his pilgrimage.

Age and Time to Become

There is no time and age to become religious and a spiritual person. I used to entertain my thoughts that old age is the best age to step in to religious and spiritual mode after enjoying the fruits of three fourth of life. Many seem to have similar notions. But process training exposure at early age made a great difference to my being and becoming. If I connect many such examples of Hindu mythology and illustrations of Ramkrishna Parmhansa's discourse to Vivekananda, time and age has no bar to step in to the search of ultimate peace and happiness.

"If God is the epitome of ultimate peace why wait for the old age when you have little time to serve the society and move to karma that gives ultimate happiness and joy" Swami Shivanada spoke to his disciple in his Ashrama. So is journey of self search in process centric learning programme. The quest of spirituality and religious practices in search of God may begin from childhood as well. Story of Bhakta. Prahlada as a child is known for intense devotion for Lord Vishnu. His demoniacal father tried all in his power and authority to drive him to worldly pleasure. But the brave and the courageous boy fought with devotion and faith. Finally God came to his rescue and asked him to seek the blessings whatever he wanted. Prahlad asked, ***"my Lord, should thousands of birth fall to my lot, may I still always possess an ushakable and unflinching devotion to Thee". In Gospel of Shri Ramkrishna the idea of yearning of God is stressed very much. Whatever path you follow, Whether, Muslim, Hindu, Christian, Sikh or Jews – the vital point is***

the state of restlessness that one gets in touch with. If we are in touch with our inner self in search of our being ;the guide within will take us to destination. The fact is we must be restless to go for an experience in search of God. In Islamic scripture- Quran, Khuda (prophet) is in abode of khud (self). Sayanmbhu is lord shiva's ultimate abode is inner peace and ultimate joy.

Those who seriously struggled for spiritual life and those who have surrendered themselves to Divine need not fear. Divine is always with us. Infinite is always with us.Jesus Christ is always with us.. Lord Shiva is within that is embodiment of my faith, energy and eternal power. Many in small group work seek love by giving love to others. and in return they keep expecting love and warmth from others. Manifest behaviour of individual members would be to protect and deal with their anxiety of over help towards others quite often. They get hurt very soon for not having received love and affection from those to whom they protected and supported. I have noticed such an acute pressure of self denial as if they do not need to love themselves but to keep expecting from the world to shower love to them. Loving oneself is loving the God within and getting in touch with inner core.

Lessons: Towards Spirituality

This is what we need to learn while reflecting on this experience and think of other similar religious insights like the holy trip to Mecca or Ajmer sharif or Tirupathi hills etc, I am quite convinced that these experiences were meant to be *individual meaning-making experiences and not mere rituals that belong to any one religion*[49] or the other. Since they are intrinsically dual experiences, what meaning each person derives is really dependent on what the person looks for in it and also the faith with which the person undergoes the experience.

I feel good that in India, we have such a powerful and yet very subtle and simple experiential learning tool available which, so beautifully blends nature, religion and basic human values to help us understand ourselves and learn to work with others. Faith that evolves within a person leads to Sankalpa (the resolve). Jainism preaches for anuvrata (micro resolve).Taking small resolve on any habits drives us to move

[49] Ibid (For details read 'Bhakti school of Vedanta' by Swami Tapayananda published by Ram Krishna Math ,Madras Jan.1990)

towards bigger resolve. Sankalpa rolls down in to creation firstly like ripples from which words are created. Higher domain of Sankalpa as an outcome of lessons learnt from faith and conviction that shows the power of sattawa(absolute truth)[50].As we go down the process, this truth gets enmeshed in ripples like waves of rajas(power lust) and lowest to bottom rung inert and inactive tamas(toxic feelings and act). How do we create such a faith for meaningful life is a process of self discovery through rigours and and self descipline. Religion does teach us to bind our self in doctrines of values and quest for ultimate peace. Let me quote what Mother Teresa used to speak very often to her colleagues;

"The fruit of silence is prayer
The fruit of prayer is faith
The fruit of faith is love
The fruit of love is service
The fruit of service is peace"

Those who have learnt a great deal of understanding of human process, their fear, underlying assumptions values and inner- dynamics of inter-personal understanding need to set a common goal of service to humanity. Questions loom large for process trainers, should they desire to nurture collective social excellence through right human values for peace, happiness and harmony in the society. We must use our religious insights and virtues to build bridges amongst people from different ethnicity, race, caste and creed. Of course, if we have sown the seed of spirituality in their race towards self exploration and process understanding of human dynamics at an early stage in life there is a greater possibility of having spiritual attitude later in life. In my opinion, sensitivity training, in our kind of programmes[51] addresses all that pertains to our learning from senses but there is more to that where applied behvaioural science and process learning converges with spiritual awakening of a person. Nevertheless, managerial world in organizational frame work is constrained to such an spiritual awakeing process that blocks their pace of sustained learning to influence dynamic change process. Most of them, therefore make cosmetic change instead.

"Modern man in search of a soul' has touched the core of self integration with universal spirit Jungeon philoshphy has described 'ego-centric

[50] Pt R K Sharma, Eternal Solutions, May 2009

[51] Human process traning proigramme and many other similar efforts to organizations are designed to work on short term goal of human relations issues.

integration' of personality has given mastery over senses, mind and body but we fail to strive for the fullest integration. Carl Jung[52] has reaffirmed in depth that spirit of a person is Tao –the fullest truth, origin of all thing. He corresponded it with cosmic spirit. With the help of prayers and hymns and by repeating mystic words, meditating on the divine reality we do create vibrations and music in soul that we begin to rise above our little personality, our little ego, our individual consciousness. Then we get in touch with our super consciousness the superego that lies within. The deepest integration takes place when super consciousness is in touch with the conscious self– the body, mind and senses. Because spiritualized ego is rooted in the universal being the cosmic power. It remains so much in touch with mind and body that every act that a person does remains in tune with the prakriti(nature). He becomes so spiritually integrated. The faith to himself becomes synonym to faith to thyself.

I am reminded of a story of a king that a participant shared in my group on the last day of my intense human process lab. The king was jailed for 50 years and kept in the dark room by his enemy who ruled his kingdom after putting him in the prison. One fine morning on a bright sunny day kindness touched the soul of the cruel enemy king. He realized somewhere deep down that so much torture to his predecessor is not fair. He personally walked to the prison with soldiers and spoke with a sense of dignity to the prisoner King 'I want to give you freedom. That is enough for you for having lived in the darkness for so many years. I grant you the freedom. Please move out from this place and experience the world beyond this room." The prisoner king listened, pondered and began walking out quietly. Suddenly he saw the bright sunlight of the day out of his dark prison cell. He cried 'Please do not ask me to go;I can not bear so much light of the day. Send me back to the dungeon. I plead guilty do not give me the freedom. I am so much accustomed to ignorance and suffering of my darkness. I do not want a new lease of my life and resisted the soldiers who were walking along with him out of the lonely dark cell" He ran inside the cell of the dungeon that was already closed. He struggled hard and looked around to seek help. His enemy was walking away who bestowed him the freedom. It was a shrill cry in wilderness. No sooner he lost his eyesight and became blind due to the piercing bright light of the day. But indeed he got his freedom.

---

[52] Carl Jung 'Modern Man in search of Soul"published by Routleg and Kegan 1953 London,It has profusely been quoted by Swami Yatiswarnanda in his classic work on "Meditation and spiritual life" published Ramkrishna Ashrm, Banglore. 1989.

While taking it to 'here and now' I asked my participant whom do see here as enemy[53]. He said with all humility and broken voice "my cruel self that put me in prison of ignorance and it was so frightening to see the truth".

One of the days I had a chance to visit an asylum for mentally derailed old people run by an NGO known VISHWAS supported by church group in Greater Noida area near Delhi. I spent some time chatting with them and also with their lady counselor. She said none of them were victim of clinically definable neurosis but from senseless and emptiness of their lives. It might be meaningful here to revisit Ravindranath Tagore's poem from Gitanjali

Freedom is all that I want
But to hope for it my heart breaks
Will I break when I get
Yet I hate it and love it.

Paradox of Mystical Worship

The paradox of mystical worship during the pilgrimage is very intriguing and rewarding. We worship God and offer things what we have got from Him. Flowers are offered and prasadam is offered to our deities. These are the gifts of nature created by God. Devotees offer everything to God and feel elated and touched. It may be an illusion of blessing from Divine.

We say while offering, in prayer "Twadiuam Vastu Govindam Tubhyameva samarpava" Most of the religious families of Christain, Hindu, and Islam faith say before taking food, ''O God we take your blessings of the food that you have given to us. Bless us before we take it." Anything can be offered to the Divine- the dress, flowers, food and tilak etc. Very often people travel quite far to go to Ajmer Sharif to offer Chadar, they go to Vaishno Devi to offer chunri to Goddess. It may sound ridiculous on a pure scientific and logical ground but it is so emotionally fulfilling to those who have experienced the purity of being while offering their prayers at the shrine. It connects us with Divine. Our

[53] The trainer in me was caught in a hunch as if the participant had yet not addressed the authority and he saw me as his enemy in the story. But his response made me feel blessed and moved .It was one of the most touching experiences of my group work a few years back.

sacrifice and offerings make a difference to our value that is unclear and invisible. If we are ready to sacrifice our luxury to Divine we take pains to walk bare feet to offer our prayer. Can I sacrifice a part of my wealth to serve poor and needy.? Do I have kindness and care for those who can not afford the comfort s of life? Worshipping God who is speechless, soundless, and invisible infinite power through a synthetic vision,wider perspective.If we draw the joy by being with Him and happiness while connecting with Him the mystic power of our worship alleviates our being to higher level of satisfaction. Paradox is that God and the self appear to be two entities. To me it is not so. I alleviate my self while extending myself to externally symbolized Divine. He is within and I am a part of that super consciousness—*Paramatma*.

"My mind wonders
When I go for worship in a temple or a church
I choose to confess and speak to myself
Lord is a silent onlooker of my plight and intent.
I love him and he loves me
He is part of me so am I His part".

One of the most powerful interpretations of following text explains what tells the truth of our quest for ultimate purity mentioned in Mahanirvana[54]:

Uttamo Brahmsadhbahavo
Stutir japo adhmao Bhavo
Trahi pooja dhama dhama

Worshiping the idol in the first stage is better than mere repetition of holy name; and singing of divine glories. Better still is Dhayana or contemplation. But highest of all is to integrate and realize 'I am He".

Conclusion

While working in a small group as a trainer I have found the meaning of religion quite opposed to what many think it ought to be. To me when I work over hundreds of lab participant's learning diaries I discover that many people are greatly dissatisfied with themselves, the world they live in and issues that they have been grappling with in relationship. It creates conflict, confusion and question for unsatiated quest for self acceptance

[54] Ibid (Mahanirvana Tantra 14.122 has been quoted in above text) page 379.

and inability to live with their discomfort. Deep seated fear and sense of doubt coupled with low self-esteem and inadequacy has been the floating group agenda at the self level. I recall a participant stating at the end of the lab, "I knew so much about others. Perhaps I knew too much of others. But I have not known myself at all. I had image of my own and stayed in a fool's paradise. It is the search of our consciousness that gives us an idea of our true nature.

It is the super consciousness that connects us to our higher self. Such a process is led by the inner spirit, the quest for being and becoming. Spirituality is the essence of all religious thoughts provided we attempt to discover our struggle for integration between unconscious with the conscious self. Religious practices take us to prayer. We join for pilgrimage to set ourself towards purity and offer our prayers to God. Faith is the most essential thing in the prayer with submission to God. Prayer is the means of such discovery that takes us near God provided we connect our heart and mind to the hidden energy of God within. Spirit or the passion that takes us to stability in calmness despite our indulgence in Karma. The spiritual aspirant realizes and feels it most poignantly, from the depth of his heart and cries to the Lord within.That is the beginning of his self confrontation. The depth of a devotee is love for God. Gita says "Relinquish the path of formal religion ad take refuge in Me. I will liberate thee from all sins. Grieve not "Many People keep grieving and blaming the past in the hope of living in the present. Neither they create a future of their choice nor they enjoy the present but keep on lamenting on the past that drives them to misery. Therefore, it is the purity of owning all the sins and evil that I possess that are part of me leads to self acceptance. My doing and my being merges so deep and so well, as stated in Upanishad below[55] that takes me to pure divine self

"Charanam Pavitram Vitatm Puranam
Yen putastrati duskritani
Ten pavitran shudhen puta
Atipapmarati tarem"

"Being purified by the holy, all pervading and eternal presence of effulgent.. Being,, man gets rid of evil. May we too go beyond the touch of sin, our great enemy, being freed from impurity by every Holy spirit 's presence within that purifies all." The process of self confrontation does

[55] Mahanaryana Upnishad 1.11

the cleansing of all sins, through authenticity, genuine understanding of relationship with little differentiation of being and doing. "I am curious to search that merger that seem to be evolving within in pursuit of my process learning journey. I find my religious beliefs and values do not hold boundaries of one and another. It is more inclusive than before yet I have miles to go" Sujit spoke in a small group work during the closing phase of the lab. "We knew that a noted process trainer of his time was more an atheist than, however, his belief and values had great impact on me during my early days.[56] Self can not be seen by visible form. It can be felt and experienced in its purest form. The law of karma and doctrine of transmigration is applicable to those who are caught up in to the triangle of mind, body and ego. Our religious faith and belief drives us to deepest value to help integrate within and beyond the percepts of our sensitivity. Our senses remain coloured and adulterated that does not view the connectedness of cosmic universal self rooted within- that is Swaymbhu (Shiva), Khuda or Budha. Our religious journey has been devised socially to encourage the self purification process. Yet there is a virtual journey that we can take within through our self exploration process.

The next chapter takes us to the clarity on sensitivity traning and trainers' dilemma confronting their assumptions and apprehensions. Self awareness and our growing convictions to bring change in society is rooted in changing oneself.

[56] Late Sujit Bhattacharjee one of the founders of ISABS had a deep passion to pursue the darker side of invisible self during intrapersonal exploration. Somnath chattopadhyay has been another master facilitator who made a great impact on reshaping of my being on such delicate balance of doing versus being. (An Intern diary and learning journal 1981 Delhi).

Chapter VII

Sensitivity Training and Group Process–Challenges and Dilemmas of facilitators

Group dynamics training has its own jargon like any other discipline.. several schools of thought operate in this direction but sensitivity training has acquired special thrust on concept of self and interpersonal exploration primarily through 'here and now' than that of 'there and then' learn to live in todays' reality is an easy task for many of us if people are grounded and hung up in the past issues, it is very difficult for them to move ahead nor accept the truth of the present. They hardly learn to deal with challenge of today's complexities of life. They are hung up on the residue of past so badly that reality of today looses the essence of living in today's world. Thus' laboratory training' popularly known as sensitivity or T-group training (small group process training) has emphasized on the essence of a process of "living to day," as here and now agenda. Others believe that learning to live in a current reality is always a misplaced notion of coping with cemented past due to one's inability to learn from the past. Some facilitator believe I am not afraid of dealing with past issues of learner in the T-group setting. After all past crucial of his presence. Why do we deny from his being?" a very experienced trainer reacted. T-group cannot described as only here and now focus cdentric' therefore, psychoanalytical approach of understanding self and one's interpersonal relation dynamics also assume critical significance in here and now. However, common notion of T-group training has been here and now is fundamental to group exploration for self learning. group is thus, the resource to steer the self exploration and thereby enhance greater self awareness. Therefore, trainers of T-group have been advocating the principles of "here and now' during small group work with no blend of psychotherapy, no counseling and other tools that drives learners towards greater self awareness and group understanding.

T-Group Training or Sensitivity Training

T-group is relatively an unstructured group in which individuals participate as learners. The data for learning are not outside these individuals or removed from their immediate experience within the T-group. The data are transactions among members, their own behaviour in the group, as they struggle to create a productive and viable organization, a miniature society; and as they work to stimulate and support one another's learning within that society. it is participants centered. it accepts the participants as they are and draw upon them as resources for working in the training laboratory. a major goal of the sensitivity training is to contribute towards personal growth of the participants, particularly through increased self awareness and interpersonal competence. alongwith the personal growth the T-group contributes towards understanding of the group dynamics and the process of group development. these in turn are expected to help the participant in working effectively in groups and organizations.

Let us broadly examine emotional issues that are very common in T-group. This may encourage many trainers to shift from here and now agenda in their anxiety to deal with the emerging emotional issues impinging individuals state of being during the group life.

- ***The problem of identity***: *who am i in this group? Where do i fit in? What kind of behaviour is acceptable here?*
- ***The problems of goal and needs***: *what do i want from this group? Can the group goals be made consistent with my goals? What have i to offer to the group?*
- ***The problem of power, control, and influence***: *who will control what we do? How much power and influence do i have?*
- ***The problem of intimacy***: *how close will we get to each other? How personal? How can we trust each other and how can we achieve a greater level of trust?*

Psychoanalysts strongly believe that the 'present' has been the outcome of one's past. The kind of personality that has evolved is that of yesterday's creation. Therefore, how can we ignore the dynamics of life and its issues that impacted a great deal in our making. If it is true, most of us believe it is. So why do we discourage it to address in our T-group lab setting work? One may debate and ponder over the issues. But logic of both sides are quite convincing. Puritans of T-group believe otherwise. But Indian have gone (particularly-ISABS trainers) crazy. At one level they carry on process work endlessly inside and outside the small group until the event is over. And over the years they have become highly normative in mode of design setting for every act of small group and large group activity. That seem to be discouraging several innovative blend except that of sunrise and special sessions.

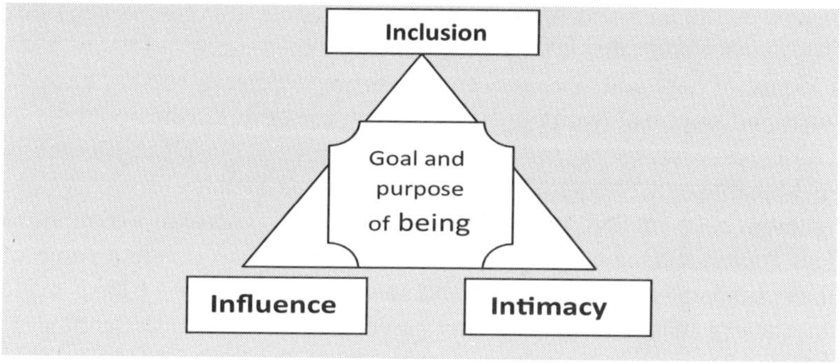

Above four issues stir the person in the group to work on himself or herself tirelessly. If that is so how can we support only group centric intervention in the name of 'here and now' or wait for a moment to advice him to work for the unclocked issues somewhere else. If he does not get a chance he remains high and dry or gets totally derailed person – neither here nor there. There are many such cases in the life of learners interns who have decided not to return back to learning group fold after having undergone final phase experience. I think we are very unfair and unethical to the professional and the emotional health of people at large, if we overdo or undo something that we are not capable of, nor sincere of doing what we ought to. On the contrary we stir the person through the process and leave it high and dry. We need to expand our own vision and values, where T-group occupies importance in the center position. Here and Now therefore occupies one of the most crucial place in addressing T group mode of training.

Puritans of T-Group

The puritans take strong view on that but facilitators of human process lab, in general, have mixed opinion on its velocity and orthodoxy in a human process lab of different nature. The paper discusses the insights and operating dilemmas of the current practices and process on here and now in small group work. From oriental stand point of our Vedic belief we do know that-

> *"Avyaktadini bhutani vyakt madhyani bharta*
> *Avyaktandhinameva tatra ka paridevna"*

Gita defines that past is not visible nor the future is in our sight. Therefore, why to lament and worry for these two. It is the present that lies in the centre of the past and future that is seen, visible and comprehendible. Today is the truth that is evident, and being experienced right now. Thus concept of here and now in T-group learning seems to be very close to such philosophical reality of life. That is what Lord Krishna-epitome of consciousness preaches to Arjuna during the time of his self confrontation in Mahabharata. We symbolize Arjuna as a passionate learner, whose ignorance is fuelled by underlying dilemmas, several assumptions and apprehensions on human understanding. Let us examine some of these inherent contradictions of human process learning. I have made an attempt to share my thoughts based on my own understanding of T-group learning as a student of group process over the years. While I do appreciate the merit of 'here and now 'in lab setting but avoidance of person centric intervention in order to stay on here and now might delay the pace of learning for many learners and group might escape the issues of critical importance for personal exploration until pressure mounts on the person. This hypothesis, of course, is debatable. Some of us may not agree with this at all.

I have also noticed many trainers jumping for person centric intervention opposed to group centric intervention in a typical T-group training to deal with deeper intrapersonal blocks. It is very clear that T-group demands skillful trainer who have patience to deal with contextual reality of 'here and now' with a great degree of patience and endurance with themselves But I have seen many T group trainers running away from the deeper dive on self awareness since they are incapacitated to move in the intrapersonal blocks that has been impacting the relationship in here and now situation. Individual interpersonal relationship issues are dealt inadequately nor the issues are resolved at the self level. Eventually learners are advised to go for 'Advance Human Process lab' time and gain after one lab or other in their journey of PDP.

Let me play 'devils advocate' on this issue. Why can't professional T-group trainers handling phase B or Phase A make reasonable creative intervention at intrapersonal level to enable the group experience of unblocking the residues of those a few who are hung up with inner blocks but have moved to higher level in PDP stage. In the name of here and now fixation, are we setting standards with poor self level work at the early stage or even at higher stages of professional development.

Those who are in great hurry to sharpen their tools of psychoanalytic process and empathetic ability they make quick internvention on person centric issues instead group driven agenda like norm setting role taking etc. That does bounce since group feels dependent on fascilitator.

Logic of using creative interventions in T-group situation are driven on following premise.It demands blend of 'person and group' centric intervention as the time requires. Behaviours produced in T-groups for channelizing emotional energies may be placed as below.

- **Dependency – counter-dependency:** leaning on or resisting any one in the group who represents authority, especially the trainer.
- **Fighting and controlling:** asserting personal dominance, attempting to get own way regardless of others.
- **Withdrawal:** trying to remove the sources of uncomfortable feelings by psychologically leaving the group.
- **Pairing up:** seeking out one or two supporters and forming a kind of emotional sub-group in which members protect and support each other.

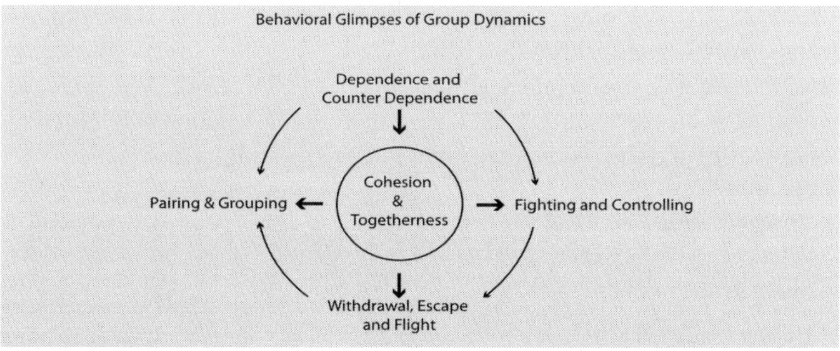

Such emotional issues of person within remain unresolved that emerge on surface again and again when they become trainer. It is obvious that many such trainers find inadequate to address intrapersonal issues that has never been dealt adequately in the learning phase of small work life. I believe here and now syndrome need not compromised on development of skill of self confrontion,self acceptance and self denial that is deeply rooted impacting interpsonal behavior in the group in a person. It leads to escape tendency amongst learner to avoid touching the core and move on superficial interpersonal issues of group life in the garb of her and now focus.

Dilemmas on Learning to Live in the Moment

Let me take the logic otherwise in favour of burying the past. The common belief is that human beings learns to live in the illusion of his past glory or in the shackles of its past depression. The present reality does not encourage individuals to break their pastmaster syndrome easily. In every learning moment they tend to look back their issues and events of the past to emphasise how bad or good things used to be that had impacted their current reality. It is quite common scene with elderly people who would lament the past and beat their drums of past glory accusing that today's life has degenerated in many ways. Why can not we learn from the history of life cycle? Has history become so redundant that we do not want to peep in to draw lessons for the present in shaping our future? A clinically strong trainer raised this question to a group of T group trainers in faculty meet quite some time back during time of Sujit, Pulin[57] and many other veterans of seventies.I was a young observant of the process." Is it our inability to go in to the depth of intrapersonal issues while developing interpersonal and functional skills of facilitators. Intrapersonal work through Gestalt and other therapeutic mode of intervention has significantly slowed down in PDP work. We claim we are doing NTL copy cat but that is not so. Yet NTL is much different than what we are and they have their own reasons to adopt a design.

[57] Sujit Bhattachrjee one of founders of ISABS ,with whom I had a long association. A veteran of T-group evolution in India had a sharp difference on the 'here and now' philoshphy of treating past as untouchable by trainers. He believed that it is the depth of intra-psychic work through self exploration and self analysis would strengthen the competencies of T-group trainer before he learns to delve in to issues of 'here and now'. If we do not offer strong foundation of intrapersonal work how can we help the facilitators become effective to deal with the task of complex human beviour in T-group.

Sociologically speaking generation gap is rooted in such a belief. They live in the illusion of the past and fail to accept the reality of today, where they stand. If we connect this social process in laboratory learning, an interesting dynamics may be experienced. The 'here and now 'focus in the T- group setting, drives the members towards growing orientation of self explaination to address their present behaviour through their past events.. Following statements would endorse an interesting paradigm that may need serious attention by facilitators while running T group lab.

Abhishek, an intelligent engineer executive joined the large public sector company and was attending a cousin lab. "I have never been spontaneous and extrovert from my childhood. I was an introvert. The youngest sibling with five sisters elder to me always over protected and overpampered. I used to play and study in family children network than building any new relation to external world. My interpersonal behaviour orientation got highly influenced due to my early upbringing. " He said in a small group sessionwhen group commented on him on selective pairing in the group.He was very choosy to relate and unwilling to explore inspite of repeated feedback by the group. Later, he went to his withdrawal and resisted to examine himself. The group decided to drop him.The facilitator raised the issue through various mode of group level direct and indirect intervention. But he was unwilling to work on here and now unless he was provoked to revisit and relive his past experience." Facilitaors dilemmas was to steer his attention on what is that he is doing to himself in current situation. He persuaded him to stop explaining but to focus as to how does his behavior has been impacting others in the group. Abhishek kept speaking 'this as his natural style. People did not understand him.

"Tell me what should I do?" he asked.

"I guess you know what should be done by you." Facilitator quipped.

"No, I really I do not.. please help me" Abhi appeared to be serious.

"Why do not you see around and check with the group aren't they helping you and trying to reach you? If you believe their intent you may begin working with them to seek your answers and help your self."

Facilitator statement touched the magic zone of Abhi. He began moving forward. Yet he was a hard nut.

Facilitator left this process to the group to address the issue and expectations of Abhi. This was typically a here and now group centric intervention.

In early stage Abhishek never yielded to the pressure of the group rather his anger was on the trainer and on group members that was quite perceptible.. ***Dilemma of the group was to help him through letting read out the pages of his past or push him to examine i.e his present reality. But trainers' observation made the difference to change the course of action.***

It could also be trainer's dilemma and his intuitive assessment of the situation. Orthodox T group trainer would leave it to group to decide. Participant thus would feel high and dry and carry a strong self rejection and accuse himself for having come to such a learning event. But trainers with multiple skill with a focus on particiapnt's inability and learning goal, may choose to modify the nature and quality of his intervention into a blend of self and group intervention as below. Both the design of intervention had it's own pay off to learning the outcome. Let us examine another case.

Sonali sought repeated help from the group looking at the trainer again and again.

"Why are you asking me to help? I do not think you need any help," Trainer added.

"It is unfair to say, I do need. I trust you more than any one here",she said to trainer.

The trainer diverted her attention to the group." It would be wise if you trust yourself more than trusting any one here. Say what you want to say directly to the group. I sense many of them want to reach you for quite sometime. But you are not sensitive to their initiative and manifestation. Check with the members sitting in the group here.'Facilitators encouraged her to look around.

Sonali became silent and tense. She was willing to step in to a dependence where trainer's authority was safer to have any label. Peers feedback was likely to be more uncomfortable, she thought. The intuitive understanding of the trainer on here and now may vary. The facilitator was willing to confront her directly by putting himself on the mat. He did nothing of that sort. He decided to take her to the group and thus placing her on here and now track.

I believe facilitators' gut level feeling and intuitive act on the agenda has a lot to do in such a situation. Of course, his values do matters. Do I want to take on the person right away out of my impatience, concern and anxiety? It needs to be responded by me before taking a plunge as facilitator. What is bugging me, is more important than what is happening to a person(s) in the group at a given point of time.

Myths of Learners Differential Assumptions

The belief that any errant behaviour of today has to be understood by delving in to the past. The myth that if it is hystertical in the lab it must be historical. Of course trainers or learners may find difficult to get out of the syndrome yet it is desirable to have it done. Therapist would prefer to go backward to have control over the learner the client. But the very belief is mythical in T-group –with a clear 'here and now 'focus.

Participants assume that if facilitators listen to their past they are well understood. many facilitator feel the same way. Modern puritans in T group discourage this practice. They are of strong opinion that going backward is not about creating change. It is the present alone that would shape the future of the person. Therapeutic interventions are generally discouraged in T group yet many facilitators with mixed skills do apply at some point of participant's blockages. Choice may be left to facilitators to intervene while assessing the group life.

Dilemma of immobility in 'present and journey forward' towards future versus understanding the person 'through his past through journey backward' has always been a matter of debate.

In order to accept the past or while coming to terms with life, understanding of the past is important. But are we in a business of encouraging change process in the life of participants or just understanding to help him in the cyclic life process.? That is too cumbersome I guess. I agree that there are many unresolved issues that remain invisible under the carpet. People would like to speak out. They would search for a space to ventilate their pain and unstated stereotypes and apprehensions. We need to choose and make a choice as a facilitator which one is better for the participant. And which one suits his skill and position of comfort.

Many facilitators feel that over emphasis on 'here and now' gives the participants adequate scope to escape and fend for themselves and not address their core issues of self denial, self acceptance, self worth, and identity etc unresolved over the years.. Therefore, they are referred back time and again to undergo ALHP to work after having completed, Phase A and Phase B during ISABS[58] professional development journey. Some of us convert it as a political issue to escape the deep intrapersonal work in the race of becoming a certified T group trainer. Many of us have become good fighters on such political agenda due to prevailing conceptual ambivalence on the promotion and granting of a professional membership after PDP. Ironically we need to yearn for inner fighting or self work as a qualitatively growing facilitators than to fight for building our caucus team and disciples. Whatever may be the case, I strongly believe that T group work on here and now does not and should not dilute the quality of intrapersonal work at any cost in our design. Nevertheless, the 'here and now 'orientation is far more desirable and powerful approach than to jumble in to too many things in T group training. Issue is not of puritans versus non puritans. The most important issue is to help the participants on what he or she wants to work for not what we want to offer.

Assumptions while addressing here and now -	**Assumptions while addressing Past issues**
Learning to live in present reality builds foundation for future changes.	Self disclosure and sharing the past enables the person to unload the junk.
Struggle to relate in here and now helps build skills of giving and receiving the right feedback in group to expand one's blind window of personality.	Understanding the past would help build clarity of the whole person.
Working through 'here and now' agenda is less threatening to work with self and others than to focus on self with clinging past.	If person is hysterical something is historical. Whatever is happening today to me my past is responsible for it.
There is no point clinging to the past for understanding the present and building a new future.	It is very meaningful to connect 'here and now' agenda with issues and processes of the past to have clarity of intrapersonal cyclic processes.

There is a popular story of what comes first –egg or chicken? We know the answer yet most of us dwell in ambiguity. Is it the past that builds the future karma or the present karma that shapes the future. Answer is

[58] Indian society of Applied Behavioural science (ISABS) has well established system professional development programme (PDP) that encourages budding T group trainers to go three rigorous staggered time plan courses for several years with specific guidelines.

straight nothing but the present that builds the future. So here and now must assume central position.

Implications

If we examine the above conceptual frame from our current practices we need to learn a great deal for our future strategy for developing professionals. For example advance human process lab and basic human process lab depict two different orientation and expectations of learners. Therefore, one can not operate on same orthodoxy Let us examine as to why do we send back almost 30-40 % upcoming professional to undergo advance human lab experience in ISABS setting? Most of us attribute for inadequate work done with self in early stage of professional development career. Basic lab participants prefer to learn about each other. On the one hand the focus of the leaner on self is deluded by strong emphasis on contextual reality of here and now. It takes long time to bring self on the mat for self examination. However the work on advance human process must be central to intrapersonal hang-ups without compromising the here and now reality. The corollary of the past issues connected to present would evolve into a clear link of there and then issues with here and now. Can we draw a parallel between the two both as a participant and a facilitator to make new meaning of the relationship between past and present. Isn't true that the 'present' has taken birth from the embryo of the past? So why do we get bogged down to the present that does not encourage to learn from the past at all nor wants to peep in? In order to empower and shape our future the present assumes significance. Let us not steer ourself to be what we want to be, but struggle to become what we were meant to be. Challenges are enormous for a facilitator to be or not to be. Here and now is the essence of a process that drives individuals to the quest of being. Yet the journey of internal self exploration has to assume priority in pursuit of self and interpsonal awareness. This need not be diluted nor compromised in the name of bringing professional excellence in T group. There are other schools of thought that are legitimate and hold equal importance towards our common goal. We must encourage innovation, autonomy and experimentation that has been value of human process learning. Therefore setting boundaries would limit the pace of learner in human process and group dynamics training.

Section – III

Trainers Identity, Methods and Implications

I have learnt that unlearning has most painful process in my training and development career. I did learn yet many things I could never unlearn. My faith ,analysis and my commitment to self with my self image has direct relationship with nature of methodology and skills thereof. The method where I find my comfort is crucial .Challenges of T-group trainers in to day's complex world are enormous and I find it would remain to be relevant in time to come.

Chapter VIII

Trainers or Facilitators –An Identity Search

Styles and Their Methods

It is difficult to hypothesize that identity of a person is closely associated with his choice of training methods and tools used in a learning setting. Particularly, in a given unstructured training set up or T- group situation or process training methods. Its nature of preferred intervention may have some bearing on identity that one has evolved over the years. No such research has been formulated to examine such question in depth. Following piece of work raises some genuine examination on related issues.[58]

Training aims at change in a person. It is re-education, reinforcement and inculcation of knowledge, attitudes and skills in a group or in a person. An overview of contemporary literature, in the area of training and development, indicates a striking phenomenon with regards to the concern for the development of trainers. In fact, there is a major shift in the emphasis on the trainer as a valuable resource for improving the training process. While earlier, the term `training' usually implied training courses and training methods employed, with comparatively little or no significance on the long-term effects of training and the implied contribution of the trainer. Now there has been an increasing

[58] Nagendra singh, the core research team leader had taken up the study to connect with his earlier frame reference that he has been pursuing for quite some time at his own cost with no extra support from ISABS.

realisation that the development of trainers is crucial to develop training as a discipline (Odiorne, 1970). Trainers' behaviour their knowledge skills and attitude have been a critical factor in creating an impact on the learners. Therefore, `trainer' is regarded as central to the process of learning climate (Lynton and Pareek, 1999).

How the trainer handles the situation effectively is open to observations and examination provided the trainer himself has a mental preparedness to do that.

Layers of Trainers Identity

The layers of identity are understood from the concept of self. The self-image is a part of one's opinionated layer; deeper level is that of attitudinal layer whereas the deepest level is that of one's value and belief of a person defining the ground of self-esteem and self-concept as such.

The concept of trainers'[59] development does not stop at merely training qualified individuals in the techniques and skills of training or in accumulating knowledge. Regardless of the knowledge in his field of specialisation, the trainers' motivation, personality characteristics, functional styles and attributes determine to a large extent the quality of training and its impact on the trainees. Trainers behaviour during training could therefore, be the resultant of various related factors to his self-concept both as a professional trainer and also a person. Study of identity layers have touched the depth of search process in a given frame role as trainer. The question of being a trainer and study of their dormant psychological needs would determine the layers of their identity.

Each individual has multifold concepts of himself or herself, who he is, what he does, what he believes, what he values, what he likes etc. It is his frame of reference, personal reality and a screen through which he sees, evaluates and understands everything else. These perceptions of the self vary in clarity, precision and importance from individual to individual.

---

[59] Singh took up this project sometime during early eighties as part of ISABS research initiative where MDI and ISTD were contacted to partially support the effort of the author. The researcher had proposed to examine the cognitive frame (see his case in this chapter). This piece of the document has been modified with recent data base collected to meet the added objectives of the project with new professional members outreach. Therefore the comparison of time frame may not be possible nor desirable .The focus of the project has radically moved to new process insight from the piece of work that was taken up during early eighties.

A person's self concept is the most important factor that affects his way of communicating with others. While situations change, people's beliefs about themselves are the determining factors in their communicative behaviour. While a strong or positive self-concept is necessary for a healthy interaction, a weak or a negative self-concept on the other hand generates a feeling of inadequacy and insecurity.

A weak self-concept proves to be a handicap while communicating with others. Such people find it difficult to express themselves, accept constructive criticism or voice opinions contrary to others for fear of being disliked. They lack confidence in their own opinion and ideas. (Perscot 1945, Lynton and Pareek 1967).

How far trainers' self-concept is related to their role efficacy? What implications it can have with regard to their choice of a particular training methodology? What training style would be preferred by a trainer who operates on a particular assumption about himself? The study envisaged here, aims to examine the inter-relationship of one's style, self-concept and pedagogical preference in a training situation.

Objectives of the Study

In the light of the above, the specific objectives of the study were as follows:

(a) To examine the various behavioural styles of trainers reflecting their concern during training process.

(b) To determine the attributes and self-concept of trainers in the training – learning situation.

(c) To study the inter-relationship between trainers styles and their preferences in relation to training methodology.

(d) To examine the overall impact of the interactive mechanism of trainers, their attributes and pedagogical preferences in the context of pre-training, training and post-training situations.

(e) To explore the determinants of facilitating skills in small group process learning task, and to present the critical learning lessons of par-

---

* Indian Society for training and development

ticipants from varieties of trainers.

Methodology

A survey questionnaire was administered to ISTD* trainers using the purposive sampling technique.

The questionnaire was mailed to 1000 trainers on All-India basis of which 180 responses were received. However, in order to have a larger sample and diverse group of trainers, a few established institutions were also included in the sample. Some of the institutions were MDI, New Delhi, NISIET Institute Hyderabad, as well as the participants of trainers development programme of the ISABS. Thus, additional 70 respondents were also included in the study sample size. The total sample size was 250. A few in depth interviews of trainers were also conducted to enrich qualitative dimensions of the analysis.

Table 8.1: Response from Different Sample Size

1. Corporate structure training client	50 Multi-training agencies (ISTD put training freelancing)1985-1990
2. Social organisation	60 Post capacity building agencies (ASEED-IDMAT)2001-2003
3. Public sector	40 Established training institutions 2001-2003 (MDI, BIRD, NISIET)
4. Mixed participants from corporate/MNC & INGO	100 ISABS 2001-2003
Total	250

Note: Sampling has been drawn from a blend of multiple sources and it does not fall in to common time frame. Therefore, comparison between sub-set of different sample universe may not be statically correct method. However overall view of the trend and behavior may give us adequate insight to the issues raised and objectives defined. Original study by the author (Singh 1985) has been connected to support the hypothesis stated above and to bring in the process dimensions.

Trainers Background and Orientation

Author's own case study and his cognitive mapping on trainer's role may be an interesting shift to bring in a new dimension process insight of trainer self.

Contextual Frame

Since early twentieth century, innumerable research studies have been conducted on trainer's excellence (Singh, 1981). Researchers have looked into trainer's traits, attitudes, abilities, values, behaviour, voice and many other characteristics; trainer effect has been judged by students themselves, administrators, practicing teachers and by themselves. The quality and effectiveness of training is primarily dependent upon the feelings that the trainer communicates to the participants through his behaviour. Thus, understanding the background and orientation of the trainer assumes greater significance.

One of the important pre-requisites of a good trainer is that he must be trainee oriented, in the sense that not only he is aware of the behaviour of trainees but takes actions suited to the emerging training situation. This chapter deals with the trainers' professional background and orientation with particular reference to the training – learning situation. (Lynton and Pareek, 1967).

Professional Affiliation and Experience

Many trainers look for multiple professional associations in order to search their sense of satisfaction and colleagueship in given areas. There is a need to relate and establish one's own identity, there is a gradual move towards fellow feeling amongst trainers of diverse background.

Generally, trainers have wide professional background. A diverse multi-discipline group ranging from 2 years to 15 years training experience covered the sample distribution. Categorization made on the basis of responses collected covered almost all the professional specialisation viz. behavioural science, banking/finance, quantitative area, marketing and material management and general management. Professionals from finance, technical and quantitative area shared more than 35 per cent (59) of the sample size, whereas behavioural science trainers represented only 20 per cent of the sample size. It was revealing to note the diversity in background of trainers in the sample (see Annexure I). Length of experience in training profession had seemingly an equitable proportion in the sample finally adopted for the study. Subsequent analysis of the data is largely based on three categories of experience according to its length viz. high, moderate and low. There was no such deliberate strategy to distribute the size of respondents in different categories, however, it fell in place as above. It is worthwhile to locate the basic educational back ground of professional members of ISABS where hardly 10-15 percent are from basic discipline of Psychology, rest of them are from management, HR background, engineering and other social sciences.

Professional Affiliation (PA):

PA of a trainer normally measures his interest and relationship with several professional bodies relevant to his field of specialisation and work.

Table–8.2: Sample Distribution A/C to Experience and Professional Affiliation Score

Experience	Aff Mean Member-ship office Bearer Score (PAS)	Total Sample Size	(a)	(b)	(c)
High	1.5	72	15	25	32
Moderate	4.0	82	11	23	48
Low	3.4	96	15	25	56
MS	2.8	250	41	73	136

Note-The PAS determine the number of membership acquired by virtue of Maximum obtainable Score = 5, Minimum = 0

As evident from Table–8.1, no relationship was found between the length of experience of trainer and his PA score. Nevertheless, a possibility of reverse relationship was perceptible (not significant at T-test). Trainers with moderate length of experience had secured highest PA mean score followed with those who had the shortest range of experience. However, it was the new group of trainers who had shown higher interest in the office bearership and membership of such organization (34). While majority of such office bearers were young trainers, they hardly held any key position in the organization.

Executive and key positions of the professional bodies are still manned by 'elders' who have already passed through the grill of a long career, and some of them lost interest in their own professional growth and in the growth of the organization (professional bodies) they head. Analysis indicates an emerging postulates:

(a) *That tendency to affiliate with several professional bodies has been higher among budding trainers.*

(b) That experienced trainers continue to hold the 'forte' as key executives of such organisations.

(c) Affiliative relationship to such bodies reduced gradually with the growing length of experience of a trainer except where involvement has been more on a continued power position of the member.

(d) Dysfunctionalities in the operation of several professional society has largely been due to an emerging conflict on a stereotype leadership (perceived by new trainers) at the top by the old (who have no time for the organization) and the enthusiastic and creative young people who form the future foundation of an association.

Table–8.3: Professional Affiliation Score A/C to Background and Experience of Trainers

Sl.No.	Particulars	PAs	Total	(a)	(b)	(c)
1	Behavioural Science& Personnel Area	2.5	60	8	20	32
2	Accounting & Finance Area	1.8	40	10	20	10
3	Quantitative Area	2.1	55	8	20	27
4	Marketing Area	1.66	65	22	18	25
5	General Management & Misc. Area	2.8	30	5	10	15
	Total	10.8	250	53	88	109

(a) Stands for Membership, (b) Stands for membership and (c) Stands for office bearership.

It was observed therefore, that the trainers desire to affiliate with the professional bodies as much as possible, was primarily to enhance their professional recognition and for seeking mutual acceptance with each other. Analysis according to specialisation revealed that trainers in marketing had the lowest PA score and even low profile in the struggle for office bearership. Contrary to that, those in quantitative and behavioural science area were more concerned of professional affiliation, as evident from the table.

Is it that the trainers in these two areas are yet in the process of building their own professional identity in the training world? Whether trainers with finance and marketing background attained the saturation stage in professional identity? Or, they hardly need such a struggle for themselves. HR/personnel and behavioral science people appear to be more inclined and strive to such a goal.

Findings do not answer these questions, instead, they pose leading questions to all those engaged in a trainers development. Whether the professional affiliation provides a sense of enrichment that trainers look forward to is a matter of debate? Most of the trainers saw their affiliative needs satisfied more than their task and professional needs through such associative process.

Perceived Learning Pattern and Interaction

Learning pattern was operationalised in terms of the trainers' dominant sources of learning on his job of training. The pattern of perceived learning influenced their nature of interactive processes inside and outside the class-room setting. Three basic components of learning were chosen for the analysis.

Training Environment

Majority of the trainers perceived that they learnt more through the macro environment from which the trainee hails from. The situations that are known to the trainer by 'his own understanding' of a trainees environment, could be based through his consulting, his own experience of working as manager etc. And thus, they could integrate their experience while training.

Trainees

There is a subtle difference between learning through trainees themselves and learning through their environment. For the purpose of analysis, it was separated. Nevertheless, trainers found it difficult, generally, to discriminate the two (revealed during the case interview). While clubbing the response structure of the sample in above two categories, it was observed that trainers learnt more from the subject matter (reading and preparation for the class). It substantiates the earlier theories in training; that trainers learn more from the trainees and their environment than the subject matter itself.

Nevertheless, it would be interesting to examine further as to what self-image and styles really make trainers think that they seem to be learning more from the subject matter itself. Interestingly, trainers with low experience fell in that category. It appears that trainers who have not grown as experienced trainers, their primary source of learning has been through subject matter. However, 20% of trainers, regardless of their age and experience perceived subject matter as the learning source. It substantiates the hypothesis above, that the grown up trainers generally tend to learn the least from the subject per se than trainees' and their environment.

Interactional Emphasis

Dominant interactional pattern during the training were identified to be of three types viz. (a) trainer and participant, (b) participant and participant, and (c) trainer and subject matter.

While examining the pattern of our sample, it was discovered that 71 of them preferred to encourage interaction between trainers (themselves) and the participants. It does give a positive thrust of 2 way communication in trainers' own belief. However, it was revealing to note that sizeable proportion of trainers had the belief of confining to the subject matter itself. Whether such trainers had perceived similarity in their pattern of learning, is doubtful. There seems to be a deeper incongruity in trainers' perception of his source of learning and his interactional pattern during training. Because, only 50% of them attributed participants to participants interactive mode as the higher sources of learning whereas only 20%.of them kept emphasizing training to subject matter (T-S) as desired interactional emphasis. Nevertheless, trainers' own belief in his learning and interaction had a great bearing on his evolution of self-image (see subsequently in this report).

Table 8.4: Interactional Pattern and Goal Congruity[60]

Emphasis	Total	MS	Congruence (satisfaction level high)	Neutral Level of satisfaction	Low satisfaction level
T---P	91	2.1	56	15	20
P---P	51	2.5	30	7	14
T---S	108	1.4	48	17	43
Total	250	1.8	134	39	77

It was also evident from the Table–IV that majority of the trainers (88) were satisfied with their career goal as a trainer. Nevertheless, 62 of them (including neutral ones shared dissatisfaction towards their career. Emerging observations were:

1. *Greatest dissatisfaction with their own career (as trainer) was observed among those who preferred the trainer to subject orientation. This is also defined as self directed emphasis during training.*
2. *Group directed trainers (P – P) felt the highest satisfaction in terms of their career as a trainer (14 out of 21) as also evident from the mean score (2.5).*
3. *Equal proportion of 'TOT' oriented trainers – who were the largest in sample drawn also shared highest satisfaction with their own profession.*

Summary

The professional background of trainers depicted their depths of involvement in the training career. Whether professional affiliation provided a sense of enrichment that trainer look forward to was a matter of debate. However, majority of them experienced their affiliative needs satisfied more than that of their professional needs through such associative process.

Analysis of dominant interactional pattern among trainers was that of

[60] The operational meaning of goal congruity is trainers of own belief, desired mode of learning source and expectation that he has set from training function in general qualifies the sense of one's goal congruity..Clarity of learning goal and style of handling the process also determines the goal clarity.. Thus the source of learning and its degree of compatibility with nature of goal is critical to add on the degree of contribution.

trainer-participant. Majority of them, therefore, were found to be task oriented (77 out of 150) and 58 of them were group-oriented trainers. The subsequent chapter deals with relationship of one's self image with their training orientation and performances to training methods.

1. *It was rather difficult to make sure the length of experience and professional specialisation on the basis of sample list provided by ISTD. Nor we could determine in advance, the kind of diversity in sample size. Proportion was determined on the basis of the responses received.*
2. *Three components, Trainees, subject matter and Trainees' environment were selected on the theoretical model propounded by 'Lynton and Pareek (1967)'.*
3. *Trainer – participant interaction indicated the trainers interaction with participant satisfying participants & one's own professional need during training, regardless of the feeling and climate of the group. Therefore, it is defined as Task Oriented Trainers. Task oriented trainers have greater concern of accomplishing the task, irrespective of the training climate.*

Group oriented trainers are generally concerned about participants – participant's interaction. They would encourage a group to evolve its own culture and norms conducive to their learning. Self-oriented trainers are those whose entire focus is on depicting their control and command over the subject, regardless of the need and expectation of the participants.

Chapter IX

Methodology and self image of trainers

Contextual Frame

The concept of training function together with training methodology encompasses a broad spectrum of learning situations. Training methods of a wider variety, both traditional and experimental, have gone a long way in determining the focus and direction of training, thereby, significantly enhancing the utility of the training itself.

Decision on particular training method largely depends on what a trainer thinks about himself and his ability to control the situation. Each method has its own uniqueness in terms of its merits and demerits. Nevertheless, trainers' option to adopt a particular method might be due to a situational force. A particular training situation might influence one's decision to select a method. In some cases, the training climate has a great role in the pedagogical preferences of the trainer or group of trainers (Dayal 1970, De 1978 and Randall 1978).

Training method is as important as the other training input, but the stress and focus tends to vary, depending upon the institution of the instructional situation. There are methods for each type of training implicit to any training function. For instance lecture method, case method, role-playing, in basket, business games, syndicate and critical incident method etc. are found to be very useful and applicable in most management development programmes. On the other hand, methods of training like job rotation, on-the-job or implant training have been used in different types of training programmes. Just to reiterate, there are as many methods as the objectives and types of training programmes.

Another equally, if not more, significant factor that determines the choice of the training method, is the extent of control the trainer feels he needs on his participants. Trainers who resort mainly to lecturing, are those who like order and feel a need to talk, are generally afraid of losing control and exposing themselves under testing questions. Lecturing tends to satisfy these needs. However, the relationship between behaviour, personal needs and choice of training methods may not be so direct. Infact, it can be inverse where the need to control may induce the trainer to advocate permissive methods. He may do so to avoid acknowledging his need to control and lack of spontaneity are the characteristics of such trainer. This part of the report discusses the analysis of the data made thereafter.

Trainers' Orientation and Self-Image:

Those with higher self-image score were found to be generally group oriented trainers. It was revealing to note that self-oriented trainers had the lowest self-image score (2.8) amongst all. Task oriented trainers saw themselves as more knowledgeable, adaptable self confident and imaginative. Group oriented trainers saw themselves as highly imaginative, more adaptable and powerful too. Their need for power was higher, but their awareness to high sense of security to opt for group oriented approach was glaring through data. Such trainers might opt for more permissive training method because they think that they can handle the situation. They felt assured of their position in a classroom setting. Subsequent case studies in this report substantiate this analysis.

Table–9.1: Trainer's Orientation and their Self-image

	Particulars	Task Oriented	Group Oriented	Self Oriented
	Overall Image M.S.	3.6	4.2	3.4
1	Knowledge of subject matter	3.8	4.0	4.8
2	Imaginative power	3.9	4.5	2.8
3	Adaptability	3.7	3.9	2.7
4	Friendliness	2.9	3.5	3.0
5	Forceful & aggressive	3.1	4.1	3.1

6	Self confidence	3.8	4.6	3.0
7	Relaxed and free	3.3	4.7	3.8
8	Cooperative and helpful	3.5	3.8	4.0

Maximum obtainable score was 5.0 and lowest was 1.0. Rating was on 5 point continuum (N=250).

Major clarification of the sample is based according to the orientation of the trainer's relationship with their self-image to training method. Overall mean score indicated that group oriented trainers considered themselves generally more positive than that of the other trainers. Questions that needs to be examined here are:

Whether choice of the method is largely dependent and rooted in trainer's assumptions about himself? What he thinks of himself might lead him to generally opt for structured or unstructured methods of training. Because his assumptions are closely associated to the overall training orientation.

Preferences for Training Methods

As evident from Table-VI, there was an apparent disagreement in the preferential rank of trainers with regard to various training methods. However, trainers generally agreed on the preferences of case methods, except those who were self-oriented trainers*. Task and group oriented trainers preferred case method to be the most preferred one followed by simulations and games, whereas self-oriented (or egocentric) trainers ranked lecture methods and lectures-cum-discussion as first and second important method respectively as their choice. But the reverse is not true, use of lecture method too, may be a situational decision by any trainer.

Table-9.2: Trainers' Preferential Rank Score for Various Training Methods

Sl.	Particulars Oriented	Methods Oriented	Task Oriented (T-P)	Self (T-S)	Group No (P-P)
1	Structured	(a) Lecture Method	6.8(8)	1.27.2(1)	7.5(8)
		(b) Lecture-cum-Discussion	4.1(3)	2.5(2)	5.7(5)
		(c) Case Method	3.5(1)	5.2(4)	1.5(1)

		(d) Panel Discussion	6.0(6)	4.7(3)	6.8(7)
2	Semi-	(a) Simulation/ Games	3.8(2)	6.0(5)	2.5(2)
	Structured	(b) Role Playing	5.2(5)	6.2(6)	3.4(3)
3	Unstructured	(a) Open Session	4.3(4)	7.1(7)	6.5(6)
		(b) Process Work & T-Group Technique	6.5(7)	7.8(8)	4.0(4)

Max. obtainable score = 10
Min. obtainable score = 01
W Test: Significance at. 05 level
Figures in the parenthesis indicate the ranking of item.

It was revealing to note here, that the dominant choice of structured methods was generally by those who were more egocentric and self-conscious. Such people were more concerned of "their knowledge of subject matter". Similarly, task oriented trainers were found less prone towards unstructured training methods against those of group oriented trainers.

Analysis of the data revealed a significant difference in the preferential ranks of various trainers, 'lecture method' was the least preferred among the task and the group oriented trainers*.

Table-9.3: Preferential Score and Trainers' Orientation

Orientation	Structural	Semi-Structured	Un-Structured
Task	Moderate (5.5)	High (6.5))	Low (4.5
Self	Moderate (5.0)	Low (4.5)	Very Low (2.5
Group	Moderate (4.8)	Very high (7.5	Moderate (5.0
Overall Score	Moderate (4.8)	(18.5) 40%	(12.0) 22%

Figures in parenthesis indicate the preferential score out of 10. Higher the score, greater the emphasis on particular method. Generally, trainers preferred to have semi-structured method in most of the training situations followed with structured methods. Low emphasis on unstructured training methods indicated a different kind of trainers' orientation. The question that arises here is:

Why unstructured training methods are necessary? How many trainers in general are prone to process work and handle the group in an open house session? Unstructured methods provide substantial scope to allow the trainees to evolve their own sense of direction and freedom of thought and action. Are we prepared (as a trainer) to cope with the threat of loosing the floor?

This calls for greater amount of flexibility on the part of trainers to change the approach and styles as and when necessary. It is the perceived threat from the participants or trainers' own sense of fixation to methods and approach that he is used to. Assuming that 'process work' is normally applicable only in case of behavioural science trainers (30)* the subsequent analysis depicted the same pattern. Combination of open house discussion and process work was put together, eventually to examine the rank score of both BS and non-BS trainers.

Self-image and Pedagogical Preferences

As is evident from Table- 9.3 it was revealing to note that trainers with low self-image generally preferred highly structured pedagogical tools and methods.

Nevertheless, all those who used structured training methods were not necessarily trainers with a low self-image. It was primarily due to the fact that they perceived themselves low on relating to people (friendliness) and trying to protect themselves. Many trainers with soft and submissive behaviour perceived the group as a threat of getting swayed by them and, therefore, they preferred to use group assignments and other highly structured methods. Low and high self-image influenced the nature of self concept that trainers had about themselves. Image has been operationalised as an outcome of the opinion formed by others about oneself and one's own opinion formed about oneself.

Exhibit: Trainers own Perception and their Self Effectiveness

High Image	Low Image
Highly Effective (HE) Confident 1 Knowledge Aggressive Neutral Positive Attitude Flexible	**Less Effective (LE)** Timid 3 Insecured Highly Knowledgeable Affiliative Diffident Critical
Moderately Effective (ME) Confident 2 Very Aggressive Hostile Biased Defensive Rigid	**Moderately Effective (ME)** Low Knowledge 4 Low Control Low Imagination Tensed Negative

Study of self-image of a trainer is a partial attempt in understanding trainers self-concept. Data revealed that image helped trainers in formation of their self-concept. During the formative stage, image (high or low) can be an important variable to influence the nature of self-concept one develops for oneself (Belbin 1974).

It was established that trainers generally with high self-image were positive to the task environment. Image responses, analysed as above, were collected in relation to the task environment. Task environment of trainers were of diverse nature, however, uniformity could be drawn since the task *per se* (of training) was common to all. It ranged from the organization and conduct of the course to the actual handling of the session. Pedagogical preferences were also found to be associated with trainers level of overall effectiveness in that method. Few trainers were very effective in handling a case method, because of their experience and practice and tended to use that very often. Their belief about the positive learning impact of case method of teaching was unquestionable. Some of them were so rigid about a method that they used to decide the 'method' prior to their understanding of the group and subject matter.

Compatibility of a method with the level of participants and with the effectiveness of the trainer was equally important variable linked with the trainers' image. His effectiveness was determined by the process of compatibility drawn by the trainer between the level of participants (trainees) and the method in the training situation.

It is not important that he considers himself flexible but others too should (trainees) perceive him as a flexible trainer. Whether others see him changing his stance, open to feedback and criticism and able to relate to them at an equal plane is a question worth investigating.

Table-9.4: Low Self Image Trainers and their Methods

Sl.No.	Dimension	Image	Score	Highest Preferred	Remarks
1	Knowledgeable	2.5	(S)	Lecture Methods	not able to apply
2	Imaginative	3.1	(S)	Panel Discussion	
3	Friendliness	2.8	(S)	Group Discussion	
4	Controlling and	3.0	(US)	Group Discussion and Case Method	Interfering
5	Protecting and	3.9	(S)	Lecture Method	Insecured of Group
6	Relaxed	2.5	(US)	Field Visits/Syndicates	
7	Sensitive	2.8	(S)	Job Training, Lecture Method	
8	Cooperative Helpful	2.2	(US)	Panels Syndicate	
9	Soft and Submissive	3.8	(S)	Group Assignment Highly Structured Method	

Overall Mean score = 3.6
'S and US' stands for structured and unstructured methods respectively.

Summary

This chapter examines the orientation, image and pedagogical preferences of the trainers. Those who found themselves comfortable with the rigid and explicit task situation largely preferred the use of structured methods. Clarity of training task, greater control on training environment facilitated task oriented trainers to choose a midway approach of choosing semi-structured methods.

Image analysis substantiated the hypothesis that trainers with low image did not like to opt for flexible and open training situation hence they preferred structured training method. Low image trainers were found most ineffective in usages of particular training methods and also in making a learning impact in the class room.

Image is an opinionated assumption (checked or unchecked) about oneself. The opinion that an individual has about himself. It is associated with nature of attitude he has formed within himself about any object and in turn to himself. Image and one's own attitude is deeply related to one's own value system.

Chapter-X

Trainer's Style and Implications

Trainers' styles are basically a set pattern of behaviour in an individual. In this study, trainers' styles have been operationalised as the latent motivational pattern of trainers in their task environment. This describes briefly the trainers styles and their associated behaviour.

Contextual Frame

Motivational syndrome of a trainer determines his styles. Motivations are rooted so deep in our thoughts, emotions and actions that our manifest behaviour tends to get patterned over a period of time. Their styles have thus been classified into three catagories viz. Result, Influencing and Intimacy. Those trainers generally concerned with results, excel in quality and performance are 'result styled' people. Influencing trainers are more concerned of impression, influence and control. Intimacy trainers are generally tilted towards making and maintaining relationship with the participants. It is significant to note here that none possesses only one of the styles. Styles are necessarily an outcome of a particular combination of such patterns. It is the dominant one that determines the nature and intensity of style.

Sample of trainers in our study were asked to respond to a self-rating questionnaire (Annexure II) that depicted their motivational force determining their styles. Some of them had hardly developed a pattern as it was difficult to discriminate one amongst various styles. Following subcategories were made out of the three major styles:

Exhibit: Trainers' Styles and their Assumptions

Manifest Behaviour and Assumptions			
Result Styles	Coach	I teach others do good	
	Pace Setter	I do good	
Influencing Styles	Authoritative	I impress and listen to People	
	Coercive	I control and they have to listen to me	
Intimacy Styles	Emotive	I like them (participants) close to me	and they become
	Participative	They become cohesive as to encourage them	

The exhibit reflects the assumptions that trainers have about themselves. The instrument developed for the study had high reliability (item Interco relation test. 85) and validity. Pair comparison method of analysis revealed that trainers in general, had mixed styles.

Experience, Methods and Styles

It was evident from the analysis that the length of experience of trainers had some relationship with their choice of methods and dominant styles. Nevertheless, trainers with longer experience were seemingly more tilted towards coach styles.

Coach Styles

Coach trainers were those who preferred to stimulate trainees to think and contribute to the ideas. They encouraged intervention and interruptions by the trainees at any stage of their discussion in the class. They believed that trainees spontaneous reaction would enrich the quality of their (trainers) task. Dominant coach styled trainers were generally liked by their co-trainers because they helped their juniors to grow and take up training jobs.

Case – Suresh

Suresh was the chief of training department of a training institute. Naveen, his junior colleague was to take a class, particularly on a subject in which he was not very well exposed. However, he was adequately briefed by Suresh as to how he had to cover the subject matter in the class. Suresh could sense the fear of Naveen but he insisted Naveen to take the plunge. He encouraged Naveen to experiment with himself. Suresh went with Naveen in the class and joined him in beginning sitting away from the trainers floor. That made Naveen comfortable before his 'take off' in the session. After a while Suresh came out of the class, leaving Naveen to his take off stage. As evident from the table the group orientation of the trainers was found closely related to their coach styles.

Suresh in the above case, portrayed a coach character whose concern to help Naveen was more self-directed. Suresh helped him explore a direction for himself in the group without belittling Naveen. Trainer with this style were generally fond of unstructured methods like simulation and group process. Thus relationship between their styles and methods of training were found to be quite meaningful.

Case – Ravi

Ravi is highly known young group trainer. He enjoyed taking up unstructructed and session structed gap session organisation asked him to do three days lab for senior staff. His mode being a coach style. His co-trainer had absolute freedom to make intervention of his choice. He never belittled his co-trainer inspite of the fact that several mistakes were made by him during the process Ravi kept building upon the gaps.

Table – 10.1: Percentage Distribution of Sample

According to their Overall Orientation

Styles	**Self Orientation**	**Group Orientation**	**Task Orientation**		
Result					
Coach	16.50	24	19.5	Pace Setter	29.5 46.0
16.0	40 16.5	36.0			
Influence					
Authoritative	4.6	19.0	20.5		
Coercive	15.4 20.0	16.0 35.0	21.5 42.0		
Intimacy				Emotive	21.0
	9.5	10.0			
Participative	13.0 34.0	15.5 25.0	12.0 22.0		
Total	**100**	**100**	**100**		

Graphic Presentation of Trainers Style

According to Experience

Pace Setter Styles

Result-styled trainers were equally conscious of their performance, quality and its excellence. Their assumption about themselves was that they were the doers, model setters, and therefore, they should 'do' as far as possible. 'Doer' concept is also linked with the belief that 'others are not able to set the pace'. His need to prove his excellence was found increasingly high. Inspite of their competence, many of them were found to be dissatisfied with their group, therefore, sometimes with the training environment.

Case – Mohan

Mohan as a senior training officer wanted to take every session by himself in his programme. His colleagues felt left out in due course. He thought 'I alone can do this session in the best possible manner' others have to observe and learn slowly. Incidentally, he was effective in his class. Very soon his colleagues ignored this fact and started relating and concentrating their energy in some other non-training activities. Later on he felt shocked to note that his colleagues were not at all interested to observe and learn from his sessions although trainees and participants were very appreciative of his class, apparently. One heard him saying "others are jealous of me since my feedback rating is good".

Authoritative and Coercive Styles

These styles reflected concern of trainers to influence and make an impact on the group. Trainers were found trying to influence and impress co-trainers. Tendency of authoritative trainers was to give more of appreciation and reward both to trainers and supportive training staff than to control. Of course, their need to control and induce discipline was no less important, but at appropriate time.

Coercive trainers had greater amount of rigidity in their programme design and were more concerned of bringing 'decorum and discipline' in classroom. Their nature of relationship with the pears and co-trainers was generally found to be coercive. The reason was not their anxiety of providing task excellence, but fear of being dominated and controlled by others. Their need to induce control and discipline was more due to fear of loosing control over trainees.

Case – Rao

Mr. Rao was a knowledgeable trainer. He, however, never encouraged his co-trainers to look at his training design. One of the participants questioned his sequence and content of the programme, of course, with all modesty. Rao was hurt because he saw it as an insult before other co-trainers sitting in the class. He felt like responding to the question of the participant but his discomfort did not make him do so. "I kept watching that fellow during subsequent inputs of the programme and finally found his fault in one of the class assignments and pulled him up in the class", the trainer said in a tone of great satisfaction during the interview sessions.

Coercive trainers generally perceived aggressive participants as a threat and it became difficult for them to accept their strengths. Whereas, authoritative trainers saw them as a potential resource persons and drew strength for their discussion. As both (authoritative and coercive) styles are offshoot of trainers influencing styles, the former was more acceptable and liked compared to the latter.

Emotive and Participative Styles

Emotive styles, essentially indicate the affiliative concern of trainers towards trainees. Their need to build rapport and maintain relationship with them during or before or after the training. They get emotionally involved with the participant's problem and concern, hence difficult to detach their feelings from task even at a critical stage. Chances are that participants would take undue advantage of such concerns of trainers. Emotive trainers were liked by the participants as persons but not rated as good trainers. Participative trainers are, of course, affiliative but moderate in their intense emotional relationship with the participants. Generally they are attached with the participants but wherever necessary they could detach themselves.

Karan a growing, industrious trainer used to get so close to the training group that every group was like his intimate family. He used to go even to receive them and see them off to the station in the early days of his joining. Very soon he discovered that he just cannot fulfill their demand nor could satisfy their needs in toto. His need of seeking acceptance from them as a 'nice good human being' overpowered his styles and methods. Even a slightest rejection of his self by them would make him disturbed and uncomfortable.

Trainees Perception

Many trainees were asked as to "what kind of trainers influenced you the most?" The common response (55 per cent) to that was:":***Trainers who had control over the situation, could handle difficult, probing and divergent questions with caution and confidence without getting swayed by the questions. His ability to keep the group in harmony with his styles and involvement was also appreciated."***

Other kind of response was (25 per cent)" That the trainers who could behave well, listen to trainees' personal problems and be human to them. They were considered as 'nice trainers' irrespective of their ability to control the situation or knowledge of the subject matter."

This indicated that the behaviour of the trainers was most significant variable in making a learning impact on trainees. Because it could facilitate listening and attentiveness towards trainers. This was true more in case of some (semi-structured and unstructured methods). Trainers who had predominantly, been using particular methods. Trainers, with highly structured methods were of course, found regimental, but their command on subject and way of presentation alone would come to their rescue in establishing their impact.

Table – 10.2: Perceived Highest Influence on

Trainees by Trainers

Sl.No	Item	% (N=250)
1	Subject Matter (Knowledge of Trainers) and its application	11.11%
2	Ability to establish relationship with various aspects of training and behave well	22.22%
3	Ability to control emerging situation in class and exhibit high sense of confidence and conviction	55.56%
4	Appropriate combination of all three (1,2,3)	11.11%

Nevertheless, influencing authoritative trainers impressed more than others, but effectiveness was in real sense, where styles matched the need and level of the trainees. Those who failed to match themselves with the trainees' need and expectation were psychologically rejected by them. Hence, low listening and learning in the group. The objective of the study, however, did not focus on the above aspects in depth. Attempt, therefore, was to cover a selected (relatively smaller group) trainees group to establish the linkage between trainers and trainees' perception.

Inter-Relationship of Self Concept, Styles and Methods

Several case histories and subsequent analysis of trainers and trainees of the sample size indicated that three variables viz. trainers' self concept, their styles and methods are closely related to the trainer's being.

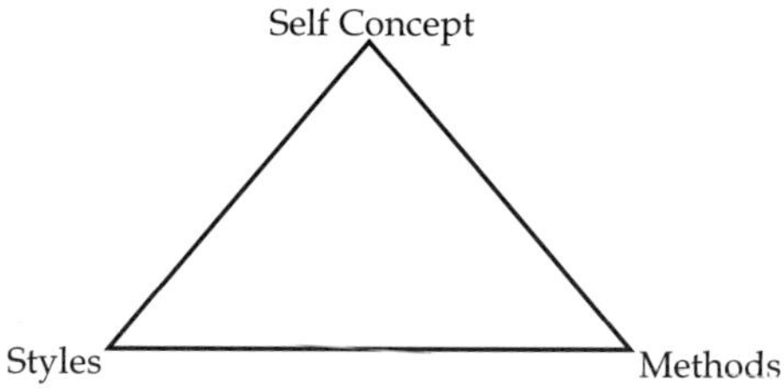

The nature of impact had a differential meaning to different trainers. One of the respondents mentioned;

> *"success to me was a source of satisfaction derived from groups recognition of my work with them. Initially, I was working in the training group to produce the expected consequence. No sooner, I realised that I was, therefore, more concerned with attaining the result than sharpen and clarify the objectives of the session".*

Result styled trainers did get into this dilemma and found difficult to deal with the situation. Whenever results were not produced as per trainers expectations such discomforts were unmanageable. A budding trainer shared his experience;

> *"I remember how uncomfortable I used to be in the class in the early days. However, I had manoeuvered myself to look comfortable through deliberate jokes and spending time on lighter issues. The methods chosen were nevertheless, group discussion but my fear of getting floored out, loosing control on subject directed me to hang around seemingly group orientation but for affiliative purpose."*

The manifest orientation did not reveal the authentic concern of the trainer. It should be his manipulation for survival in the class. Whether such manipulative orientation necessarily would lead to greater learning amongst trainee is a question for deeper probing. Some of the trainers shared their apprehension during the interview and one of them aged 45, stated his assumption:

"participants did not accept me as such unless I could influence them through my session prepared by all seriousness, in combination with visual aids……….. Later I discovered I have been dealing with my anxiety of influencing the group instead of creating a climate of learning for the group. Trainees started appreciating my knowledge, but not my training styles. I am, of course, knowledgeable but no so friendly, social and adaptive. Over a period of time, in 10 years of my training career, I have learnt that I cannot learn unless I decide to do so. My methods chosen for influencing the group were hardly integrated with my belief on learning."

The data and case studies revealed that there was a close linkage of trainers' self concept, their styles with their opted training methods as stated earlier. Impact of styles at the outcome level was perceived to be activated by other factors like his self concept in pursuit of his (trainers) own psychological needs. Question that arises here; whether the role of a trainer provides a situation where I detach my being from the role ? Is it an illusion to be a non-being in the task situation and manipulate myself (and the group) or get manipulated by a particular training method? Is it really possible. Analysis as above, in this study accepts such possibilities and the assumptions thereof. Nevertheless, illusion of a trainer, many a times, overpowers the trainers' styles and his pedagogical behaviour.

It was seen that the trainers with academic and content bias would focus more on structured session preferably lecture-cum-discussion. Even preferential sitting arrangement for the group by a trainer would define his perception about the training situation, his role and himself.

Future of Group Process Training

Future of group process training would take a momentum with fast pace of new technology and changing economy. Time is going to be priceless constraint for many. Many would choose to cut short their option for shorter modular packages in the caption of group process than desired option of depth and width. Future is for those who love floating than diving across the waves and current. Application of human process learning and applied behavioural science for the corporate to impact their work life is going to be critical day by day. The fierce competition both at global and local level, speed and innovation is going to force people to build bridges than to stay isolated. In such a situation clarity of human process, sensitivity and new alliances would demand the understanding of better relationship management.

Group Process trainers today and tomorrow

Modern group process trainers are the product of ISABS and ISISD driven modular approach. There are many such organisations who are offspring of ISABS like Sumedha, Astha and several other consulting entities. These offspring's are committed to process learning mode with their own derivations. Whereas quite a few are getting exposed to current NTL design than old mode of NTL program that used to conduct very long duration stretched over a fortnight and months together[61]. History of NTL reveal that dozens of Indian social scientists like Dharni, Udai, Ishwar, Abad and Somnath etc have done early grounding and foundation courses with NTL before they could help evolve ISABS into an organisation. But tomorrow process trainers are fully Indianised and modernized with varieties of tools and equipments exposed to new multivariate training intervention. Moreover, T-group training technique has undergone sea change with heavy conceptual input demand on one hand and application of pscho-anlytical process on the other. Some are strongly opposed to any such mode but focus on *here and now* by encouraging the learners derive their learning agendas at their own without any conceptual input from books or from outside source. Study taken up during late eighties and mid nineties revealed interesting findings in response to the following questions posed to select respondents during the ISABS event. Respondents were those who sponsored their nominees for several courses announced by ISASB at different points of time.

[61] National Training Laboratory is world known process driven learning organisation based in USA which has trained large number of T group trainers all over the world. .ISABS founding members are product of NTL.Today quite a few members are closely associated with both NTL and ISASB programme. Historically speaking NTL has begun its programme on extended mode for a long duration for almost a month on stretch to create new breed of trainers. Later it discovered that programme on staggered mode would be more desirable.

Table: 10.3 Perceived Mode of "T- group" Training Currently in Practice in India (1995-2000)

Does T-group training being followed in India at the orgnisations level has gained acceptance?	Low acceptance 30% organisations out of 250 respondents using on piece meal basis 65% of respondents' organisation knew nothing of T group ; but 5% did know and were using it quite often with select trainers of their choice. Most of them were corporate sectors. (Corporate respondents, N=40).	Select few gone in to OD mode intervention in organisation through group process training.
Does T-group training has gained acceptance in social sector target audience (Non Government Organisation)	Moderate acceptance(N=30)	Very Limited use of pure T group intervention, inadequate trainers.
How far trainers are willing to modify and transfer their learning of T-group with organisational context?	Quite far and reasonably good in work life with ability to transfer their learning in any different context. Corporate learning setting very high application. Social learning setting moderate application possibilities. Government sector least application of T group learning.	Majority found it a meaningful exposure even if they did not go through complete internship phase work due to several constraints. Yet 18% of ISASB exposed respondent did not like T group kind of training at all so they did not came back. There could be several grounds for having disliked the process driven ISASB training.

Following three sectors have been exposed to T-group learning over a period of time by ISABS. ***Government Sector(GS)*** ***Social Sector(SS)*** ***Corporate Sector(CS)*** ***Education Sector(ES)***	***GS=Very difficult to transfer the learning value of group process since it does not match with nature of governance and its practiced value.*** ***SS=Has similar value of openness and authenticity so application possibility is willingness.*** ***CS=The corporate sector prefers to buy 'T' group driven human process learning knowing brand image of the programme already established.*** ***ES= education sector there is limited exposure to such training - teachers of university colleges neither from pvt. Management institutes have shown little interest in this training.***	Education sector has highly structured teaching system hence openness and innovative way unstructured orientation is least preferred method for university system. Social sector has scope to accept such process but high cost of training demands special subsidy and support to attract their attention. Corporate sees it as an opportunity of career. for their employees and also to give them stress free time in five star luxury setting of learning time.

Source: Data was collected during 2002 by professional and associate members of that period (N=35) in addition to other group of trainers comprising total 250

Above analysis indicates that future of group process in next decade is bright in terms of career option for professional development. It is also evident from the analysis that future of group process is deepening and many with long term perspectives would prefer such exposure and many with short term and quick fix formulae would look for other cosmetic modules emerging in the market. Every day new modules are coming up with strong focus on process orientation but are not typical T group program. Such modules are highly welcome by new trainers the future therefore lays varities and blended module of training at one level and highly specialized module of shorter duration with focus on cognitive and process depth. Time being a constraint for the organisations the focus of long duration process orientation modules have lost the demand and would loose its market value tomorrow.

Knowledge Economy Versus Knowledge Society

One can foresee the trend that time is brighter commercially for those who have grip over the process learning as against those who are caught up with content issues. Growth is not the agenda of tomorrow. Without stimulating development, growth as such is meaningless for the nation. Therefore, benefit of process learning orientation is going to be very critical. The company and social organisation have taken positive interest in last few years to understand the value of process issues than content and strategic issue for their developmental programmes. But there are several sectors like education and government sectors which are least sensitive particularly in Indian context.

One can explain the reason that those who are keen on maintaining *status quo* are not enthusiastic to buy the meaning and relevance of process learning. But those who are struggling to change to meet their demand of organisational goal and task have no choice but to have gripping insight on process issue to survive. It is going to assume more attention as we progress along with complex technological era. The knowledge economy may not last long without building a knowledge society. The gaps are visible. Economy alone will not make the sustainable change in spite of the fact it has incredible impact on a short term gain. The process science therefore increasingly felt to be most advance subject in HR and OD field which may not be easier for every body to step. However the exposure of the process science[62] seems to be gaining importance by leaps and bounds. There could be several explanations to this process. Undoubtedly, this is the age skepticism and materialism. Knowledge era has tempted the world to acquire wealth like a deceptive mirage. Greater the knowledge in society, with increased intelligence[63] without morality and spirituality, higher would be the tendency towards self destruction due to completeness, and conflict originating out of the greed for wealth.

It is interesting to note the variance of approach adopted by NTL and ISABS way of handling group in general. Of course each trainer is different, therefore, he or she has own way of handling the lab. ***Variance and innovativeness is key of ISABS way of running it. However one would question the lack of uniformity and ambiguity details on one weak process work that is left to the trainer to a large extent. The model differs from trainers to trainers instead of organisational standard***

[62] T-group leaning lays foundation of knowledge about one self that is driven to change as we move forward. India revolution on spiritual awakening at some level shows subtle but strong and dormant on the need of society to look forward on deeper issues beyond economics of living. This is evident in America and else where as well. Society is not satisfied and happy with all that it has even today. It is working a gripping fear for its own survival on its own economics of living. Recent debate Knowledge economy is raising critical issues of digital dive and so on (Nagendra Singh, Knowledge economy is alien to society- need for development leadership, Paper presented during National symposium at IMI Delhi 2006).

[63] Swami Shivanada, "Bliss Divine" Divine Life society, Rishikhkesh, India 2004.

with given chronological sequence strongly approved by the internal authority system. It may have cultural variations too between India and America or European frame of mind where system and clarity of task assumes greater significance. Thus client orientation is taken in to account with greater precision with accepted standard of modular sequence.

Summary

Trainers' styles are rooted in his motivational syndrome. The psychological needs that get satisfied in the trainers role described the nature of style a trainer has developed over the years. Result, Influence and Intimate styles of trainers indicate concern of task excellence, task impression and impact and concern for establishing better relationship with participants respectively. Choice of method and trainers self concept was also found closely associated with their styles. Nevertheless, the outcome was largely dependent upon nature of self image, assumptions and the belief trainers had formed about themselves. The process orientation of trainers reflect their competencies on group process training and dynamic relationship. It is revealing to note that corporate sector seems to have higher interest and involvement in such a programme than any other sector. The value of training is deep seated and brings incredible impact on one's value re-examination and driving individuals towards search for one's own identity. The education and government system is too closed to learning process that is so open and self testing mode. Thus, T-group training has generally been attracted by corporate sector professionals. Though most of professional members are drawn from academia and corporate with their current occupation association with social sector as well in different capacity.

There has been an increasing realisation that the development of trainers is crucial to develop training as a discipline. How the trainer handles the situation effectively is open to observations and examination provided trainer himself has a mental preparedness to do that.

A trainer's self concept is the most important factor that affects his way of communicating with others. While a strong or positive self-concept is necessary for healthy interaction, a weak or negative self-concept, on the other hand generates feelings of inadequacy and insecurity.

As stated earlier, the questionnaire was mailed to 600 trainers on All

India basis. We could get total sample of 250 for the final analysis. Out of which sample got randomly distributed from different background and subset the patterns of findings revealed the following:

1. *The professional background of trainers depicted their depths of involvement in the training career. Whether professional affiliation provided a sense of enrichment that trainer's look forward to was a matter of debate. However, majority of them experienced their affiliative needs satisfied more than that of their professional needs through such associative process.*

2. *Analysis of dominant interactional pattern among trainers was that of trainer-participant. Majority of them, therefore, were found to be task oriented as against those of group oriented trainers. Number of process driven trainers are quite a few in number nationally*[64]*.*

3. *Use of structured methods was largely preferred by those who found themselves comfortable with the rigid and explicit task situation. Clarity of training task, greater control on training environment facilitated task oriented trainers to choose a midway approach of choosing semi-structured methods.*

4. *Image analysis substantiated the hypothesis that trainers with low image did not like to opt for flexible and open training situation hence structured training method. Low image trainers were found most ineffective in usages of particular training methods and also in making a learning impact in the classroom.*

5. *Trainers' styles are rooted in their motivational syndrome. The psychological needs that get satisfied in the trainers role described the nature of style a trainer has developed over the years. Result, Influence and Intimate styles of trainers indicate concern of task excellence, task impression and impact and concern for establishing better relationship with participants respectively. Choice of method*

---

[64] ISABS and few other process biased professional bodies have limited professional members in India. ISABS has about 150 professional certified members till date..

* Sudhir Agarwal and Mahaveer Jain op cit. Series of edited publication for Parth Sarathi and Mahaveer Jain have compiled interesting articles on related issues (for details see annual handbook facilitators published by initiative and intervention 2010-2011)

and trainers self-concept was also found closely associated with their styles. Nevertheless, the outcome was largely dependent upon nature of self-image, assumptions and belief trainers had formed about themselves.. It was in this context that self image and identity of several trainers of ISASB orientation were examined to relook at the manifest behavior of professionals. Of course the study taken up quite some time back need to be directly correlated with other studies as placed in different chapters of this book.

Review and reflections touched interesting insights of learning group behaviour during encounter session as reviewed in this book by ***Sudhir and Mahaveer*** in their early work.*

"Number of situations arose during group work experience and gave us insight on different pattern of many trainers. However, the first intervention by the trainer after the group started working was "Group began by introducing themselves. Cycle was over. Group did not know what to do thereafter. They have done their job of knowing about each other. Some of them felt that self awareness is almost done in a half day interaction. I raised the question, "What the members wanted to know from their introductions that would help them to work together later in the group? This intervention underscored the difference between a T-Group and others groups and emphasized the member responsibility for group progress. After a few minutes of interaction the trainer shared his perception that members had introduced their organisations rather than themselves. This sounded punishing to the group and elicited strong defensive remarks by members attacking the observation. This intervention created a subtle understanding by the members about the pattern of exploring the consequences of any action in the group. The trainers' intervention made it possible for some members to talk openly about their reactions to power and authority (status symbol) and generated dependency and counter-dependency statements directed towards the trainer. The trainer accepted the attack calmly and did not nod for supporting statements. This could serve as a model for handling the feelings expressed in the group. When the trainer was asked by a member to help them as to how they can go about, he responded through the intervention that he was in a dilemma as to whether to respond to a direct question and how to respond to that direct question. The trainer had tried to model open expression of personal dilemmas and motivation when this was important for the group."

Styles of trainers and their learning as examined in the aforesaid study has revealed that very often there is an effort to select a leader visible in the group dynamics. They also select a leader "by selecting a leader to what extent they could solve their problems?" The very role of trainers' intervention objective is to enable the group to learn from its own course of action than to create a dependence in group learning climate. How do we create a sense of personal responsibility to deal with their problems and their prerogative (right) to seek help from anyone whenever they feel like than to ask the so called leader or the trainer. The study has not gone in to depth due to inadequate sample size but throws new areas of research on related theme. For new horizons of research it is desirable to unearth the deeper areas of search from the group process data available from interns diary who have gone through professional development learning diary.

The findings draw attention of trainers and learning those engaged in trainers development activities. Notwithstanding, the focus on particular functional area, growth of the trainer as a person is the most critical variable in making him effective. Findings are definitely suggestive of the emerging thrust and emphasis on various trainers' development programmes. Institution need to examine as to what design can help build or produce better trainers. With the expanding network on training institutions at various level and for different purposes, the quality of trainers, their orientation and skill assume the greatest significance in today's context.

Chapter XI

Review and Reflections: T-Group Theories and Practices

Review by different readers in their journey of internship gave an interesting insight to conceptual frame of T-group. Knowing the fact that T-group cognitive frame has been evolved by rich experiences of eminent facilitators and researchers. Our effort to collate their review and reflections we were enriching and refreshing.

Most of the interns and upcoming professional members were expected to make intense review of Process centric books during the journey. Following review compilation by **Mahaveer and Sudhir** gave an interesting glimpse of T-group related depth and meaning drawn from different published sources. For example Bradford, Gibb and Benne's original work **on T-group theory had its own significance** touched new meaning on the. Ramlingam's effort of review and reflections[64]. Ramu's insight of the book had strong emphasis on self reflections whereas Somesh dwelt upon author's view quite elaborately. For example Ram's writing is self explainatory. Of course, we complied several of such reviews but only few of them have been selected for this book with modifications·and change to suit the objectives of the book. Let us look at the notes from different readers and their insight

[64] T-Group theory and Laboratory Method By L P Bradford, J R Gibb & K D Benne above review was compiled by Sudhir Agarwal and Mahaveer Jain as a piece of their book review effort.

which are so touching. Let us begin with what Ramlingam writes: *"I started reading this book in 1991 when I entered Phase – A. By reading this book I am able to perceive the human processes by observing the contents (events in the group) and conceptualise (generalize) the processes by reflecting on what is observed. I prefer to read this book again and again as I am undergoing experiences in groups to gain insights into experiential learning processes.*

It was an account of the accumulation of knowledge, skills and wisdom in relation to T-group training, The resources of developing the T-group methodology have been generated from experimentation by using the action-research model of changing. In a T-group, the objective is to mobilise group force to support the growth of members as unique individuals simultaneously with their growth as collaborators. The members learn to help the facilitator as he assists in the development of individual and group learnings. A training laboratory is a community dedicated to the stimulation and support of experimental learning and changes. The experience in T-groups help members to plan change efforts in associational life outside the laboratory.

As a member of the T-Group, I collect data about my behaviours; I analyze the data with the experience, which generates the behaviours. My learnings are tested and generalized for continuing use. I learn about my motives, feelings, and strategies in dealing with other persons. I learn of the reactions I produce in others as I interact with them. Form the confrontation of intentions and effects; I locate barriers to the autonomous functioning in my relations with others. I develop new images of potentiality in myself and seek help from others in converting potentialities in actualities. I increase my abilities to respond, interactively and adaptively to situations. I achieve concurrent growth in personal autonomy and in social effectiveness.

Increasing awareness of sensitivity to emotional reactions and expressions in oneself and in others.

Improving ability to perceive and to learn from the consequences of one's actions through attention to feelings of his own and others.

Stimulating the classification and development of personal values and goals consonant with democratic and scientific approach to problem-solving in personal/social decision and action.

Developing concepts and theoretical insights which will serve as tools in linking personal values, goals and intentions to actions consistent with inner self and requirement of the situation.

Developing behavioral skills to support better integrations of intentions and actions- achieving behavioral effectiveness in transactions with one's environment.

Helping to transfer new learnings to back-home situations ;- applying the new ways of behaving with typical ways of behaving in home settings.

Learning how to learn;- Analysing one's own process of learning.

The facilitator needs to be continuously aware of that he is working with group members towards re-education. Everyday in a laboratory he is full of episodes of relearning, of reorganization of precious learnings. I confront my old patterns with new possibilities. The above objectives of T-Group involve examination of the relation-ships between old and new experiences, between old and new learnings, and the arduous process of achieving some viable choice or synthesis between the old and the new.

Barriers of change and behavioural modifications

(i) *Seeking easy, early answers to the problems. The laboratory must be prepared to cope with shock and initial resistance.*

(ii) *Conflicts between the familiar and the unfamiliar. The trainees will have conflicts between holding on to familiar patterns of behaviour and trying out the unfamiliar.*

(iii) *Resistance to breakdown of compartmentalisations within the individual. The participants may believe that role behaviours on the job and at home are determined by the situation and not by the individual's personality.*

(iv) *Reluctance to expose thoughts and behaviour to others. Laboratory conditions must encourage collaboration and trust among members and thus reduce the threats inherent in self-exposure.*

(v) *Defensive reactions resulting from lack of individual security. If the individual defends his present patterns against all changes, little learning will take place.*

(vi) *Lack of skill in assessing behaviour. The members may not have had an enabling environment for trying out new behaviours..*

(vii) *Lack of conceptual structures to plan the direction of change. Members may think that behaviour is just a human nature.*

(viii) *Hesitation to accept or to offer helpful reactions. Members may not have previous experience, which legitimizes feed backs from peers as a learning process.*

(ix) *Lack of connection seen between laboratory and potential utilisation. The laboratory training must include assistance in planning the application of laboratory learnings.*

The six situational case episodes narrated by L P Bradford throw light on the rationale and impact of the interventions the trainers had made in of trainers' intervention

- *The trainers observe hand-clasping experience to widen gradually in building trust and comfortable feeling of protection among the group members. Competition when becomes a conflict, trainers refrain their entry as their intervention might create more dependency.*
- *Moreover, group conflicts. belong to the group and so the trainers refrain from early intervention as otherwise the group would be deprived of an opportunity to deal with the conflict. When the competition or conflict blocks the group action the trainers intervene for facilitating group movement.*

<u>*Situation one*</u>: The above insight does reflect a pattern that many trainers would tend to accept. However, the first intervention by the trainer after the group started working was "What the members wanted to know from their introductions that would help them to work together later in the group? This intervention underscored the difference between a T-Group and others groups and emphasized the member's responsibility for group progress. After a few minutes of interaction the trainer shared his perception that members had introduced their organisations rather than themselves. This sounded as a criticizing remark to the group and elicited strong defensive remarks by members attacking the observation. This intervention created a subtle understanding by the members about the pattern of exploring the consequences of any action in the group. The trainers' intervention made it possible for some members to talk openly about their reactions to power and authority (status symbol) and generated dependency and counter-dependency statements directed

towards the trainer. The trainer accepted the attack calmly and did not need for supporting statements. This could serve as a model for handling the feelings expressed in the group. When the trainer was asked by a member to help them as to how they can go about, he responded through the intervention that he was in a dilemma as to whether to respond to a direct question and how to respond to that direct question. The trainer had tried to model open expression of personal dilemmas and motivation when this was important for the group.

Situation two: When the group starts working after initial introduction of the group many issues arise;Whether the group could tolerate ambiguity and lack of structure to solve the fundamental problem of group building. I recall one group confronted the trainer vehemently seeking his role and clarity of purpose. They failed, so they selected a leader in the disguise of a trainer who appeared to be Mr. know all.

When an effort to select a leader was thrust forward by some members, the trainer raised the question "By selecting a leader to what extent they could solve their problems? "and" was a leader a crutch upon which the group could lean?". The intervention creates an awareness among members about their personal responsibility to deal with their problems and their prerogative (right) to seek help from anyone.

Situation three: Trainer's own statement:

It was an interesting scene to study the group behaviour...for example,when a member dominated the process and the other members tended to reverse some decisions in the group, I intervened, "whether he was setting standards for the group and where his sanction had come from". (Standards set by strong members can immobilize the group).

Though there was no immediate response from members, I felt that it would be picked up later by the group. Only as the group analyses its own process and the behaviour of its members including the trainers could the, group develop and learning takes place. The interventions have to guide the members towards an analyses group process and members' behaviour and toward their appropriate behaviour in tune with this decision.

Situation four: On the threshold of the middle phase of the group one intervention by me helped to the emergence of a group value that "there should not be private experimentation with motives not openly expressed") one dominant member aroused two other members to secretly change the places of name cards on the table during lunch break).

This helped the group to examine manipulative behaviour (action) in the group. The process helped to build more open and trusting relationships. The members became aware of some of the ethical issues involved in manipulation.

Lessons drawn

Above review depicts as to what exactly has gone wrong in what kind of group process. Though the original author Bedord and his team are veteran T group facilitators experience and insights may be seen similar in our own case. It is to be noted that the development of the group will require members' feedback to one another to move forward in order to build relationship.

- *Normally, in a T-group members keep resisting feedback on the group that it would be hurting. The trainers seem to try, from time to time, to relate the discussion to the actual data about the event, but these interventions are brushed aside.*
- *Some members convey that no learning would come to them if data about their performance is withheld by the trainers. They expect internally that trainers should share their feedback to them as how they have been doing in the group work. The issue of seeking authority's approval and validation is on surface for quite some time unless trainers decides to confront authority issue in the group.*
- *Sometimes trainers voice their own feelings of what they have been facings during the last few days or in here now setting. This is just opposite to group's expectation since they want direct feedback as to what has been their performance.*
- *Subsequently members do make self-disclosures and seek feedback from everyone. That leads to some amount of openness.. Most of the members tends to give feedback so that others learn to take them earnestly. Sincerity of feedback and its authenticity is very important in giving and receiving feedback during group work.*
- *If there is a planned method to give and receive feedback and it is a part of group self directed intervention, trainers may use it a powerful tool to reinforce the group learning. Then the group could*

go through the planned process of inviting and giving feedback smoothly. After a while, it might become the norm in the group.

- *The group willingly practices the norm encouraging free discussion about the need for feedback, its immediacy, ways of feedback and encouraging trials might have produced effective results, the trainers thought later to take it forward to relate the dynamics and process owned and developed by the group.*

Interpersonal Encounter:

Somesh made an interesting review on the encounter process in an interpersonal setting. The role of "Trainer' explains the trainer interventions with their intended effects during the beginning, middle and final phases of a Group's life. The importance of helping the participants understand the relationship between the training experience and real life problems is, according to the author, an important role of a trainer. He also emphasis the trainer's role in terms of 'making it happen' as contrasted to; 'letting it happen' so that participants can benefit maximum from the training experience with a caution that the trainer does not takeover to create dependence in the group.

While examining the policy Issues like selection of; participants (especially with a view to keep the participants with mental problems out of the Group), Group composition and subgroup Formation' (eg. subgroup on the basis of caste, gender, age, region, and so on) and 'Contracted Aspects' (Contracting his role with the participant right in the beginning).

How much 'safe' is the 'psychologically safe' environment in the group and why is it? Has been discussed with a view that some element of risk is always there and participants must be aware of this fact. The author also mentions the uses and abuses of gimmicks (i.e. management games, exercises, role plays and so on) which trainers sometimes bring in to fulfill their own fancy.

While examining the ethical issues T-group on his/her own. The fact that in their commitment to liberate participants from their blocked expressiveness, the trainers act as role-models and in fact tell 'others how to feel and how to behave has been brought out with considerable emphasis.

The author is of the view that training is relevant for those who function as 'helpers', whose work involves the facilitation of learning and development in others, the list is long including teachers, nurses, physicians, judges, community workers, managers, supervisors and so on. He has given same excerpts from such training with groups of psychiatrists, judges, managers and executives.

Finally it summarises the contents of an interesting section on 'social action and training' emphasising that training is not a panacea for all problems faced by the society. He is also critical of the 'over claim' from which training organisations usually suffer. Training if pushed as 'first aid' for employee distrust or low morale due to poor administration may be considered as an obnoxious instrument of control or an unwanted influence. Somesh wrote:

"One important use has been that I am now more aware of the necessity of a trainer to help the participants understand relationship between the experience(s) in the group and back home real life problems. Some times I used to conduct an exercise and leave the participants to understand its relation with back home situations. I thought that my doing so may prevent participants from leaning on their dependence."[65]

[65] The current trend in ISABS present clarity by professional excellence guidelines have brought freshness. A professionally excellent member will also demonstrate congruence in practices as a person in spaces in ISABS and life outside and role model the values of the institution. Members on the path of excellence will be also be contributing to knowledge building and sharing through concept presentations, writings and publications with some regularity and demonstrate continuous learning. (Shanker, ISABS readings 2011).

Annexure

Questionnaire
(Used for Research Project)

A

1. Name: Sh./Smt./Kumari ------------------------------------

2. Date of Birth ------------------------------------

3. Educational Qualifications ------------------------------------

4. Job Experience:

   Name of Employer/ Position DurationNature of Teaching

   Institution held Work Experience

5. Area of Specialisation Past Present

   in Training.

6. Professional Affiliation.

   Name of the Professional Member Office Bearer

   Societies/Association.

7. Which element of learning as a trainer is more important to you, during training (Rank I, II and III).

   Rank

   Trainees

   Subject matter

   Trainees-environment

8. What kind of interaction you prefer to encourage while handling a session (Rank I, II and III)

Rank

Participant ....Participant

Trainer .... Participant

Trainer .... Subject matter

Any other ....

9. What interaction you normally discourage while handling a session (Rank I, II and III)

Rank

Participant .... Participant

Trainer .... Participant

Trainer .... Subject matter

Any other ....

What would you like to be in your career?

(i) professional trainer

(ii) reputed academician

(iii) unique researcher

(iv) university teacher

(v) field practitioner

(vi) any other

10. How do you find your role as a trainer in congruence with your career goal stated above. (please tick (ü) mark).

Satisfactory Somewhat unsatisfactory

Unsatisfactory

11. Where do you get the maximum satisfaction in your present training activities (Rank I, II and III)

    Relating to participants

    Interest in subject matter

    Act of teaching itself

    Any other

12. Which of the training methods mentioned below do you generally prefer to use while conducting a programme (kindly rank in order of your preference out of the following).

    (a) Discussion

    (b) Lecture Method

    (c) Case Method

    (d) Unstructured group

    (e) Games and simulations

    (f) Lecture-cum-discussion

    (g) Role playing

    (h) Panel discussion

    (i) Conference and syndicate method

    (j) On the job

13. Given the opportunity and your interest, in what area of training methodology would you like to specialize?

14. How good are you in your training activities? Following are the dimensions of training for your self-rating.

You have to assess yourself as where <u>you are</u> (ü) and where you want to be the ideal one (O),on the same continuum.

Indicate where <u>you are</u> by '✓' (tick mark)

you want be 'O' (encircle the number)

High Av Low

1.	(i) knowledge of the subject matter	5	4	3	2	1
	(ii) knowledge of training methods (techniques)	5	4	3	2	1
2.	Imaginative power	5	4	3	2	1
3.	Practical application of knowledge and illustration	5	4	3	2	1
4.	Practical application of knowledge	4	3	2		1
5.	Adaptable (adjustability with new trainees' group and trainers' group)	5	4	3	2	1
6.	Friendly (among trainees & co-trainers)	5	4	3	2	1
7.	Control (controlling the group by means of intervention)	5	4	3	2	1
8.	Forceful (aggressive during control of group and while supporting his point of argument)	5	4	3	2	1
9.	Self confidence (before and during handling a session how strong you feel)	5	4	3	2	1
10.	Protecting (reassuring and defending your self on point of controversies)	5	4	3	2	1
11.	Relaxed (not tense during discussion accepting others point of opinion)	5	4	3	2	1

12.	Enthusiastic (having high interest and desire to do better in training)	5	4	3	2	1
13.	Sensitivity (to self and environment and ability to empathize with others)	5	4	3	2	1
14.	Sociability (tendency to be social and encourage interaction)	5	4	3	2	1
15.	Extent of openness (attempt of being ormal or informal with the group)	5	4	3	2	1

B. TRANS-CHECK I

Given below are some statements each with alternatives 'a' and 'b' Encircle the item you choose as shown in the illustration.

(a) I feel training is necessary in a situation where feedback has been established.

(b) I prefer the shortest course of action out of the alternatives that come up in performing the trainers role.

Please respond to each pair there are no right or wrong answers.

1. (a) I may extend responsibility to my programme assistant for various training functions but take it away if performance is not forthcoming.

   (b) When trainees' suggestion or information is inappropriate, I stimulate them to re-think and come up with another idea.

2. (a) I may extend responsibility to my programme assistant for various training functions but take it away if performance is not forthcoming.

   (b) I prefer to recognise and appreciate the trainee's contribution and feel that snubbing them for their interventions during the session has little effect.

3. (a) I may extend responsibility to my programme assistant for various training functions but take it away if performance is not forthcoming.

   (b) When a trainee disagrees with me: I am tactful in responding and justifying what I really want to say.

4. (a) I may extend responsibility to my programme assistant for various training functions but take it away if performance is not forthcoming.

   (b) I develop close personal relationships with trainees because I believe this marks out to be a good trainer.

5. (a) I may extend responsibility to my programme assistant for various training functions but take it away if performance is not forthcoming.

   (b) When a trainee is wrong on a certain point or has failed to perform the exercise, I let him know my feelings in a firm and reasoned manner.

6. (a) I may extend responsibility to my programme assistant for various training functions, but take it away if performance is not forthcoming.

   (b) I am available to the trainees as a consultant and advisor when it is agreed that they need help.

7. (a) I may extend responsibility to my programme assistant for various training functions, but take it away if performance is not forthcoming.

   (b) I expect the trainees to follow my instructions closely.

8. (a) I may extend responsibility to my programme assistant for various training functions, but take it away if performance is not forthcoming.

   (b) I reward good work and feel that punishment for non-performance has only a limited use.

9. (a) When trainees suggestion or information is inappropriate, I stimulate them to re-think and come up with another idea.

   (b) I prefer to recognise and appreciate the trainee's contribution and feel that snubbing them for their interventions during the session has little effect.

10. (a) When trainees' suggestion or information is inappropriate, I stimulate them to re-think and come up with another idea.

    (b) When a trainee disagrees with me, I am tactful in responding and justifying what I really want to say.

11. (a) When trainees' suggestion or information is inappropriate, I stimulate them to re-think and come up with another idea.

    (b) I develop close personal relationships with trainees because I believe this marks out to be a good trainer.

12. (a) When trainees' suggestion or information is inappropriate, I stimulate them to re-think and come up with another idea.

    (b) When a trainee is wrong on a certain point or has failed to perform the exercise, I let him know my feelings in a firm and a reasoned manner.

13. (a) When trainees' suggestion or information is inappropriate, I stimulate them to re-think and come up with another idea.

    (b) I am available to the trainees as a consultant and advisor when it is agreed that they need help.

14. (a) When trainees' suggestion or information is inappropriate, I stimulate them to re-think and come up with another idea.

    (b) I expect the trainees' to follow my instructions closely.

15. (a) When trainees' suggestion or information is inappropriate, I stimulate them to re-think and come up with another idea.

    (b) I reward good work and feel that punishment for non-performance has a limited use.

16. (a) I prefer to recognize and appreciate the trainees' contribution and feel that snubbing them for their interventions during the session has a little effect.

    (b) When a trainee disagrees with me, I am tactful in responding and justifying what I really want to say.

17. (a) I prefer to recognize and appreciate the trainees' contribution and feel that snubbing them for their interventions during the session has a little effect.

    (b) I develop close personal relationships with trainees' because I believe this marks out to be a good trainer.

18. (a) I prefer to recognize and appreciate the trainees' contribution and feel that snubbing them for their interventions during the session has a little effect.

    (b) When a trainee is wrong on a certain point or has failed to perform the exercise, I let him know my feelings in a firm and reasoned manner.

19. (a) I prefer to recognise and appreciate the trainees' contribution and feel that snubbing them for their interventions during the session has a little effect.

    (b) I am available to the trainees' as a consultant and advisor when it is agreed that they need help.

20. (a) I prefer to recognise and appreciate the trainees' contribution and feel that snubbing them for their intervention during the session has a little effect.

    (b) I expect the trainees' to follow my instructions closely.

21. (a) I prefer to recognise and appreciate the trainees' contribution and feel that snubbing them for their interventions during the session has a little effect.

    (b) I reward good work and feel that punishment for non-performance has a limited use.

22. (a) When a trainee disagrees with me, I am tactful in responding and justifying what I really want to say.

    (b) I develop close personal relationships with trainees because I believe this marks out to be a good trainer.

23. (a) When a trainee disagrees with me, I am tactful in responding and justifying what I really want to say.

    (b) When a trainee is wrong on a certain point or has failed to perform the exercise, I let him know my feelings in a firm and reasoned manner.

24. (a) When a trainee disagrees with me, I am tactful in responding and justifying what I really want to say.

    (b) I am available to the trainees as a consultant and advisor when it is agreed that they need help.

25. (a) When a trainee disagrees with me, I am tactful in responding and justifying what I really want to say.

    (b) I expect the trainees to follow my instructions closely.

26. (a) When a trainee disagrees with me, I am tactful in responding and justifying what I really want to say.

    (b) I reward good work and feel that punishment for non-performance has a limited use.

27. (a) I develop close personal relationships with trainees because I believe this marks out to be a good trainer.

    (b) When a trainee is wrong on a certain point or has failed to perform the exercise, I let him know my feelings in a firm and reasoned manner.

28. (a) I develop close personal relationships with trainees because I believe this marks out to be a good trainer.

    (b) I am available to the trainees as a consultant and advisor when it is agreed that they need help.

29. (a) I develop close personal relationships with trainees because I believe this marks out to be a good trainer.

    (b) I expect the trainees to follow my instructions closely.

30. (a) I develop close personal relationships with trainees because I believe this marks out to be a good trainer.

    (b) I reward good work and feel that punishment for non-performance has a limited use.

31. (a) When a trainee is wrong on a certain point or has failed to perform the exercise, I let him know my feelings in a firm and reasoned manner.

    (b) I am available to the trainees as a consultant and advisor when it is agreed that they need help.

32. (a) When a trainee is wrong on a certain point or has failed to perform the exercise, I let him know my feelings in a firm and reasoned manner.

    (b) I expect the trainees to follow my instructions closely.

33. (a) When a trainee is wrong on a certain point or has failed to perform the exercise, I let him know my feelings in a firm and reasoned manner.

    (b) I reward good work and feel that punishment for non-performance has a limited use.

34. (a) I am available to the trainee as a consultant and advisor when it is agreed that they need help.

    (b) I expect the trainees to follow my instructions closely.

35. (a) I am available to the trainees as a consultant and advisor when it is agreed that they need help.

    (b) I reward good work and feel that punishment for non-performance has a limited use.

36. (a) I expect the trainees to follow my instructions closely.

    (b) I reward good work and feel that punishment for non-performance has a limited use.

Bibliography

1. Belbin, R. M. and Belbin, Eunice (1974). *Problems in Adult-retraining*, London, Heinemann.
2. '*Bricks of Foundation*' edited book on behalf Indian society of Applied Behvioural Science 2002 New Delhi.
3. Bob Garrat, "*The Learning Organisation*": *Developing democracy at work*, UK 200, Harper Collins.
4. Brockhaus, R. H. (1982). *The Psychology of the Entrepreneur* – Encyclopedia of Entrepreneurship, Englewood Cliffs – N. J., Prentice Hall.
5. Carland, J. W., Hoy, F., and Carland, J. (1988). Who is the Entrepreneur? Is a question worth asking. *American Journal of Small Businesses.*
6. Chris Cook, Powel, A., and Sims, A. (June, 2009). "*Spiritual and Psychiatry*", Published by Royal College of Psychiatry.
7. Dayal, Ishwar (1970). *Management Training in Organisations* (Text, cases and simulated exercises), Prentice Hall of India Pvt. Ltd.
8. De, Nitish R. (1978). Training for Public Enterprise Managers: Relevance of Organization Development. *Economic and Political Weekly*, **13**(47), M-115–125.
9. George, Kent (1973). Training is a System. *Training and Development Journal*, **29**(9), 10.
10. Golembiewski Robert, T. and Arthur Blumberg (Eds.) (1973). *Sensitivity Training and the Laboratory Approach: Readings about Concepts and Applications.* 2nd ed. Itasca, IL, F. E. Peacock Publishers, Inc.
11. Green Thad, B. and Raymond T. Butkus (1999). *Motivation, Beliefs and Organizational Transformation.* Westport, CT, Quorum Books.

12. Lynton, R. and Pareek, U. (1967). *Training for Development*, Richard Irwin.

13. Kets De Vries, M. F. R. (1977). *The Entrepreneurial Personality: A Person at Crossroads*.

14. Karim Aly Kassam (April 2010). "*Development in Practice*" **20**(2).

15. Lewin, K. (1997). Defining the "Field at a Given Time." Psychological Review. **50**, 292–310. Republished in *Resolving Social Conflicts & Field Theory in Social Science*, Washington, D.C., American Psychological Association.

16. Lewin, K. (1946). Action research and minority problems. *J. Soc. Issues* **2**(4), 34–46.

17. Lewin, K., Lippitt, R., and White, R. K. (1939). "Patterns of aggressive behavior in experimentally created social climates". *Journal of Social Psychology* **10**, 271–301

18. Back, Kurt W. (1987). *Beyond Words: The Story of Sensitivity Training and the Encounter Movement.* 2nd ed. New Brunswick, NJ, Transaction Books.

19. Michelet Jules (1877). "Bible of Humanity", Translated by Vincenzo Calfa, New York.

20. Mahaveer Jain and Parthasarathi' (2010). *T group II:* Annual Handbook of group facilitators, New Delhi, Manak.

21. Marsh, Arthur (Aug. 1977). Tailoring IR Training to the Manager and his needs. *Personnel Management*, **9**(8), 26–27, 35.

22. Ordiorne, George S. (1970). *Training by Objective: An Economic Approach to Management Training*, London, Macmillan Company.

23. Prescott, Lecky (1945). *Self-consistency: A Theory of Personality*, New York: Island Press, pp. 92–93, 103, 107.

24. Parth Sarthi (2008). 'Enhancing Effectiveness of Training: A systems Approach, New Delhi, Manak.

25. Randall, John S. (Sept. 1978). You and Effective Training: Part 5 – "Planning Your Sessions". *Training and Development Journals*, **32**(9), 42–43.

26. Lewin, K. (1922). *Der Begriff der Genese in Physik, Biologie und Entwicklungsgeschichte.* (Lewin's Habilitationsschrift).

27. Singh, Nagendra P. (1981). Trainer me, Role and Implications. *ISABS Journal*, **6**, 1–2.

28. Singh, Nagendra P. (2005). 'Repositioning ISABS (ed)'. Published as proceeds of ISBAS seminar, New Delhi.

29. Singh, Nagendra P. (2005). 'Rhythem and Rhymes (ed)'. Compilation of poems from life T group experience, published by ISABS, New Delhi.

30. Sinha Dharni (1991). "T group Training", New Delhi, ISABS.

31. Sinha Dharni (2009). "Laboratory Education in India" Trends and Needs (from Stones to milestones, Mahaveer Jain and Parthsarthi (ed)), New Delhi, Manak.

32. Swami Sivanada (2004). 'Thought Power', Divine life society publication.

33. Subhas Sharma, (2006). Management in New Age, "Western Windows and Eastern doors", New age international publishers.

34. Smith, Norman R. (1967). The Entrepreneur and His Firm: The Relationship between Type of Man and Type of Company, East Lansing, Michigan State University.

35. Swami Abheyananda (2005). *Life beyond death, RK Mission.*

36. Swami Tapasyananda (1990). *Bhakti School of Vedanta, Ramkrishna Math Madras.*

37. SGI quarterly (July 2011). *-A Buddhist forum for peace, culture and education*, number 65, pp. 12–13.

38. Schumpeter, Joseph A. (1931). Economic Theory and Entrepreneurial History, Aufl, Munchen Und Leibzig.

39. Swami, A. C. (1995). *Bhakti Vedant "Shrimad Bhagvad Gila"* published on behalf of Bhakti vedant, Book trust.

40. Udai Pareek (2002). 'Process the Neglected Dimensions in the Organisations'. Brick of foundation (ed.), published by ISABS.